The Integrity of the Body of Christ

The Integrity of the Body of Christ

Boundary Keeping as Shared Responsibility

ARDEN F. MAHLBERG &
CRAIG L. NESSAN

CASCADE *Books* · Eugene, Oregon

THE INTEGRITY OF THE BODY OF CHRIST
Boundary Keeping as Shared Responsibility

Cascade Books
An Imprint of Wipf and Stock Publishers
199 W. 8th Ave., Suite 3
Eugene, OR 97401

www.wipfandstock.com

Paperback ISBN 13: 978-1-4982-3536-5
Hardcover ISBN 13: 978-1-4982-3538-9
Ebook ISBN 13: 978-1-4982-3537-2

Cataloging-in-Publication data:

Names: Mahlberg, Arden, F., and Craig L. Nessan.

Title: The integrity of the body of Christ : boundary keeping as shared responsibility / Arden F. Mahlberg and Craig L. Nessan.

Description: xii + 224 p.; 23 cm—Includes bibliographical references and index.

Identifiers: ISBN: 978-1-4982-3536-5 (paperback) | 978-1-4982-3538-9 (hardback) | 978-1-4982-3537-2 (ebook)

Subjects: LCSH: Pastoral theology. | Pastoral care. | Clergy. | Pastoral theology—Evangelical Lutheran Church in America. | Nessan, Craig L. | Cooper-White, Pamela | Cooper-White, Michael. | Title.

Classification: BV4011 M35 2016 (print) | BV4011 (ebook)

Manufactured in the USA

Contents

Foreword

IN OUR CURRENT CALLINGS, we serve at historic institutions of theological education. On July 1, 1863, the bloodiest battle ever fought on U.S. soil took place on and around the campus of Gettysburg Seminary. In the previous days, Robert E. Lee and the Confederate army had crossed the Mason-Dixon line, the border between Maryland and Pennsylvania. Lee believed that his advance into northern territory would overwhelm Union forces, cower the civilian population, and lead to a swift victory and permanent division of the nation. The Civil War was all about borders and boundaries; it was about who would govern which territory, whether a *United* States would prevail or the young country would be divided into two or more loose federations of autonomous and largely independent states. Above all, it was about whether or not boundaries would forever be established between races—an elite and superior (white) class ruling it over an enslaved, rights-denied underclass of African Americans and presumably other people of color as well. Would whites be allowed at will to cross personal boundaries, lay hands and legal claims of "property" upon persons of color?

A few decades later, near the end of the nineteenth century, a different kind of boundary battle took place at the still young Union Seminary in the City of New York. Though it was founded by Presbyterians in 1836, some six decades later Union's leaders had to make a determination of where doctrinal lines would be drawn and who would ultimately govern the school. Upset with teachings by one of the school's faculty members, who embraced the radical notion that not everything in the Bible might be literally true and verbally inspired by God, church officials deemed his teachings heretical and demanded his release from the school. Standing on the principles of academic freedom, scholarly self-determination, and a commitment to embrace and honor a wide spectrum of beliefs, Union's leaders decided to declare their independence from the Presbyterian

Church and become a freestanding, independent, and broadly ecumenical school for the preparation and formation of ministers and other leaders in church and society.

Throughout their illustrious histories, these two great institutions have had to engage in continuing discernment (and often hotly contested, prolonged debates) about boundaries. How rigidly would theological and confessional borders be drawn? Who would be allowed to teach? Could women as well as men, persons of color as well as whites, be allowed to become students and even faculty and senior administrators? Who would determine the style of worship at chapel services, and who might be allowed to preside at such services? What would be the nature of the relationship with other schools? Would it serve seminaries well to join with colleges and universities as the movement for accreditation gained steam? Could our schools accept the constraints and careful governmental monitoring that ensues in becoming eligible to administer U.S. federal student loans? What policies would guide governing boards as they steward endowment funds? Are some promising investments "off limits" by virtue of company products or labor practices?

Over the course of human history, persons, families, tribes, organizations, and nations have recognized the necessity of setting and stewarding borders or boundaries—those places where one individual, group, community, or public entity ends and another begins. Establishing and tending boundaries requires careful attention and constant vigilance. Many boundaries are good; they protect persons, other creatures, and property from being overrun, abused, and denied their rightful place in the universe. Some boundaries, like those within which and for which the Confederacy was established, cannot be allowed to stand and must be torn down, if they are allowed to be set up in the first place. Since its inception, humankind has had to engage in discernment regarding boundaries: Which are good and which are bad? Where should they be drawn, and with what degree of clarity? How rigidly should they be enforced? How do those in power enforce boundaries of their own making, and how are just boundaries reestablished when tyranny and abuse reign? Currently, our nation and others with the greatest resources are engaged in heated debates about how national borders should be monitored and patrolled, opened or closed. In sharp contrast to the spirit of the Statue of Liberty in New York's harbor, whose torch beckons and invites in the "huddled masses yearning to breathe free," some current politicians' campaign slogans shout, "Build a wall; keep them out!"

This is a book about stewarding borders, establishing, tending, and sometimes changing boundaries. Its authors—Prof. Craig Nessan and Dr. Arden Mahlberg—bring to bear their collective wisdom on a vast array of topics related to personal and professional boundaries. Each author in his own way has assumed a *calling* in which boundary tending lies at the very heart of the profession. A pastor, professor, and longtime seminary academic dean (Nessan) and a practicing clinical psychologist (Mahlberg) lead readers gently but insistently down a path into some of the most complex and vexing dimensions faced on a daily basis by their peers in many professions. Heeding their own counsel that boundary keeping is a communal endeavor, they reach beyond their own experience and insights to draw heavily upon the wisdom of others; readers will do well to follow the many tributaries that lead to other resources cited in the extensive footnotes.

The book is deeply *theological*; it makes the claim that God cares about how we relate to one another as individuals and communities. The Hebrew Bible portrays creation as a divine boundary-establishing activity. At creation, God "separated" things and beings. Where there was only an amorphous glob of borderless nothingness (*tohu va bohu* in Hebrew), God drew boundary lines between day and night, darkness and light, earth and sky, plants and animals, male and female. When boundaries were crossed, pain, enmity, and alienation occurred through the eating of fruit from a tree "across the border." But when some boundaries became oppressive and no longer served God's beloved, they had to be crossed. Jesus and his followers got in trouble when they transgressed some of the overly rigid religious laws that had become death-dealing rather than life-giving. St. Paul declared that in the overarching unity in Jesus Christ "there is neither Jew nor Greek, slave nor free, male nor female." (Gal 3:28) Explicitly Christian at its core, the book's insights and practical implications will nevertheless be relevant to readers of any faith tradition, and to those who ascribe to no spiritual creeds or religious beliefs.

As educators engaged in the formation of future "ministers" (we use the term broadly to embrace a wide range of vocations in which today's seminary graduates live out their callings), we are well aware that our institutions' and ecclesial bodies' requirements for "boundary training" courses or workshops are often met by sighs, groans, and eyerolls from our students. Such reactions frequently reveal resistance to engaging with difficult and challenging topics, some of which touch sensitive nerves within fledgling religious professionals. A significant percentage of students (especially women) have themselves been victims of boundary violations at the hands of family members, neighbors, strangers, teachers, clergy, or others least suspected of such crimes. Some who find their way to our schools have been on the offender side of a boundary violation and must come to terms with their culpability, which can provoke profound guilt and should result in serious self-examination regarding fitness for a calling in which temptations and opportunities to repeat such behavior will appear at every turn. Mahlberg and Nessan walk the fine line between a legalistic approach and an overly tolerant stance that has all too often marked the church's way of treating boundaries and boundary violations. Later chapters offer quite specific guidance on a vast array of issues that every person will encounter with some regularity, with particular focus on those unique to religious and therapeutic professionals involved in what prior generations of pastoral theologians commonly referred to as "the cure of souls."

The authors recognize that boundary tending is *contextual*. In our work with seminarians, clergy, and congregations over the decades, we have often witnessed colleagues get into trouble as they move from one ministry to another. Such troubles arise from a failure to recognize that boundaries are drawn differently in different places. Whereas unannounced drop-in pastoral calls may be appreciated and even expected in some contexts (we have tagged along with a "community promoter" on her round of spontaneous visits in Central American *campesino* villages), in other settings such a practice will be met with horrified looks and a chilly reception at the door. Just as preachers must exegete a text of Scripture (that is, must draw out of a passage its original meaning and what it might mean for us today), so pastoral counselors and other helping professionals must exegete their context to determine what words and actions are appropriate in that particular setting. Being a careful student of "where the boundaries lie" becomes particularly acute as one engages in cross-cultural ministry. As one example, direct eye contact in some cultures is the norm for conveying respect and authenticity; in other contexts such eyeball-to-eyeball exchange is regarded as presumptuous, offensive, or even flirtatious, particularly with a person of the opposite gender.

While every context undergoes change over time, the landscape for professionals has undergone seismic shifts in recent years with the advent of smartphones, with the dizzying array of social media, and with other developments made possible by the electronic revolution. Should one "friend" students, parishioners, or members of a youth group on Face-book? Do I widely disseminate my mobile phone number? How does one "keep sabbath" and "turn off and tune out" from time to time when serving among folks, who may launch search and rescue operations if a text message does not receive response within minutes? If Robert Frost's legendary poetic assertion is true, that "good fences make good neighbors," how does one even begin to conceive of building fences in the cyberspace neighborhood? No book can anticipate every boundary-tending matter that will be encountered in daily life and the exercise of a profession, but this one offers enough of a road map to help readers avoid many danger zones.

Boundary tending, as we have suggested, is deeply theological and highly contextual. While, as the authors delineate so compellingly, it is communal, it is also profoundly *personal*. Each of us brings our own history and unique set of life experiences to bear in our relationships and professional responsibilities. While there are no inherently gender-specific ways of responding to events and occurrences, socialization tends to shape women and men in different ways; this too varies by cultural context. Among the many gifts offered in the chapters that follow is a heavy dosage of attention to the whole matter of self-care. Often ignored if not outright derided by ecclesiastical officials frustrated at hearing anecdotal stories of the rare clergy who refuse to respond to a true emergency on a day off, this area should receive the kind of careful and compassionate attention the authors signal. While the "wounded healer" is an apt description of all who engage in spiritual and therapeutic callings, there are limits to just how much hurt and pain one can endure and manage in a redemptive fashion that may serve others.

Among the boundaries most difficult to reinforce among those of us in the helping professions are those that pertain to respecting our own human limitations and temptations, as well as the power conferred by our professional role. We hold a *fiduciary* trust—from the Latin word *fides*, which means both trust and faith! If airline crews and long-distance truck drivers must abide by strict limitations of time spent in the cockpit and cabin or behind the wheel, should enforced periods of rest and renewal not be even more rigidly monitored for those whose sharp retort or careless comments may cause someone in our care physical, psychological, and *spiritual* harm? No less than is the case for other professionals entrusted with high-level responsibilities, personal well-being and stewarding of the self is a life-and-death matter for those of us who engage in spiritual and mental caretaking. Some boundary crossings may appear mutual, but it is always the responsibility of the professional to maintain the appropriate line of familiarity—to cross sexual boundaries with a member of one's congregation, or to exploit a parishioner financially, is not only boundary crossing but violation.

Nessan and Mahlberg herein offer a solid foundation on which to build personal and communal codes of ethics. Good communicators that they are, the authors set forth a broad range of issues in an accessible manner devoid of "insider language." Even as the book will serve well in the classroom and professional gatherings of the clergy or counselors, so it can provoke lively conversations by parish councils as they set policies and fulfill their responsibilities to ensure that congregations are safe places for all. Doctors Mahlberg and Nessan invite us into honest and open conversations about matters that, despite receiving heightened focus in recent years, merit more frequent and in-depth examination. May such conversations flourish and help us all develop and sustain integrity and wholeness in our callings!

Pamela Cooper-White
Christiane Brooks Johnson Professor of Psychology & Religion
Union Theological Seminary, New York

Michael Cooper-White
President
Lutheran Theological Seminary at Gettysburg

Introduction

"You shall love the Lord your God with all your heart, and with all your soul, and with all your mind." This is the greatest and first commandment. And a second is like it: "You shall love your neighbor as yourself." On these two commandments hang all the law and the prophets (Matt 22:37–40).

WE WROTE THIS BOOK after years of hearing people—clergy, seminarians, and their spouses—ask for a comprehensive resource on boundaries in congregational life. We wrote this book both for people who have violated the boundaries of others and for people whose boundaries have been violated. Readers have wanted to know how to create common language and how to establish common understanding about boundaries. They want to develop a shared recognition of what boundaries are and of how to think through boundary issues. Clergy and seminarians want to know how to speak up to insensitive colleagues within the seminary or church context.

While this is a book about boundaries and boundary keeping, it is, more fundamentally, a book about love. Perhaps there is something paradoxical about that. While boundaries sound like constraints and boundary keeping sounds constricting, boundaries do far more than constrain. Boundaries serve as doorways opening to wonderful experiences of love that are not otherwise possible. Only within the safety, mutual accountability, and permission of love is free expression of our most creative selves possible. When we monitor the health of our relationships with persons, things, and functions (including with our own roles), we find that some actions build relationships, some actions harm relationships (or have potential to do so), and some (neutral) actions have little effect, one way or the other, on our relationships.

1

We can group our actions into good, bad, or neutral in terms of their effects on our relationships. We might also color code our actions, just as traffic lights are color coded. A red light means, stop! A red action is one that if we do not stop it will do damage, or at least damage is possible. A green traffic light means, go! Do these things! They are good for relationships. Think of things that are good for a marriage, for example. Successful couples are willing to follow green-light practices and avoid red-light practices.

A yellow light means proceed with caution and be ready to stop. Professional drivers who see a yellow light want to know if it is fresh or stale. How long has the light been yellow? In relationships, yellow-light issues are those that require caution because you are being motivated by feelings, urges, and desires that may or may not be appropriate, may be helpful or may be harmful. Relationships succeed because people let green trump yellow most of the time—not necessarily all the time but much of the time. That is, we do not let our feelings dictate whether we will go to work in the morning, or whether we are willing to do what the job calls for. But relationships also succeed when folks are willing to slow down and prepare to stop at a stale yellow.

Boundary keeping is surprisingly difficult. You would think that good intentions would lead to constructive behavior. Most of us believe that because our motives are good, what we do is therefore justified. Or we think that when we do "the wrong thing" but nothing bad happens, it was not a bad decision. There is plenty of evidence that most of us want to do the right thing, but it has long been recognized that doing the right thing is not always that easy. Fortunately, today we have the benefit of some helpful research that we can apply to our own boundary keeping and that of our congregations and colleagues in ministry, whether ordained or laity.

Paul decried the fact that he did not understand why he acted contrary to what he wished he would do (Rom 7:15). Since World War II, social scientists have made laudable attempts at understanding how it is that people commit atrocities on the one hand, as well as how some people are able to do the right thing under adverse and threatening circumstances. In our approach to boundary keeping in this book, we hope to apply some of the things that have been learned so we can all do better, at least with boundary keeping in congregational life. Of course, we hope that the benefit will spread beyond our congregational lives, but we are confining our scope in this book to congregational relationships and functions.

Within congregational life, we set out to address with the broadest possible all relationships with persons, things, and roles. We do this because it is the health of the entire system that best shapes the health of the individual parts. For example, while the discussion of boundaries in the church rightfully gives prominent attention to sexual boundaries, especially the responsibility of clergy to safeguard from harm all those with whom they relate, the context that supports and enforces this involves focusing on the well-being of the other rather than how the other person can help you have pleasurable experiences. This means never objectifying others, not seeing them as a means to an end, and never misusing power at all, not just in the area of sexual gratification.

In our discussion we start with the fact that our judgment and decision making can only be as good as our awareness. We cannot respect a boundary that we do not recognize, nor will we effectively counteract an unhealthy personal motive that we do not recognize. Our awareness also shapes our sense of what is important and what is not important. We quickly make the point that once we start looking for them, we find boundaries everywhere, important boundaries, in all aspects of congregational life. We will examine the factors, such as time pressure, stress, and social and cultural dynamics, that routinely limit our awareness. We will look at ways to expand and clarify our awareness so we can act more lovingly, even in stressful circumstances.

We want it understood at the outset that boundary-keeping decisions in congregational life, which protect the well-being of others, can jeopardize one's own self-interest. To take a common example, we all want to be liked; in fact, it feels like we "need" to be liked. This is fine until that need overpowers boundary reasoning, which it easily can do.[1] Keeping and promoting good boundary practices may risk the loss of social support, the loss of friends, the loss of support from coworkers or colleagues, and even the loss of one's employment. In more minor circumstances, our setting boundaries may diminish our freedom and pleasure. Healthy interpersonal boundary keeping can bring loneliness instead of social resources that are precious to many people, especially clergy. Thus, to be a good boundary keeper one must be ready to sustain loss of resources and be comfortable with vulnerability. Virtually

---

1. Kerns, "Why Good Leaders Do Bad Things."

all boundary keeping involves loss, and virtually all boundary violations involve the acquisition of resources of one form or another, including the resource of power. Jesus was right: we must become willing to lose things for the sake of love, even love of self. In the Parable of the Sower (Matt 13:18–13) Jesus notes that "the cares of the world" choke the word of God to the point that it does not yield the fruits of love. These concerns can dim our awareness of the well-being of others. However, we will discover that when we are willing to take a loss on one level, other very important things become possible—for others and sometimes even for ourselves. We will invite you at various points in this process to reflect on your own motives, which can conflict with your own awareness of and prioritizing the needs of others.

How can we possibly counteract these strong forces? We bring to this discussion insights from the relatively new field of behavioral ethics, which is the scientific study of why we act ethically and why and how we act unethically. Most of this research has been done in the field of business. The task for the individual is the same regardless of the setting. We must live more consciously and intentionally, not letting the perverse forces of the psyche or the external organizational culture control us. We must recognize and understand what we are dealing with when we try to love consistently, one moment to the next, in all circumstances and with all people.

As we will discuss at various points throughout the book, living ethically requires that we learn when not to trust our own judgment and what to do instead. Our judgment, according to the research, is often shaped by forces beyond our conscious awareness, in the deep, primitive parts of the mind, where urges and desires activate our outward behaviors, sometimes before conscious decision making can even begin to occur. Ethical decision making is a much slower process than what it takes to generate feelings and urges. Often by the time the conscious mind gets involved, the train has left the station, and the conscious mind is left to construct a rationale for what we are already doing. The result is often self-deception rather than self-revelation.[2] The ego wants to preserve a positive image of the self. So researchers have come to characterize our ethics as being egocentric in nature.[3] Much of what we hear in boundary and ethics discussions is actually ego-based ethical reasoning, even when

2. Tenbrunsel and Messick, "Ethical Fading."

3. Epley and Caruso, "Egocentric Ethics."

it is couched as being based on compassion. For example, a pastor who is uncomfortable with conflict or distress in others will try to justify not insulting a person by requiring a background check. While it sounds caring to do so, it avoids the self-interest that it serves for the pastor.

When we do engage the conscious, rational process of ethical thinking with awareness of our own urges and desires, the result can be what Bazerman, Tenbrunsel, and Wade-Benzoi brilliantly characterize in the title of their article as "negotiating with yourself and losing: making decisions with competing internal preferences."[4] Bazerman and Tenbrunsel note: "Behavioral ethics research supports the argument that most people want to act ethically. Yet we still find ourselves engaging in unethical behavior because of biases that influence our decisions—biases of which we may not be fully aware. These biases affect not only our own behavior, but also our ability to see the unethical behavior of others."[5] So in many cases of decision making about ethical issues, there is very little internal negotiating going on. The self-interest of the ego takes off and musters the support of the rest of the self before our ethical, rational self even knows what is happening. As the phenomenon of ethical fading reveals, the ethical dimension of the self often is defined out of the situation entirely. Sometimes it is stress, especially time pressure, which limits our awareness and excludes ethical considerations. In order to get real negotiating to occur among the various parts of the self, we have to change our relationship to what occurs inside ourselves. In this book we will make this point both early and often.

We can become more consciously aware of what is going on inside ourselves, in order that these events have less control over us. One powerful approach we recommend is some form of meditation or prayer designed to increase awareness. This is different from what many people do for meditation when the motivation is relaxation. Relaxation can help with some things that seriously restrict awareness and thereby also ethical decision making, such as stress and time pressure. On the other hand, relaxation and stress release without increased awareness can simply assist a person in persisting with a life that is not well considered, in the same way that various forms of "numbing out" relaxation do. The purpose of increased awareness is greater self-control and freedom of choice, no longer being controlled by unhealthy habits, urges, or desires.

4. Bazerman et al., "Negotiating with Yourself and Losing."
5. Bazerman and Tenbrunsel, *Blind Spots*, 99.

With comprehensive awareness, we notice our urges and desires and how they contrast with our deeply held values. We have awareness of the present, past, and future. We have awareness of self, others, and God simultaneously.

Behavioral ethics researchers have some recommendations that have guided us in writing this book. Bazerman and Tenbrunsel, for example, conclude from their research that organizations will benefit from standards of practice that identify separately what is unethical from what is ethically desirable.[6] We will highlight how our biblical heritage is a resource for the church to do just that. We will pair "thou shalt not" with a positively stated alternative. In our final chapter we will summarize recommended practices. Bazerman and Tenbrunsel recommend a zero-tolerance policy for unethical behavior in order to reduce uncertainty. Furthermore, they also recommend continuing to move the standards to higher levels, which challenges us to grow ethically. Without that, as their research suggests, there is a tendency for standards of conduct to degrade—something we can identify also in the church. We note how Jesus raised the standards of the Ten Commandments. While there can be value in seeing the gospel as relief from the law, in fact Jesus raised the bar considerably in characterizing the alternative kingdom of God—particularly in the Sermon on the Mount.[7]

Bazerman and Tenbrunsel also note the following risk factors for unethical behavior within organizations: uncertainty in the system, isolation, and time pressure. Many of our churches and church leaders rate high on these risk factors. We recommend, as does the research, deliberately referring to the ethical standards in routine ways, in order to keep them in our conscious awareness. We also recommend particular practices that can help accomplish this same goal. Mary C. Gentile adds another useful approach from the business realm.[8] She teaches people to practice speaking up when they encounter ethically questionable practices, in order to increase the likelihood that theirs will become more

6. Ibid.

7. The authors choose to employ the term "kingdom" as the primary translation of the New Testament word *basilea*. Readers should note that in many places we employ the term "shalom" as a synonym for "kingdom." While "kingdom" may seem antiquated to some, it preserves the comprehensive claim and political character of what Jesus meant by God's kingdom activity in the world. In the New Testament, the kingdom is not a place but a mode of God's transforming presence and rule over all creation.

8. Gentile, *Giving Voice to Values*.

ethical communities. As Gentile notes, confidence that we can address unethical behavior in others and in our organizations will help us be more consciously aware of the ethical violations happening around us. This makes good sense psychologically. Her approach is elegant and brilliant. Gentile and others make the observation that the people who stand up to unethical behavior are people who were taught to expect that they would have to at some point in their lives. For Christians charged with living the alterative kingdom of God, how could it be otherwise?

James L. Bailey speaks of the alternative kingdom of God as a "contrast community."[9] The findings of behavioral ethics support the value of making explicit the contrasts between self-interest and best practices in our decision making. We recommend that readers begin to practice examining their ethical lives according to best practices while reading this book. When making decisions that affect others, ask yourself these questions: (1) What do I want, based on my feelings and desires? (2) Why do I want that? (3) What would it do for me? (4) How strongly do I desire that? (5) How important does it feel to me? (6) Why do I feel so strongly? (7) What best practices are called for and why they are they needed? and (8) Why are these best practices so important? By asking these questions before engaging in potentially unethical behavior, we let the rational, ethical part of the brain have a better chance of influencing our behavior. Throughout the book, and especially in our final chapter, we offer best practices as a resource to help guide us in good decision making.

It is hard to live in contrast with our environment, especially the contemporary social environment. We are strongly influenced by the social norms around us. For this reason behavioral ethicists recognize the need to create an informal culture of high ethical standards in our organizations (congregations, in the case of this book) in all aspects of their functioning. Formal codes of ethics and conduct, while essential, have less sway on us than the informal culture. You, our reader, are co-architect of the informal culture of your congregation and in the larger church—you, your coworkers, friends, colleagues and peers. We welcome your interest and participation in helping make our congregations more healthy and vibrant centers of love.

We express our heartfelt appreciation to those who reviewed our manuscript and offered constructive suggestions that have enhanced our work: Robert Albers, Wayne Menking, and Gary Schoener. We also

9. Bailey, *Contrast Community*.

are deeply grateful to Michael Cooper-White, President of the Lutheran Theological Seminary at Gettysburg, and Pamela Cooper-White, Christiane Brooks Johnson Professor of Psychology and Religion at Union Theological Seminary, for sharing their insights in the foreword and offering constructive advice for improving the book. We also offer thanks to the many people whose work we have built upon (as represented in references and bibliography) as well as to countless unnamed others from whom we have learned. The authors express our special gratitude to Halcyon Bjornstad for her assistance in proofreading and indexing. The editors and staff of Cascade Books have been excellent to work with in the editing and publication process, and we are grateful to each of them. The authors especially desire to express thanks to their wives: Arden to his wife, Linda Mahlberg, for her patience and support through the process of devoting many hours to this book; Craig to his wife, Cathy Nessan, for her steadfastness and support. We dedicate this book to those who have requested a resource like this, in the hope that it will contribute to forward movement for an ethical church. We especially dedicate this book to our children, whose generation calls us to accountability for bequeathing to them a church that more adequately demonstrates the integrity necessary to serve as a life-giving community for them, their peers, and future generations: Nathaniel and Nora Mahlberg; Benjamin, Nathaniel, Sarah, Andrew, Jessica, and Mary Nessan.

PART 1

Defining and Protecting Integrity through Boundaries

1

The Necessity of Boundaries for Creating and Sustaining Identity and Effective Mission

SCENARIO ONE: PASTOR A AND PASTOR B

EARLY IN HER MINISTRY at Grace Church, Pastor B. began to visit members who were unable to attend church. She was the new Associate Pastor and was eager to meet everyone. The pastor rang the doorbell at one of her first calls. A frail yet spirited elderly woman came to the door. "Are you Dottie?" Pastor B asked politely. She introduced herself and asked to come in. When they sat down, she said: "Everyone has told me, 'You will enjoy getting to know Dottie.'"

"Actually, Pastor, my name is Dorothy. I've always loved that name. It was my grandmother's name, but everyone calls me Dottie."

"Well," replied Pastor B, "Dorothy is a beautiful name. And, actually, I prefer to be called 'Pastor Blanchard,' if you don't mind."

Pastor B. realized that she was in the same boat as Dorothy. Her name was Susan Blanchard. When the call committee decided to extend her the call to be Grace Church's first Associate Pastor to work with Pastor Alvez, a member of the committee declared excitedly, "Now we have a 'Pastor A' and a 'Pastor B!'" Everyone laughed. But the names stuck! When Pastor Blanchard raised her disquiet in private with Pastor Alvez, he brushed it off. He thought it was cute. She, however, felt uneasy, like she was not in control of her own identity. Should she assert herself over this issue with her new colleague and congregation? "Pastor B," in

11

contrast to "Pastor A," was by definition second-best. It was not that she needed to be first, but according to her understanding this was supposed to be a nonhierarchical copastorate.

Pastor Blanchard came to discover that many of the members of Grace and also many members of the local community had been given nicknames by others, like "Stub," "Baldy," "Skinny," and "Nutsy." When she began to inquire in private, many of them did not like their nicknames but nonetheless had resigned themselves to them.

"She'll always be Dottie to me," the church secretary said when Pastor Blanchard told her about Dorothy's preference. Names convey messages and communicate images. "Dorothy" does not evoke the same meanings and images as "Dottie." Pastor Blanchard did not like the implications of being labeled "Pastor B."

Who has the right to decide what one is called? This is a boundary issue of great significance. The question about who has the right to define one's core identity in life leads us into the central theme of this book: the myriad boundaries questions we encounter in Christian community. Naming others can be a form of domination. Conquering cultures routinely rename those they have come to dominate, instead of using the native people's own names for themselves. Cult leaders often rename their members as part of asserting their control. Bullies engage in name-calling to intimidate their victims. One of the first steps leading to dehumanization and violence is stealing the name of another person or group and substituting a degrading epithet (for example, "cockroach" or "vermin") for their valued name.

As Pastor Blanchard considered the issue of naming more fully, she became disturbed by the realization that she, Pastor Alvez, and their clergy colleagues had been educated, trained, and socialized to label parishioners. As Pastor Alvez was orienting Pastor Blanchard, he said: "We do have three alligators in the congregation and one clergy wannabe." He proceeded to identify the people he felt had a history of criticizing their pastors in ways that did not seem could ever be satisfied except by their removal; he also talked about those members who sometimes could be satisfied with specific things but who were preoccupied with figuring out how they could always get what they wanted. This type of labeling (alligators, clergy killers, and clergy wannabes) reduces ambiguity and complexity. It makes us feel like we have got the person figured out. But once we have categorized another, we see and relate to the label and lose site of the person in all of their rich complexity. Therefore, labeling is a violation of a person's identity boundary.

BOUNDARIES, BOUNDARIES EVERYWHERE!

Boundaries are fundamental structures that establish and preserve identity. Boundaries protect the essential nature of things, while also contributing to their definition.[1] *A guiding question for respecting boundaries is, who does this belong to?* The Ten Commandments begin with an identity boundary. We are commanded to know and acknowledge who God is, as well as to remain clear about who God is not. It is God alone who defines God's nature, not us. We are neither to construct our own image of God nor to behave as if anything other than God is God. We are not to use the name of God in ways that diminish God's being or identity. We are to use God's name to preserve God's being and identity for us and for others. God's identity belongs to God, not us.

Similarly, we are also commanded to respect the identity of others. Bearing false witness is one form of creating a false image of the other. This includes saying a person's name with a negative inflection. We are also enjoined to respect our own identity as a person created in God's image.[2] Jesus encouraged each one of us, "Let your light shine!" In the Parable of the Wise and Foolish Bridesmaids, when the women who let their lamps go out came to join the party, they were told, "Truly I tell you, I do not know you" (Matt 25:12). Attitudes and practices that protect and nurture our core identities are essential to living as Christ calls us to live.

One of our deepest longings is to express who we are: to be known, understood, and accepted just as we are. When other people project their own images upon us and have agendas for who they want us to be, we feel unsafe and withhold who we really are. By adolescence, most children who are still creating stories or artwork as a form of self-expression have stopped showing them to anyone else. It is so easy to form our own images of others and to justify them to fulfill our own agendas. For example, a pastor might peg a young person as a future pastor and become overinvested in that outcome. The young person would not want to disappoint such an influential person in his or her life. When others act like they are authorities about who we are, on some level we feel we are unsafe, even if

1. Cf. Olsen and Devor, *Saying No to Say Yes*, 4–7.
2. Harbaugh et al., *Covenants and Care*, 119–21.

their image of us is flattering: "I can tell that you are the kind of girl who will make a man very happy." On the other hand, when others criticize us, they attack our very being. One's identity is unsafe in either case. Who does one's identity belong to?

While we are quick to form impressions and to set agendas for others, a part of us longs to know others deeply for who they are. Allowing the self to be "self" and the other to be "other" establishes the delightful conditions for the meeting of an I and a Thou. How we treat a stranger respectfully becomes the model for how we treat each and every person, since here we approach the other without presuming already to know who they are. We ask their name and invite them to tell us about themselves. We err in such encounters, however, if we too quickly form an impression, thereby creating a false image, one based upon our own construction. Exploring who others are in deliberate conversation by listening to them gives us the benefit of an entirely different way of seeing things, something wholly "other" from our own hasty perceptions. While the impulse of the anxious mind is to reject what is foreign and different, the secure and open mind responds to differences with respect, fascination, and curiosity.

Respecting boundaries is so essential to the spiritual life that it is a key part of the prayer Jesus taught his followers: "and forgive us our trespasses, as we forgive those who have trespassed against us." This is territorial language, the language of boundaries and borders. While the translation can be "sins," "debts," or "trespasses," we note that the major thrust of the Ten Commandments has to do with disturbing or violating established boundaries, which the word "trespass" reflects.

Various types of boundaries are associated with different parts of our being, as we will explore in the chapters ahead. We have a physical boundary that protects our health, which, if violated, will result in death. We are commanded not to kill. Life does not belong to us—it belongs to God. It is not ours to take. We are not to take from others their possessions or their loved ones. We are even commanded not to steal with our imaginations—not to covet or desire what others have. Does it not feel like a kind of theft when we have something precious and sense that someone else wants to possess it instead of being happy for us? "Do not commit adultery!" Again hear the warning about a boundary violation. With marital infidelity, you are not just going where you do not belong (even if invited); you are stealing from your own marriage what rightly belongs to it—vital energy whose absence damages the marriage, even if the partner is not consciously aware.[3] We are also commanded to protect the boundary around sacred time—to keep the Sabbath holy, uncontaminated by thoughts about work, outside responsibilities, or the secular values of the dominant culture that distract us from the sacred values of the culture of God.[4]

The commandments have to do with respecting boundaries. So they tell us what not to do instead of telling us what to do. Thereby, they delineate boundaries in ways that would not be as clear, if the same content were merely put in positive terms. For example, "Do not covet what belongs to your neighbor," clarifies a boundary. Taking the same content and putting it positively could translate as: "Be grateful for what you have." This may communicate somewhat the same idea but misses the lesson about boundaries: To whom does this belong? Put even more positively, God could have commanded us to be happy for our neighbor for the good things they have to enjoy. Again this surely is a part of what it means to fully love our neighbor, but it misses the truth about boundaries.

Beyond the discipline of boundary keeping, translating the commandments positively as did Jesus *builds bridges across boundaries* that would not be possible without first respecting the boundaries for what they are. The commandment to "love the Lord your God with all your heart, and with all your soul, and with all your mind, and with all your strength" (Mark 12:30) builds a bridge to God; God is accessible and can be totally engaged. To "love your neighbor as yourself" (Mark 12:31) reveals the bridge not only between people, but between us and Christ. To recognize that how we treat the least important person (Matt 25:40) is the same as how we treat Christ requires both a boundary and a bridge. Boundaries beget bridges. Respecting the boundaries defined in the Ten Commandments, while adding love, strengthens each person's uniqueness, their capacity to love, serve, celebrate, and create, giving us the conditions ripe for spiritual community.

Spiritual community depends on bridges between and among us. Paul taught the followers of Jesus to understand themselves as a mystical body, the very body of Christ. Each one has a unique and important function that when linked to others is like the complex organism of the

---

3. Harbaugh et al., *Covenants and Care*, 123–24.
4. Brueggemann, *Sabbath as Resistance*, chap. 1.

human body.[5] To live as members of Christ's body requires both the ability to be a unique person, on the one hand, and the capacity to unite with others without damaging them, on the other. The standards are high and the challenge significant.

We all know what it feels like to be violated. If you have ever had a purse stolen or your car broken into, you have felt violated. If you have ever had people say hurtful things about you to others or misrepresent you, as happens in gossip, you have felt a boundary violation. Gossip is by nature problematic when it comes to boundaries. Barbara J. Blodgett defines *gossip* as "informal, evaluative discourse about someone not present who is a member of the speaker's social group. These features—the informality, the absence of the person being talked about, the evaluative or judgmental nature of the discourse, and the relational context—are ones I take to be necessary and sufficient features of gossip."[6] Perhaps you have experienced even worse violations. It is now widely recognized that abusive violations of a person's integrity can wound that person in profound ways for a very long time.[7] As a consequence of abuse, parts of the self can be cut off and the individual can turn against themselves or others. Among the many consequences, the abuse can so negatively impact a person's relationship with God that it impairs their capacity to trust the gospel.[8]

A car that has a few things wrong with it can run safely at forty-five miles an hour. When you try to drive it ninety miles per hour, however, it will perform badly and may even be dangerous. The demands of the godly life are at least that challenging. Every part of the vehicle needs to be in top condition. Therefore we can cultivate awareness of and care even for subtle boundaries, not just the obvious ones. As scientists learn more about the impact of boundary violations on our lives, they coin new terms: "microviolations," "micro-insults," and "micro-incursions."[9] These are the kinds of behaviors that are not easily detected but do have significant impact on our sense of safety, our willingness to disclose ourselves freely, and our ability to do our best work. These relatively small, apparently minor, violations damage our spirit, especially when they are

---

5. Nessan, *Shalom Church*, 34–36.

6. Blodgett, *Lives Entrusted*, 88.

7. See Fortune, *Love Does No Harm*, 35, for reflections on the meaning of "harm."

8. Fortune, *Is Nothing Sacred?*, 110–11.

9. Cf. Sue, *Microaggressions and Marginality*.

persistent. What we would call toxic environments at work, home, or church result from accumulating subtle violations. Such events seem so small that people can disagree about whether one person is being overly sensitive or the other person is being overly insensitive. Is it something, or is it nothing?

Before mechanical sensors of air quality were invented, coal miners would bring a caged canary with them into the mine, because canaries are more sensitive to dangerous gasses than humans. As long as the canary was singing, the miners were fine. But as soon as the canary stopped singing, the miners knew to get out fast. Like the proverbial canary in the coal mine, some people are more sensitive than the rest of us when it comes to toxicity in the psychological and spiritual environment. These persons are more strongly affected by attitudes, language, and behaviors that are actual boundary violations, though these violations may not be so obvious to others. Others might regard these people as being thin-skinned or overly sensitive, especially with regard to behavior that seems to have become the norm. People who grew up in family systems where boundaries were not respected can become numb to violations of their own boundaries and to their violating the boundaries of others.[10] The sensors inside us need to be cleaned, repaired, and activated to their full capacity.

How many rabbis and priests in Jesus's time had some minor, nagging qualms about money changing in the temple? Undoubtedly there were some, but most would have been shocked by Jesus's bold assertion that the integrity of the temple was being violated by commercial activity that had become routinized. Habituation dulls our capacity to sense harmful elements. As rust weakens iron, so microviolations weaken the spirit and impair our capacity to do God's work, especially when they are allowed to continue unchecked. Attending to micro-issues proactively allows us to get better and better at Christ-like community. We will not "let our light shine," as Jesus urged us, if we fear someone around us will disrespect or invalidate us.[11]

Respecting others involves a sense of the sacred. The apostle Paul tells us that the human body is the temple of the Holy Spirit (1 Cor 6:19). My body is not wholly mine. We are advised to approach the body as sacred space. Thomas Merton also spoke about the sanctity of human

10. Halstead, *From Stuck to Unstuck*, chap. 3.
11. Bailey, *Contrast Community*, chap. 3.

subjectivity.[12] Our subjectivity is central to who we are. It is the experience of interior dwelling that we have been given, and which we create and occupy. It includes our attitudes, values, impressions, perceptions, beliefs, feelings, and thoughts. It also includes our sacred experiences, entrusted to us by the Holy One. We treat our own subjectivity as being sacred, when we do not contaminate our state of consciousness through negativity toward self or others.

Dorothy accurately detected that her identity boundary had been violated when people renamed her instead of granting her the simple courtesy of asking her how she wished to be called. She respected her boundary by telling Pastor Blanchard how she wished to be called but failed to protect her identity boundary with others, perhaps sensing that her preference would not be respected. The result: Dorothy was not as fully at home in Christian community as she might have been. Nor was Pastor Blanchard, who also chose not to make an issue of her moniker after she failed to get the support of Pastor Alvez. Because of his expressed attitude, Pastor Blanchard faced the risk of alienating him and others in the congregation simply by exercising the right to choose her own name. The result? She also became tentative in other areas of self-expression. She treated those people differently, whom Pastor Alvez labeled as alligators and clergy wannabes, interpreting their behavior otherwise than the behavior of those not so labeled. Even microviolations have real consequences for the body of Christ.

PROTECTING AND PRESERVING THE IDENTITY AND MISSION OF THE CHURCH

Boundary issues are pervasive in the life of the church. Often when we hear the word, "boundary," we think chiefly, if not exclusively, about sexual boundaries in ministry. God knows that maintaining clear and proactive sexual boundaries is an imperative of the first order for healthy ministry.[13] The extent and magnitude of sexual boundary violations throughout the Christian churches has permanently harmed countless victims and their families—women, men, and children—each one precious to God. The failure of the churches to hold leaders accountable for sexual abuse and to remove offenders from public service has further

---

12. Merton, *Seeds of Contemplation*, chap. 2.

13. Cf. Hopkins and Laaser, eds., *Restoring the Soul of a Church*.

complicated the church's integrity. Moreover, these abuses have brought scandal and suspicion to everything the church does. This book certainly advocates for vigilance and accountability in maintaining and respecting sexual boundaries at every level of the church's life—beginning with the ethical responsibilities of the clergy.[14]

At the same time that we insist on clarity about sexual boundaries, in this book we extend the argument for wise boundaries to encompass a broad array of church practices by *including all church members* (laity, lay staff, and clergy) and *every dimension of human life* (thought, word, and deed). For church professionals not to exploit church members for their own ends is only the beginning. In virtually every human encounter and human activity in the life of the church, we either express the identity of the church by living according to the values of God's kingdom or not. Are we being the church, or are we being something else? There are necessary boundaries that are rightly observed, if we are to relate to one another with the respect due to those made in the image of God and redeemed by Jesus Christ. What is more, it is crucial that we recognize and tend these interpersonal boundaries for the sake of preserving and safeguarding the integrity of the church's core mission of bringing the Gospel of Jesus Christ to the world in word and deed.

Boundaries can be detected at every human interface. As we have already seen, there are boundaries that involve "naming" and "labeling" persons. Furthermore, there are many boundaries involving the use of language in appropriate and edifying ways. There are boundaries involving inflection of voice and innuendo of speech. There are boundaries entailed in written communication, both private and public: handwritten notes, newsletter announcements, professional correspondence, e-mails, messages social networks, blogs, text messages, and a host of other electronic means. There are boundaries involving propriety and respect in the assembly for Christian worship and at other church gatherings for congregational, council, and committee meetings. There are boundaries involved in childcare and youth ministry. How we do these things with integrity as church will be different than how others might do them in secular society.

Pastors must follow accepted professional practices in visitation, counseling, and all other private meetings with people. There are boundaries involving a wide range of public behaviors: for example, what one

---

14. Cf. Jung and Stephans, eds., *Professional Sexual Ethics*.

buys and where one purchases it, what movies one attends and which DVDs one rents, or whether one drinks alcohol in public. Pastoral ministry is public in a way that requires careful attention to boundary crossings that might compromise the effectiveness of the pastoral role and the church's ministry.[15] Maintaining clear boundaries can assist all members of the church to preserve clarity about roles, avoiding dual relationships and role confusion. We will go so far in this book as to suggest that we maintain proper boundaries by reflecting not only on our words and actions but even on how we 'think about' others in a salutary way. This is only a beginning list of how defining boundaries affects our life together with others in the church.

Because the range of issues involving boundaries is so broad, it is important to offer a working definition of the term 'boundaries'. *Boundaries protect the essential nature of persons and things, while at the same time contributing to their definition. Boundaries are therefore necessary for the faithful expression of identity. In the life of the church, boundaries are intentional limits placed on thoughts, words, and deeds to safeguard the protection of persons and to guard and protect the integrity of the church's identity and mission. Furthermore, boundaries set limits on behavior in order to protect things of value.* What is at stake in tending boundaries is preserving the integrity of each person as made in God's image, the value of holy things set aside for God's purposes, the identity of the church as the body of Christ, and the mission of the church in extending God's reign. Conversely, boundary violations put at risk the integrity of persons, the proper use of holy things, the core identity of the church, and the church's mission.

Boundaries protect persons and thus allow for the faithful expression of their true identities as members of the body of Christ! Each person has been created in the image of God and is precious to Jesus Christ. For this reason, it is essential that we relate to other persons in thought, word, and deed with the respect owed to those with such status. It is now widely recognized that traumatizing a person by violating their boundaries through abuse can wound that person in profound ways for a very long time. Furthermore, research has shown that abusing children negatively impacts their relationship with God as adults.[16] Again, as rust weakens iron, microviolations weaken the spirit, especially when the microviola-

15. Everist and Nessan, *Transforming Leadership*, 116–17.

16. Salter et al., "Development of Sexually Abusive Behavior in Sexually Victimized Males," 471–76.

tions are allowed to continue. Even micro-incursions demoralize people's vitality. It is wise to assume that when someone objects to something, even where we see no problem at all, at least a microviolation may have taken place. Listening to those who complain or express hurt feelings is one way to increase our own sensitivity, asking questions in order to see things from another's point of view. If someone objects, it is wise to assume they have a valid point, even if you do not readily understand it. If we are the offending person, this means checking our defensiveness to consider what the other is expressing.

Moving from micro- to extreme violations, such as when a person has been assaulted, the impact is likely to include dissociation to reduce the pain.[17] Dissociation is a disengagement from what is happening. The victim of an extreme violation becomes somewhat, if not totally, unconscious and may not even remember what happened. If conscious, the victim becomes numb. As they experience the violation, they may feel like they have become an outside observer of what is happening to them, as if they are watching someone else. They may literally experience being outside their body. While this is extreme, micro-incursions have the same effect on a smaller scale. If we undergo a microviolation, to some degree we become less present and engaged. We may freeze up at a church meeting and be unable to fully participate because of the alarm that is sounding inside us in response to critical language or harsh tones.

A member might hesitate to participate fully in a fellowship after witnessing a pastor exploiting relationships with members—for example, pursuing members for private business interests. Agents at church-based insurance companies may seek privileged access to members or membership lists. Or a pastor might seek a clergy discount from a church member who works at a car dealership. Here the relationship between pastor and parishioner is exploited in the interest of financial benefit. This boundary also is obscured when church members in business voluntarily offer clergy discounts or other favors to their pastor.

Boundaries protect holy things! While not as damaging as infractions involving persons, boundary violations can also involve the misuse of property. For example, the church council president decides, without asking permission, to use the fellowship hall for a private Christmas party for her family and friends. Or a member who lives in the neighborhood borrows the church's lawn mower, and so it is missing when a member

17. Cf. Karjala, *Understanding Trauma and Dissociation.*

of the property committee comes to use it to mow the church's lawn. Or the chair of the property committee enters the parsonage when no one is home, in order to borrow coffee creamer for a church meeting. Or the pastor borrows folding tables and chairs for a family graduation party and returns the tables dirty, and one of the chairs with a broken chair leg. In each of these cases, self-interest leads to disrespect for things set aside for the church's 'holy' use.

Boundaries preserve the church's identity! What is the church? The church is the people of God, the communion of saints, the fellowship of the baptized, and the body of Christ. Each of these images points to the intrinsic identity of the church in relationship to the triune God. The church discovers its true identity exclusively grounded in God's grace revealed in the person and work of Jesus Christ by the power of the Holy Spirit.[18] The church lives in obedience to the Great Commandment: to love God with all one's heart, soul, mind, and strength and to love the neighbor as oneself. One constant temptation in the life of the church is to substitute some other identity to replace core Christian identity. Thereby the church serves as a social outlet for the enjoyment of the members, or as an organization to provide services for those who pay their dues. Or the church gets construed as a business venture that only has value when it makes a profit. Or the church exists primarily to perpetuate the building and provide a cemetery. So many false identities threaten to overtake the church's identity as the people of God in Christ Jesus! Good boundaries clarify, protect, and preserve the true nature of church so that it can fulfill its mission of living the Great Commandment.

Boundaries preserve the church's mission! The mission of the Christian church is to proclaim the gospel of Jesus Christ, to serve a world full of neighbors as disciples of Jesus Christ, and to care for God's creation as faithful stewards. The church exists not for its own self-interest but to mediate God's life-giving presence to the world through the message of the gospel and ministry of service for the well-being of others. Primary venues for the church to embody this mission are evangelism, ecumenism, global service, and social ministry. Wherever church leaders or members distort Christ's mission to serve self-interest, a boundary has been crossed and the intended purpose of the church becomes compromised. One of the great challenges that undermines the integrity of the church and its mission is the misrepresentation of the gospel by those

18. Nessan, *Beyond Maintenance to Mission*, 6–10.

who represent it publicly. Hypocrisy by church members and misconduct by clergy obscure the intention of the gospel as Christ's message of unconditional forgiveness, mercy, and grace. "If any of you put a stumbling block before one of these little ones who believe in me, it would be better for you if a great millstone were fastened around your neck and you were drowned in the depth of the sea" (Matt 18:6).

THE PURPOSE OF THE CHURCH AND ITS MINISTRY

Boundaries are essential to the life of the church and its ministry, in order to preserve the church's core identity and mission. There are a variety of ways to describe the basic purpose of the church. Consider the following affirmations: The church exists to follow the Great Commandment of loving God and loving the neighbor as oneself; the church serves as an instrument for the arrival of God's kingdom in this world; the church lives for the sake of proclaiming to others the good news about Jesus Christ as Lord and Savior of the world; the church seeks to follow the way of Jesus Christ through faithful discipleship; the church is the body of Christ in the world and makes Christ present to others. Each of these descriptions reveals aspects of the church's true identity and mission. In concise formulations, each of these statements expresses the spiritual purpose of the church: how the church serves God's intention to bring life, wholeness, fulfillment, and salvation to the world.

There are several paradigmatic ways the church incarnates this fundamental purpose, enacting its identity and mission—through worship, prayer, education, community life, stewardship, evangelizing, ecumenism, global connections, and social ministry.[19] The center of the church's life is in the communal gathering of God's people for worship.[20] At worship we reclaim our identity in Christ and become the people God intends us to be—through confession and absolution, praise, hearing the Word, voicing our convictions in the creed, praying, sharing the peace, presenting an offering, breaking bread, and receiving blessing. The pattern of the Christian life is rehearsed in the things of worship: trusting God's promises for our lives, learning to praise God, attending to God's Word, becoming those who care for the things for which we pray, shar-

19. Ibid., 8–10.
20. Ibid., chap. 4.

ing God's peace with one another and the world, generously stewarding the gifts God has bestowed, and partaking of the Lord's Table where all are welcome and there is enough for all. We are sent from worship to be agents of God's shalom in our daily lives.

The church also exists to pray for the needs of all people and the creation itself. We pray for God's mercy and healing in a broken world, where suffering threatens to overwhelm us. The church teaches members the way of discipleship as a primary educational task. At church we learn what it means to follow Jesus in our daily lives. By living with one another in community, the church learns what it means to live under the cross, where the weak and lonely, the sick and marginal ones have privileged place.[21] In this community we recall that it is the Crucified One who binds us together in love. We learn to experience Jesus Christ himself as we relate to one another in the church and as we go out into the local community to encounter Jesus Christ in the least of these. Moreover, the church knows the true meaning of stewardship, where everything we receive is a gift given to us from God's generosity. As stewards the very posture of our lives is that of thanksgiving for all the kindness God has showered upon us.

In its life of service, the church responds to God's goodness by sharing the good news of Jesus Christ in words and deeds. Evangelizing involves the church in speaking boldly, genuinely, and authentically about what God has done for us in Jesus Christ. Christian people are to testify to others about what God has done in their lives in order that others might believe (Rom 10:10–13). The work of evangelizing encompasses both personal conversations with others and testimonies given in public worship services. Glory is also given to God wherever Christians of different traditions and denominations are reconciled to one another as brothers and sisters. Beyond the scandal of denominational divisions, Jesus prays that the church be one (John 17:20–21). Therefore ecumenical relations belong centrally to the church's mission. Christians also build connections with one another across the globe in partnerships and cooperation that mutually enhances our life together. The catholicity of the church is manifest wherever Christians throughout the world pray for one another, join in worship together, participate in Christ-centered community, and live in mutual service to one another. Lastly, the church partakes in social ministry—both acts of charity to relieve human suffering and the work

21. For a pastoral approach to the theology of the cross, see Menking, *When All Else Fails*, 74–81.

of advocacy to transform the structures and policies that hold people in subjugation. Through these manifold expressions the church fulfills its God-given purpose.

Those who serve as ministers of the church—meaning both the clergy and laity—have as their Christian vocation the fulfillment of the church's purpose in the various ways described in the previous paragraphs. Biblically and theologically, these are the reasons why the church exists: to reveal the presence and the way of God to others in this world. For the laity, this means trusting the good news of Jesus Christ at the center of life, and following the way of Jesus Christ in discipleship by thought, word, and deed. The Christian vocation encompasses all arenas of life: one's family, the workplace, at church, and as member of local and global communities.[22] As a Christian, one's very identity is centered in Jesus Christ and one's whole existence is offered as spiritual worship of God (Rom 12:1–2).

Pastors have a particular calling among the baptized: to serve as ministers of God's Word and sacraments among God's people. This vocation involves faithful teaching and preaching of the Christian faith, stewardship of worship among the Christian community, and sharing the presence of Christ with others in pastoral care. Because of the nature of professional ministry and how these leaders represent God before the world, pastors and other ministers who work for the church are held to a high ethical standard. The failure to reflect the highest Christian values on the part of pastors and other ministers brings special scandal upon the church and its mission. Without expecting Christian perfectionism, there is an expectation that both Christian laity and especially Christian pastors and lay professionals represent with integrity the reality of God's own ministry in the world.

Boundaries are designed to safeguard the church's identity and mission. Worship takes place for the praise of God, not to sell products. Prayer is for entreaty to God, not gossip. Christian education is for learning the meaning of discipleship, not bragging about one's accomplishments. Christian community is for the mutual strengthening of the members in the faith, not cruising for a date. Stewardship is about gratitude to God, not for tax benefits, gaining influence with the pastor and congregation, or pride about one's generosity. Evangelizing is for sharing the good news, not manipulating people with guilt. Ecumenism is for

22. Fortin, *Centered Life*, 83–84.

building up the whole body of Christ, not demonstrating the superiority of one's own tradition. Global partnerships are for mutual accompaniment in the Christian faith, not creating dependency relationships. Social ministry is for sharing with those in need, not obtaining a sense of one's own righteousness or the promotion of political agendas.

The church's central purpose—to worship God and minister to the world in the name of Jesus Christ—is undercut by thoughts, words, and actions that compromise or contradict the stated purpose of the church as articulated in this chapter. When Christians, whether ministers or laity, engage in domestic abuse, cheat on taxes, operate according to unfair business practices, discriminate in hiring, tell lies, fail to maintain the safety of an automobile, or litter in public places—each of these behaviors violates a boundary by misrepresenting the will of God for human life in the spirit of Jesus. Another cause for consternation is valuing secondary identities over the primary one. This especially includes the privileging of certain ethnic and cultural heritages over baptismal identity, whereas it is baptism that properly provides the fundamental basis of Christian community. Eric H. F. Law comments:

> To be interculturally sensitive, we need to examine the internal instinctual part of our own culture. This means revealing unconscious values and thought patterns so that we will not simply react from our cultural instinct. The more we learn about our internal culture, the more we are aware of how our cultural values and thought patterns differ from others. Knowing this difference will help us make self-adjustments in order to live peacefully with people from other cultures.[23]

Engaging in intentional processes to increase diversity in congregational life must become an urgent priority.[24] Other secondary matters also are often sources of conflict in congregations, such as conflict over music and styles of worship. Often when people feel loss about their secondary identities, they do not know who they are anymore and fall out of touch with their primary identity, similar to how a person may feel lost after retirement. Such behaviors contradict Christian identity and obscure God's purposes for the world.

Likewise when Christian pastors or ministers neglect their families, fail to pay their bills, manipulate their relationships with others out of

---

23. Law, *Wolf Shall Dwell with the Lamb*, 9.
24. Cf. Law, *Sacred Acts, Holy Change*.

self-interest, misrepresent their competence, break confidences, exhibit professional jealousy, complain about parishioners to their colleagues, or display rage in public, such behaviors contradict their public vocation as representatives of God and bring scandal upon the church in its professed identity and mission.[25] These examples illustrate the variety of ways that Christian pastors and ministers can overstep boundaries to the detriment of the church's identity and mission. The Christian life—for laity, pastors, and other ministers—is abounding with ethical boundaries to preserve the church in fulfilling its central purpose of bearing witness to the reality of God in this world.

Becoming "canaries in the church" requires us to keep our eye on the church's core identity and mission so that we can better know how to fulfill it, detect what is harmful, and keep ourselves from violating it. At the close of this chapter we have mentioned examples of how personal interests that can conflict with the church's core identity and mission. Many of these will be explored in the remainder of this book. Having introduced in this chapter particular facets of the boundaries needful for preserving the identity and purpose of the church, we next discuss boundaries in relation to the matter of entrustment: the imperative that the church be a safe place for us to be in Christian community together.

25. Bush, *Gentle Shepherding*, chap. 2.

2

Entrustment

SCENARIO TWO: CONFIDENTIALITY BREECH

THE EVENING AFTER A youth event as she was relaxing, Marge shared with her husband, Larry, how upset she was with the new youth leader. She complained that he was disorganized and immature. She did not give any details but simply shared how upsetting the youth outing was for her. Maybe she was just in a bad mood, she wondered aloud. They then went on to discuss other things before going to bed.

The following morning, Larry stopped for coffee at the local restaurant and saw Elle, who invited him to join her at her table. Elle is a member of the Youth Ministry Committee. As they talked, Elle shared with Larry how excited she was with the new youth leader and the creative ideas and talents he brings. Larry shared with her Marge's negative impressions of him. Elle asked for details, but Larry only had Marge's generalizations and conclusions to share. Elle did not like Marge and did not trust her. After the coffee, Elle promptly called Clarissa, the council representative, and warned her that Marge and Larry were trying to get rid of the new youth director. Clarissa called Marge and confronted her with the charge.

All these people were affected by information about Marge's subjective state and did different things with it. When Marge shared her feelings with her husband, Larry, she assumed he would not tell anyone else and not make anything of it. For her, venting was the end of it. The matter was so unimportant to her that she did not even clarify that she did not want Larry to tell anyone else. She just assumed that Larry understood where she was coming from and that she could trust Larry to not violate the implicit conditions under which she was sharing with him.

When talking with Elle, Larry treated Marge's sharing as something of his own, essentially hijacking it, an appropriate description even though his intentions were favorable toward Marge. The term *hijacking* applies here because he took the material she shared, which belonged to her, and made it his own, grabbing ownership, and feeling free to make his own decisions about its use. While he was not completely sure that Marge would be fine with his passing along her feelings, he believed it was important that a member of the Youth Committee know that there was some disgruntlement about the new youth leader. Larry fell prey to the temptation of "substitution of judgment." He substituted his own judgment in place of Marge's.

Elle, who neither liked Marge nor trusted her, hijacked Larry's sharing and used it for her own ends, which were controlled by her feelings of dislike and distrust. She then reframed the material with a new spin: "Marge and Larry are trying to get rid of the new youth director." Her motive was to stop them by generating negative feelings toward them. Elle believed she was doing the right thing in trying to protect the youth director.

Clarissa, the council member, also took ownership of the material by making her own judgment about what to do with it. Elle did not want her to confront Marge, suspecting that the source of the information would be traced to her.

THE NATURE OF ENTRUSTMENT

Our God-given identity is something we are entrusted to claim and protect. We are entrusted with the care of our bodies, our minds, our perceptions (insights and concerns), our passions, our spirits, and with all of the resources at our disposal. We are also entrusted with the care of others—their bodies, their minds, their perceptions (insights and concerns), their passions, their spirits and their resources—alongside other responsibilities we have assumed. We are also entrusted with God's intentions and mission for our lives. We are called to live out faithfully the Great Commission. In this chapter we will look at the process of entrustment, what it means to be entrusted, and what it takes to be faithful to that trust.[1]

Entrustment is not a process that transfers ownership and rights to another. It is a process of placing something in another's care. The rights are retained by the owner of the material, whatever the content of that material. Confidential communications, for example, belong to the person who originates them.[2] What I tell you does not become yours to do with as you please. Entrustment carries conditions. Even without an explicit pledge of confidentiality, what is shared with us remains the property of the speaker, unless it has been spoken publicly. We experience this whenever our own trust is violated. Marge rightly experienced that her trust in her husband had been violated. He had no right to hijack her material and substitute judgment, allowing his own judgment about the use of the material to trump hers. Larry rightly felt his trust in Elle was violated by her hijacking of the information and using it for her own emotionally driven ends.

Church leaders too often feel entitled to the ownership of whatever subjective and objective material is shared with them. This allows them to exercise their own judgment, a process that has led to a breakdown of trust and a reduction of material being entrusted to the church. Blodgett observes: "Confidences should not be an occasion to exacerbate anyone's vulnerability or create a power struggle . . . When one person tells a secret to another, or to a group, a trust relationship is immediately implied. Often, however, the issues of risk, vulnerability, and power relevant to the relationship are not immediately obvious."[3] Fewer souls are entrusting themselves, their children, their material resources, and their time to the care of the church and its ministers. Perhaps this is for good reason.

People in positions of ongoing trust are subject to the subtle and insidious temptation of thinking that in order to care for others, they must transcend the weaknesses of those in their care. This involves the process of "splitting," whereby one separates problems from solutions, instead of looking for both in the same place.[4] If I am entrusted to help you, I come to believe that when you are confused, then I must be clear and know

---

1. Cf. Blodgett, *Lives Entrusted*, chap. 1.

2. Everist and Nessan, *Transforming Leadership*, 135–38.

3. Blodgett, *Lives Entrusted*, 53.

4. Cf. Guggenbuhl-Craig, *Power in the Helping Professions*, chap. 7.

what is best for you. If you are feeling weak, I must be strong. If you are sick, I must be well. The result of this splitting leads me to feel not only entitled to the information you share but also obligated to substitute my judgment for yours as I search out help for you. This behavior becomes so routine that leaders no longer notice they are hijacking someone else's confidences. They truly believe it belongs to them and that they are right in exercising their own power or discretion. Not only do they believe they are right in doing so, but they believe it is necessary and faithful to do so, because in the splitting process they have come to deny the other person's strengths. The whole situation becomes increasingly distorted as they deny their own weaknesses and vulnerabilities, while accentuating the weaknesses and vulnerabilities of others.[5]

Mother Teresa made the mistake of sharing in writing her emotional and spiritual weakness and vulnerability with her spiritual advisor.[6] Several times she made it clear that she did not want her writings published after her death: they were confidential. Nevertheless after her death, the Vatican directed someone to compile materials on her life and make the case for sainthood. Her spiritual advisor turned the letters over to the care of the investigator, who in turn decided to publish some of them. His judgment trumped hers. He believed others who were struggling in faith could learn from her struggles. Perhaps he was right. But whose material was this? She did not relinquish the right to have her judgment overturned, even after her death. Her sacred and sensitive material was hijacked, albeit with good intentions. Good intentions are often the basis for bad boundary decisions. No wonder people no longer trust church authorities, even though they are full of good intentions.

ENTRUSTMENT IN THEOLOGICAL PERSPECTIVE

The Christian life begins with faith or trust in God. Entrusting one's life to the care of God is at the heart of the Christian journey. The God of the Scriptures has been revealed as a God worthy of trust. God has proven trustworthy through a history of keeping promises to God's people. God promised to Abraham against mighty odds to make of his descendants a great nation and a blessing to all families of the earth (Gen 12:1–3). God made a covenant with the house of David to establish God's kingdom

---

5. Peterson, *At Personal Risk*, 122–27.

6. Cf. Kolodiejchuk, ed., *Mother Teresa*.

forever (2 Sam 7:12–16). In the fullness of time God fulfilled the promise of sending a Messiah to fulfill the promise of establishing God's peaceable kingdom (Isa 11:1–9). The promises made by God to the people of Israel came to fruition with the coming of Jesus Christ (Heb 1:1–4). Jesus's birth fulfilled the promises made in the Scriptures of old (Matt 2:22–23). The life and death of Jesus Christ revealed the fulfillment of God's promises in a profound yet unanticipated way (Luke 24:32). From the beginning to the end of time, God's Word is "trustworthy and true" (Rev 22:6). God has been revealed throughout all time as one in whom we can place our ultimate trust.

Jesus Christ expresses to us the unwavering promise: "I am with you always, to the end of the age" (Matt 28:20). The way of entrustment begins with entrusting our lives to the promises of God. Do we dare to rely on God for favor and protection and deliverance through all the chances and changes of life? The Christian faith affirms that God is truly trustworthy, abiding with us even "through the darkest valley" (Ps 23:4). The journey of faith is always therefore the way of the cross. God's people are not spared experiences of suffering, which require cross bearing. Yet we are invited to trust in God's kindness and mercy, even when all evidence of our lives points to the absence of God's presence. Truly, our own feelings may deceive us; there are many experiences that would lead us to conclude that God has abandoned us (cf. Matt 27:46). Yet our final hope is in God's faithfulness to us, come what may. Human entrustment is predicated on our entrusting all that we are to God's promises—our bodies, our minds, our perceptions (insights and concerns), our passions, our spirits, and our resources. The testimony of the generations witnesses to God's trustworthiness, even unto eternal life.

God is trustworthy as the One who has our best interests always at the fore.[7] God is no trickster who puts us in predicaments to see whether we will stumble. The Christian insistence on the centrality of faith is based on the conviction that God is fundamentally worthy of our trust. For the church, its ministers, and members, this means that faithful ministry and mission is also predicated on our reflecting, as adequately as we are able, God's own trustworthiness. Establishing a climate of trust in the church is a high priority for credible ministry.[8] For God's sake ministers and people of faith are called to build trust with one another by inten-

---

7. Cf. Cooper-White, *Shared Wisdom*, 189–93.

8. Everist and Nessan, *Transforming Leadership*, chap. 1.

tionally relating in ways that promote the welfare of the other, not by taking advantage of another's trust in order to assume power over the other or in order to attempt to control them. Attentiveness to boundaries is a prerequisite for establishing and fostering the trustworthy environment which is indispensable to life-giving ministry in the church.

The first priority at the beginning of a new ministry by a Christian leader is to build a covenant of trust with God's people in that place. There are many core practices that can assist both leader and people to establish and nurture a trustworthy climate, reflective of the God of ultimate trustworthiness. In the following pages we articulate six key practices.

The *first practice* for establishing mutual trust is prayer. The minister takes time to pray faithfully and fervently for the people among whom one is called to minister.[9] Likewise, the people enter into the relationship with a new minister by praying earnestly for her/his welfare. Bringing these mutual petitions to our trustworthy God locates the unfolding relationships in the nexus of God's compassionate care. People of faith should not underestimate the efficacy of prayer for creating the climate in which fruitful and long-lasting ministry can endure. Prayer nourishes the new relationships in a spirit of goodwill and expectation that will bear good fruit.

A *second practice* indispensable to the building of trust involves the posture of appreciative inquiry. New relationships take time to grow. This necessitates intentionality about exploring the history of the new partner by investigating written materials and engaging in strategic conversations in a spirit of appreciative inquiry. Church histories, annual reports, minutes from meetings, and old newsletters each can provide insight into what has shaped this people to become who they are. Appreciative inquiry suspends judgment in getting to know other people by choosing to focus on their strengths and gifts rather than on their weaknesses and problems.[10] Effective engagement in appreciative inquiry takes time. Just as a good friendship deserves a serious investment of spending time together, so building trust between minister and people takes more intentionality and active engagement in appreciative inquiry than we usually imagine.

9. Lathrop, *Pastor*, chap. 5.

10. Cf. Snow, *Power of Asset Mapping*. The process of asset mapping is based on the method of appreciative inquiry.

A *third practice* basic to the art of ministry and the fostering of trust is the skill of listening. Active listening grounds all pastoral care.[11] People are hungry for a caring person to take the time to listen carefully to the stories of their lives. Active listening poses leading questions to invite people to go deeper in exploring the meaning of what has been experienced, both in times of joy and especially in times of sorrow or struggle. Good listeners then sit back with attentive ears to hear and enter into the unfolding narrative. Listening is one of the most precious gifts we can give to another person, an incarnation of the gospel. Effective pastoral care almost always involves more active listening than wise speaking. Perhaps no other practice will be more effective in building a climate of trust than the ability to enter into the stories of others through genuine listening. Listeners are able to knit what they have heard into the ongoing relationships with people as their lives continue to unfold. What has been heard endures in the memory and becomes wisdom for drawing people more deeply into life-giving participation in the faith community.

James Glasse wisely described our *fourth practice* as "paying the rent."[12] On the one hand, paying the rent involves faithfulness in ministry with and for people day after day, week after week: visiting the shut-ins, making hospital calls, ministering to the grieving, teaching confirmation, showing up at congregational events, preparing well for worship, preaching solid sermons, and giving generously of one's time and resources to the life of the church. Demonstrating authentic love for the people through steadiness over time fosters a trustworthy heart and contributes to the climate of entrustment. A trustworthy pastor invites the trust of people. Paying the rent, however, also means being a faithful steward of one's own life.[13] Attending to one's own spiritual wellness, physical fitness, emotional balance, and sharp intellect finally are indispensable to sustaining healthy ministry. Ministers are called upon to lend much of themselves to the care of others. Ministers are finite creatures who can easily become exhausted in body, mind, heart, and spirit. In order to have one's energy sustained and joy renewed, one must engage in a routine that establishes a baseline of health. Taking care of one's own health in its various dimensions is fundamental to paying the rent each day, week, and month.

11. Hedahl, *Listening Ministry*, chap. 1.

12. Glasse, *Putting It Together in the Parish*, 56.

13. Everist and Nessan, *Transforming Leadership*, chap. 9.

A *fifth practice* invites both ministers and people into a process of imagining the future together. We become what we imagine. This is one of the core convictions of Christian faith. Jesus in his ministry invited both disciples and the crowds to imagine a world in which God is alive and active, affecting who we are and what we do. Jesus described this divine involvement as the in-breaking of God's kingdom.[14] His teaching and ministry challenged people to open their eyes to see and believe what God was doing: forgiving, healing, casting out demons, feeding the hungry, bringing good news to the poor. One of the life-giving activities that most opens up the horizon of the future to congregations is imagination. Resistance to change can best be overcome as people begin to imagine themselves otherwise. As Willie Jennings describes it, "theological identity enters imaginatively into various social forms and imagines the divine presence joining, working, living, and loving inside boundary-defying relationships."[15] Juxtaposing our lives in relationship to the past—through the biblical narrative, Christian history and the story of the local church—opens up new horizons of possibility. Leaders can appeal to the imagination by telling stories from the Bible, remembering significant events in the Christian past, or recalling significant undertakings in the history of the congregation. Sometimes this process of imagining the future together can be furthered by inviting an outside facilitator to serve as midwife for the process. Living by faith in God always entails imagining what God is seeking to make of us.

A *sixth practice*, always needful, is forgiveness. What do we do when trust breaks down? Both ministers and people suffer under the burden of sin. It is not a question of whether but only of when we will find ourselves estranged from one another. Not only major boundary violations in speech and action undermine the trust necessary for vital ministry. Micro-infractions also eat away at the entrustment between pastor and people. Violations of trust can be committed on all sides of the relationship between pastor and people. We do not always keep our promises. We do not always tell the truth. We do not always interpret the behavior of others in the kindest way. We do not always turn the other cheek when offended.

Although the ritual of confession and absolution is prominent in congregational worship, the actual practice of forgiveness is rarely so

---

14. Perrin, *Jesus and the Language of the Kingdom*, 32–56.

15. Jennings, *Christian Imagination*, 291.

easy. The practice of forgiveness requires the humility to admit one's own failings. The practice of forgiveness requires mutuality of goodwill to heal the breech. The practice of forgiveness requires believing in God more than in the malice of the one who has hurt us. The realization of forgiveness in the life of the church depends in many ways on the scale of the infraction and on the willingness of the estranged parties to engage in the process of reconciliation.[16] When major violations occur, or if the parties are unwilling to practice confession and forgiveness, the climate may become so damaged that mutual entrustment is no longer possible. Such instances, for example in cases of sexual abuse, need to ensure that victims suffer no additional harm in any efforts at truth and reconciliation.

THE CASE FOR BEST PRACTICES

One of the important outcomes of the practices mentioned above is humility. Humility makes us more trustworthy because we do not just look to ourselves and our own experience for guidance in making decisions that affect others entrusted to our care. Humility leads to the willingness to look beyond one's self for direction, beginning by placing God above self. The practice of gratitude helps us to look beyond ourselves toward those to whom we are indebted. The humble, grateful person is always aware of how much we are indebted to others, even as praise may come their way. We can see this, for example, in some athletes who first give thanks to God for their talents and also for the support of their parents and coaches before they receive praise for themselves. We see this in scholars who begin their public lectures by praising their teachers and mentors, acknowledging the legacy that was handed down to them and upon which they have built. Praise and reward that is not shared with those from whom one has received such gifts results in ego inflation and a sense of entitlement, as if *I* am the source of all this goodness rather than the beneficiary or conduit. On the other hand, suffering that is not handled in a healthy way can also lead to a sense of entitlement: "I have suffered so much for the church; I have given so much. It isn't fair for me to have to pass up this opportunity for pleasure, companionship, or happiness."

16. Bash, *Forgiveness*, chap. 9.

Another important outcome of such practices is the ability to surrender—to submit our will to God and our own self-interest to the protection of others. There remains great wisdom in the Serenity Prayer:

> God, give us grace to accept with serenity
> the things that cannot be changed,
> Courage to change the things
> which should be changed,
> and the Wisdom to distinguish
> the one from the other.[17]

Without the healthy ability to surrender, one tends to denigrate or devalue best practices in favor of individual, and thereby often distorted, judgment.

Humility, surrender, and compliance play crucial roles in making good decisions. While one is always called upon to employ one's informed professional judgment in the practice of ministry, we do well to beware our tendency to privilege one's own self-serving bias with its accompanying distortions.[18] Apart from best practices, overreliance on one's own individual judgment frequently leads to destructive outcomes. In the remainder of this chapter we provide rationale for the imperative of following "best practices" in ministry as a prelude to summarizing in detail many such best practices in the final chapter. Professions that are highly entrusted with the care of others establish best practices not only to guide decision making but to override the hazards of individual judgment. Professions do this, not because they regard their members as incompetent, but out of conviction about our universal tendencies toward self-deception, which lead to bad decisions. Professionals who value best practices tend to be those who willingly recognize that their own thinking is also susceptible to error, just like everyone else's. One's own brain is an essential resource, but it is fallible and subject to systematic error. It is foolish not to recognize this, trusting instead one's own judgment in all circumstances. A big part of what we are trusting, after all, is the brain's capacity to reason accurately.

Professional airline pilots have done a great deal to understand and compensate for brain error. They learn very early that the brain can mislead them about such basic yet crucial matters as where they are in

---

17. Brown, ed., *Essential Reinhold Niebuhr*, 251.
18. Cf. Ubeda. "Consistency of Fairness Rules," 88–100.

space relative to the earth.[19] For a pilot, following best practices means recognizing that especially when flying in clouds one will be fooled by one's senses or "gut feelings." The key to staying alive, and keeping one's passengers safe, is to rely on the flight instruments and believe their accuracy. Pilots are also keenly aware of their own fallibility, and recognize the inherent risks in trusting one's memory. Best practices include strict adherence to checklists and standardized procedures; by following them a pilot is less apt to overlook critical items necessary for the safety of a flight. Pilots also learn what happens to the brain when it is subjected to a great deal of stress. Thereby they learn rules to follow under various circumstances, instead of naively following what the brain is telling them to do in any given moment.

Pilots also routinely experience the limits of information processing. In flight simulation, for example, when pilots practice dealing with emergency situations, a curious thing takes place. The flying pilot, the nonflying pilot, and the trainer occupy the flight simulator. There may also be another pilot simply observing. In the midst of an emergency, the people in those various roles take in different amounts of information. How much information the brain takes in depends on the amount of responsibility held by each person. The less responsibility you have, the more information you can process, insofar as responsibility is a source of stress. The brain protects itself from overload by setting limits on the incoming information. Unfortunately, the person who takes in the most information is the observer, followed by the trainer, then the nonflying pilot, and finally the pilot—in descending order of responsibility.

Pilots learn that stress impairs their ability to make good decisions. Therefore they learn to trust best practices even more than trusting their own brains. They learn, specifically, when and how the brain can mislead them and what to do about it. The pilot is entrusted with the safety of those on board. This is more important than the pilot's feelings.

Compare this to how the minister is entrusted with the well-being of those in her charge. In Christian community, members are likewise entrusted with the well-being of one another and of the pastor. While in the church daily boundary perceptions and boundary decisions may be less intense than for pilots handling an emergency, what we have learned through the scientific study of critical decision making can be helpful to decisions made in the parish. Good decision makers understand that

19. "Sensory Illusions in Aviation."

decision making is more about process than outcomes, even when the process involves intuition. Being a good decision maker means you use a sound decision-making process.

Many people believe and act like the only test of a decision is the outcome, not the process. This false belief can lead eventually to bad outcomes, even though it may not do so initially. For example, a young man decides to invest $1,000 in the stock market but could not decide where to invest it. He pins up the financial pages, closes his eyes, throws a dart, and buys the stock that was struck randomly. Within three months, he has tripled his investment. "This is the best decision I ever made," he concludes. But was it a good decision? When people invest in a prolonged up market, they can falsely come to believe that they are good at investing, while in fact they merely invested under favorable circumstances. Bad decisions can have benign or sometimes even favorable outcomes. The conclusion that one has made a good decision simply provides faulty reinforcement for sloppy decision making and encourages neglect of best practices that work well in both favorable and unfavorable circumstances.

Who bears the responsibility for establishing best practices? The ethics of piloting comes to mind as a good example here, as does medicine. Professional pilots and prescribing health care professionals take responsibility not only for those in their direct care but also for the safety of other passengers and patients. When a piece of equipment or a medicine does not perform as the collected data suggest it should, they give their input to those in charge. Responsibility is shared across the profession. It is not just a hierarchical system. A person lacking a participatory sense of the self will tend to act as an outside critic rather than a contributor or potential contributor to the bettering of the profession. An outsider regards responsibility for best practices and codes of ethics as belonging to "them" not "us." Such a person is also likely to regard the profession's rules as an imposition from the outside rather than an aid in becoming more trustworthy and an agent for caring for others beyond their immediate charge.

Relying on the formal exchange of experiences, such as research, gives equal weight to all pieces of information. This is an important way to counteract the human brain's bias to weigh information based primarily on where it is located in time and space.[20] The brain shows a bias of *propinquity* (nearness in space and time) in the following ways:

20. For the following, cf. Roberto, *Art of Critical Decision Making*.

1. In judging how likely a bad event is to happen to us, we give more weight to events that we have personally experienced rather than those experienced by others: "It has never been a problem for me to drive without my seat belt. I even got in an accident once and wasn't hurt."

2. If a bad thing has not happened to us, we tend to make decisions as if it never will.

3. In judging how likely a bad event is to happen to us, we give more weight to events that others have experienced when they occurred in our physical proximity, while giving less weight to the same event if it happened far from where we are.

4. We give more weight to events that happened recently than to events that happened further back in time.

Another major source of bias cited in the literature on decision making, is called the *self-serving bias*. This is extremely common, and it behooves us to recognize it in ourselves. Through the self-serving bias we take excessive credit for favorable outcomes while shedding blame when things go wrong. We also give more importance to data that support our beliefs or desires than to data that contradict us. Moreover, we are biased to believe that we are better than others (*overconfidence bias*). This is a form of bias that needs to be countered by the very humility and surrender previously mentioned.

We believe that we can succeed where others have failed. It is almost universal that people who knowingly violate codes of ethics or best practices believe that while the rule is good, they somehow will be able to manage the situation in such a way so that no one gets hurt ("I'll get the money back before anyone notices it's gone"). Or if they are willing for others to be hurt (as many are), they somehow become convinced that they will manage not to get caught. The self-serving bias also leads us to rationalize our decisions, putting them in a favorable light. A common rationalization argues that our intentions were good, even though our actions may have been errant. A self-serving bias also leads some to claim the right to forgiveness when caught in an indiscretion and at the same time to fault others for any lack of leniency and forgiveness. Again, humility and surrender are the responsible stances, not entitlement.

Internal pressure from feelings and emotions are a common impetus for bad boundary decisions. The actual desire to help is very common in the helping professions. It may seem like this is due to the pressure of another's needs or interests. Often, however, the inability to say no to an inappropriate or unworkable request is more internal to the person in the helping role than to the person making the request. The requesting person may easily accept the boundary when it is compassionately and skillfully established.

Internal pressures from feelings, emotions, and unmet personal needs can also wreak havoc. Loneliness, sadness, resentment, guilt, depression, and anxiety can override rational decision making, especially when people are not well versed in ethical and moral reasoning. Employing the concept of Marcia Riggs, we are called as ambassadors of Christ to become "religious ethical mediators": "This ministry of reconciliation is a ministry of mediation for people of faith who understand that being created in the image of God, recreated in Christ, is to live as moral beings in relationship with others as an experience of cross-cultural encounter."[21] Even with such training, however, the lust for sex (as seen, for instance, in the scandal of sexual abuse in churches), the greed for money, and endemic racism are forces powerful enough to cause great damage.[22] The unmet social and interpersonal needs for power, affiliation, comfort, support, and being understood, alongside unmet intimacy needs and prejudiced cultural conditioning, can interact with the self-serving bias to justify inappropriate actions.

The tendency is to engage in wishful thinking and best-case scenarios instead of in worst-case reasoning that best practices take into account to protect people from harm. Unfortunately, people who make boundary decisions from best-case scenarios may discover reinforcement in doing so, because their actions may make them more popular with certain people, as long as they are lucky enough to not have a bad outcome. Bad outcomes in the church often remain hidden from view for a long time, either through victims' reluctance to come forward or through perpetrators' deliberate secrecy and cover-up. By contrast, people who make decisions on worst-case thinking will cause less damage but may also be less popular in the short run, unless others are educated about the reason for best practices. Conscientious boundary keepers objectively monitor

21. Riggs, "Living as Religious Ethical Mediators," 250.
22. Gaede, ed., *When a Congregation Is Betrayed*, 25–27.

their own vulnerability and stress (factors that tend to limit awareness) and promote long-term thinking over short-term considerations.[23]

The study of bad decisions also demonstrates that social norming plays a strong role. Parishioners often encourage boundary violations without full knowledge of or appreciation for the importance of boundaries. Clergy colleagues can exercise a powerful influence against the maintenance of best practices. The power of the group is such that we are uncomfortable when our actions are different from the actions of those we are with and of those with whom we identify. If others are doing it, it must be okay. If I seem to be the outlier, maybe it is because I am just being overly cautious or rigid. Yet groups need alternative voices, or they easily fall prey to *groupthink*, a subtle group process that leads members to feel there is really only one way to think about things.

When ministers experience other ministers labeling their parishioners, gossiping about them, maintaining involvement with former parishioners, or otherwise not following best practices, the tendency is to follow suit. Behavior established by senior members of a norming group is a major factor contributing to how behavior drifts away from established best practices. This is not to say that best practices cannot change over time. Professional associations do treat codes of ethics, for example, as living standards that change as more information is gathered and conditions change.[24] But such changes are implemented through a formal process.

As members of a norming group, many clergy actively devalue best-practice standards with colleagues (and interns) with comments such as these:

- "Rules are made to be broken."

- "There is an exception to every rule."

- "It is the spirit of the law, not the letter of the law that matters."

- "Rules are just guidelines."

- "Don't be legalistic."

- "Boundary rules don't apply in small towns; you can't avoid violating them."

- "Times have changed; nobody does that anymore."

23. Cf. Cooper-White, *Shared Wisdom*, 58–60.
24. Trull and Carter, *Ministerial Ethics*, chap. 8 and Appendixes A–E.

These comments are actual invitations to disregard best practices in favor of some alternative—usually feelings and desires or local precedents—when best practices are intended to trump all of those.

This does not mean that best practices as rigid rules must always prevail, but the burden of proof is always on the side of those violating the best practice rather than on those observing it. There must be a clear and compelling reason to do something other than following the rule. Ignorance or lack of understanding are among the most common excuses for violating best practices: "I don't see why it's such a big deal; I've done it before and nothing bad happened." Note well the self-serving nature of these comments. The professional standard is that if someone is considering violating a best practice, this should only be done after consulting a person well versed in the issues, someone in a position to be objective and poised to tell them what they do not want to hear. A friend or close colleague obviously does not meet these criteria. To justify violating a particular boundary, there must be an important principle that reasonably outweighs the standard boundary, such as safety. With confidentiality in youth groups, for example, the youth may be advised to tell an adult when another young person threatens suicide or harm to someone else. As we will see in later chapters, there are situations where being trustworthy results in the consideration of different boundaries that compete for primacy. What is untrustworthy is to allow personal desire to trump best practices.

Many of the factors that lead to poor decisions came into play in the famous 1996 Mount Everest disaster.[25] Two teams with highly trained and experienced guides did not follow the established "Two O'Clock Rule" of the mountain. The rule states that during your summit attempt, regardless of whether you have made the summit or not, you turn back by 2:00 p.m. at the latest. This is not a recommendation or a guideline. It is a rule articulating a best practice established from years of cumulative experience. All Everest climbers know it. Descending in the dark or in a storm is extremely hazardous and puts not only yourself but others at risk. But in this case neither of the leaders had experienced any bad weather on recent climbs, and no bad weather was forecast. The radio chatter among the climbers was confident and mutually encouraging. They had invested a lot of money and months of preparation, and this was their last day. They knew they could do it. Though they had been schooled in the bias

25. Cf. Roberto, *Art of Critical Decision Making*.

of the "sunk cost effect" ("I've invested too much in this effort to give up now"), most did not turn back at 2:00 p.m. Only four of the thirty four climbers turned back as the rule dictated. They were the outliers in the group. Eight people died, and many others barely escaped with their lives in the brutal storm and darkness that followed.

Another factor involved in this tragedy that applies to congregations was the fostering of dependence. People who feel that others are dependent on them easily fall prey to feeling they should get their way, while those who feel dependent on them will tend to defer to the powerful person. Large contributors to the church, in time or money, may want and be given a bigger vote than others.

The temptation to violate best practices is great, even though practices are based on cumulative and wise collective experience. Those who are entrusted with the care of others hold a special obligation to be trustworthy in protecting others from harm. The lesson is to know enough not just to trust one's own judgment, because one's brain is subject to bias. No one is exempt from these biases, not even those who are most skilled at what they do. A trustworthy leader is one who understands these biases and limitations in judgment and who relies instead on established best practices. If you follow them like a reliable map, you will get a predicable outcome, not in terms of social approval but in terms of safety and trustworthiness. To expect others to trust us when we are not fully trustworthy is another expression of self-serving bias.

It is important not just to know what the best practices or rules are but also to understand the principles and reasoning behind them, because the principles and reasoning act as a steady guide, especially in murky situations. As we explore the myriad boundary issues involved in congregational life and congregational leadership, we consider both the what and the why of best practices, returning to a concluding and comprehensive articulation of best practices in the final chapter. Having here examined identity boundaries and ownership issues regarding subjective states, we turn next to the significant theme of role integrity.

3

Role Integrity

SCENARIO THREE: CHURCH BASEMENT LADIES

IN THE MUSICAL COMEDY *Church Basement Ladies*, the ladies in charge
of the funeral dinner found themselves in a quandary. The widowed
pastor's young new wife brought vegetarian lasagna. However, they are
Scandinavian. They wondered if she is Catholic. Lasagna is not who they
are. Should they serve it or freeze it for another time, running the risk of
offending her and the pastor? Which is more reflective of who they are:
welcoming and appreciating differences or ethnic exclusivity?

We know that on Sunday mornings people want to spend time with
other people who are most like themselves. If they cannot find such a
group, they may not attend church. The apostle Paul's stance toward this
dilemma was, in effect, "Go ahead and be who you are; keep your differences and don't require others to be like you."

While the initial reflex of the church basement ladies was to protect
the cultural integrity of their congregation (others in the congregation
might even see them as having that unstated responsibility!), they did
recognize that the primary role for members of the body of Christ is to
live according to the culture of God, which is radically welcoming. Whatever role one plays in one's congregation, we are called to be subservient
to the primary role of living the Great Commandment: to love God and
neighbor. When this commitment is kept alive and fully embraced, any
conflict of interest can be informed by what is most essential.

CLARITY ABOUT PRIMARY
AND SECONDARY ROLES

The healthiest and strongest organizations are those in which the primary purpose is so infused in the members and the commitment is so strong, that there is mutual accountability, which is carried out respectfully. If the preacher slips and uses ridicule in a sermon, every member sees it is their responsibility to point it out directly to the pastor. When a Sunday school teacher gets frustrated with disciplinary problems and begins to use the fear of God as a weapon, any parent will feel empowered to kindly address the matter with him. When a member of the leadership team is frequently late for meetings and arriving ill prepared, any other team member will feel responsible lovingly to address it.

We all have different identities; from them come different roles and functions. In different contexts, they carry different weight. Being clear about those identities helps inform us about which are primary and which are secondary. The church basement ladies got it right. The pastor's new wife was welcomed, and her food contribution was appreciated. The work of the kingdom goes well when our thoughts, words, and actions are informed by proper prioritizing. What is challenging to the work of the church is that very often improper prioritization makes primary roles and interests secondary to other personal roles and interests. It takes intentional effort not to act from secondary personal roles and interests.

In *Church Basement Ladies*, when Mavis was charged to recruit people to prepare and serve the funeral meal, personal interest might have led her to ask her friends and avoid asking those she found personally disagreeable. Yet when she intentionally embraced her role as a member of the body of Christ, she realized that a key feature of the culture of God is inclusion: that all are welcome and treated equally; priority is given even to the least important person. There are no cliques in the body of Christ. Mavis asked those who had not recently served and helped create a welcoming space for them.

Unconsciously prioritizing friendships over inclusion is a common reason that people are excluded from church activities. The church comes to feel like a closed circle.[1] Before and after worship on Sunday mornings, personal interests draw us to socialize with those we know and like, leaving out strangers. On church outings, this dynamic can become even

---

1. Cf. "The Parable of a Life Saving Station" originally appeared as Wedel, "Evangelism—the Mission of the Church to Those Outside Her Life," 24.

more pronounced by creating an insider group that is experienced as exclusive. When there is a free afternoon or evening on a mission trip, for example, people readily want to spend time with those whom they personally like the most. Personal friendships get in the way of serving the common good of the whole group. People can be reminded not to do that.

Dual relationships negatively affect both laity and clergy in the church.[2] When parents participate as chaperons on a youth mission trip in which their own child is a member, both the parents and child can be reminded before the trip that during these days the role of chaperon has primacy over the parental role. In fact, insofar as possible, the parental role needs to be suspended so the child can have the same type of experience that the other youth have, free from "being parented," which is qualitatively different from being supervised by an objective adult. In order to avoid boundary issues, parents in these circumstances do well to exclude themselves from disciplining their own child, leaving it to other adults. This includes recusing themselves from decisions involving the discipline of their own child.

It is common to think of these situations in terms of a conflict of interest. But this is merely a subset of situations in which multiple identities and roles can produce what we could name as the clouding of interest. In any situation of multiple roles, clouding can occur. What is called for is clear prioritization, giving priority to the role one has assumed for the church, informed by the values of the culture of God.[3] This requires a great deal of self-awareness. What hat am I wearing now? Is this the hat I should be wearing in my responsibility to the church? What role am I assuming? What role is influencing the feelings and thoughts I am having right now? With awareness often comes the realization that it may not be clear what role we are assuming.

Am I functioning as a dad on the youth trip by thinking my son should not be punished, because I do not like how that reflects on me? Am I being objective in thinking the offense is so minor that it should be ignored? Given that I am not sure, as well as that others cannot be certain whether we are being objective or not, the right thing in this circumstance is gracefully to defer to others. At every level in the church we are helped by clear understanding about situations in which a person should

2. Fortune, *Love Does No Harm*, 82–84.

3. Gula, *Just Ministry*, chap. 5.

identify their dual role and recuse themselves. All parties also may adopt a stance of mutual accountability in order to assume responsibility for gracefully pointing out perceived conflict or clouding of interest, which the other person is not able to perceive or acknowledge.

The goal is the protection of the integrity of the primary role, which includes avoiding even the appearance of favoritism, impropriety, or inappropriateness. This is one reason codes of ethics for professionals include the prohibition of behavior "unbecoming" a member of that profession. All roles in the church involve the inherent value of integrity and trust. For example, parents who drink on the youth outing compromise the effectiveness of their primary role by undermining and essentially violating that primary role. The pastor who makes suggestive comments toward a youth will not be seen by that young person as pastor any longer. While pastors in training (for example, interns) are taught to "embrace your pastoral identity," many come to resent it over time and want to "take it off" or "put it on" as it suits their personal interests, rather than serving in the primary role of pastor.

The quintessential example is the pastor who relates to a parishioner out of personal intimacy needs or interests.[4] The pastor has the primary responsibility to protect the integrity and effectiveness of the pastoral role for all concerned, including someone to whom they may be attracted. This is, of course, an obligation for all those who assume any role in the church, that they enhance and protect the integrity and effectiveness of that primary role for all concerned. The role does not serve you; you serve the role. When a pastor relates affectionately toward a parishioner, the pastor can no longer relate to that person in an unclouded way, because s/he has mixed a highly charged personal interest (that even changes how the brain functions!) with an objective professional role.

For example, Pastor Terry begins to see Chloe as a good candidate for leading Vacation Bible School when he never did previously. Before long, Chloe no longer has a pastor. If she reciprocates the romantic interest, she is no longer capable of seeing Terry as her pastor; Terry has become Terry, the romantic interest. This dynamic is even more pronounced if the love relationship is acted upon and subsequently turns sour. Now Terry is the one who hurt her, which contradicts the role of pastor. Even if Chloe does not reciprocate Terry's romantic interest but only detects it, consciously or unconsciously she also has lost her pastor,

4. Everist and Nessan, *Transforming Leadership*, chap. 10.

because she can no longer trust that Pastor Terry can relate to her within the expectations of his professional role.

If roles become cloudy by being mixed together, so does judgment. The pastor and parishioner in love may try to bargain. What if the parishioner leaves the church? Then perhaps their relationship would not be unethical? For a long time this ploy has been tried by many professionals and has been rejected by ethics commissions, who steward both the integrity of the profession and the well-being of persons. The problem is that this ploy is self-serving; it is not serving the integrity of the professional role. Upon further examination, why should the parishioner leave and not the pastor? After all, it is the pastor who has abandoned his primary role in favor of personal interest. But that still would not make it ethical. The boundary violation has already occurred when the pastor allowed himself to feel, think, and act affectionately toward the parishioner. When the professional allows himself to continue the personal relationship under different conditions, he is further invalidated as a professional, because of the failure to demonstrate the self-control that is expected of a pastor. When push comes to shove, he has chosen personal interest over protecting the integrity of the pastoral role.

We are all subject to temptations of various sorts that risk violating the integrity of our primary roles. A board member can recognize an opportunity for a relative to get a job at the church and can create an inside track. A church secretary, who is a member of the church and upset that her daughter was informed by the parish education committee that she will not be confirmed because she did not complete the requirements, is tempted to come to work the next day and complain to the pastor instead of remaining in her role and doing her work. As parent she may wish to advocate for her child, but she needs to take this up with the parish education committee. It is very difficult, if not impossible, for church employees who are members of the congregation not to contaminate their work roles with their personal concerns as members.

DEVELOPING STRATEGIES FOR MAINTAINING ROLE CLARITY

Because temptations are so prevalent, we are wise to plan for how to address them and the concomitant clouding of judgment. It helps to recognize that keeping boundaries includes watching not only our words and actions but our very thoughts. Our outer actions flow from inner sources. Taking responsibility for our actions requires an increased awareness of our inner life. Since the Great Commandment is about love, let us consider the example of anger.[5] Often people who get treatment for an anger problem feel that their anger outbursts "just happen" to them. How can they be responsible for things they cannot control? They only feel capable of controlling themselves after they have done or said harmful things. What they do well to learn (and can learn!) is to increase their awareness of the inner states that breed anger. People can learn to become more aware of the beliefs and attitudes that tell them they are in danger, which lead to lashing out to defend themselves. People can learn to recognize when they are dwelling on perceived offenses and fueling the fire with past memories and damning generalizations. People can learn to slow time down so they can intervene within microseconds to stop themselves from initiating an angry action. This is possible to learn.

Self-control begins with the control of one's attention. At every moment in time we face the decision of where to direct our attention. When Pastor Terry first recognized that he was having personal feelings toward Chloe, he was at a decision point. Such a decision has consequences. There is a saying that goes: "Where we direct our attention, the rest of us is bound to follow." A dramatic example of this phenomenon involves the state law prescribing that when you see an emergency vehicle ahead on the side of the road, you are to vacate the lane next to them. The reason is that emergency vehicles stopped along the side of the road are more likely to be hit by drivers than nonemergency vehicles. Why? Because our eyes are attracted to them, and we unconsciously tend to steer in the direction where our eyes are looking.

Self-control begins with controlling where we place our attention. Self-control means saying no to the self and taking that no as the answer.[6] All boundary keeping involves a firm no. It is the essential skill of all boundary keeping. Pastor Terry, to be faithful to his pastoral role, must prevent himself from dwelling on his feelings toward Chloe so that he does not fuel his desire through mental and emotional energy. He must not allow his imagination to explore what it would be like to be with Chloe. Dwelling on urges and desires leads both consciously or

---

5. Whitehead and Whitehead, *Transforming Our Painful Emotions*, chaps. 4 and 5.
6. Cf. McGonigal, *Willpower Instinct*, chap. 3.

unconsciously to establishing the conditions to act them out. That is the natural flow of energy that must be stopped.

There is a spiritual discipline called custody of the eyes, which is being used by therapists who work with people with sex addictions. The concept of custody of the eyes is also being used in spiritual retreats to help people learn to keep focus.[7] On a retreat (usually a silent retreat) custody of the eyes as a discipline encompasses not looking into the eyes of the other retreat participants or at any printed words, so as to keep focus on one's retreat. Roman Catholic worship leaders historically were taught custody of the eyes by keeping their eyes on the altar and cross as much as possible, both for the benefit of maintaining one's own attention on worship and for guiding the worshipers to do the same. It is hard for worshipers to be disciplined when the worship leader is not.

Custody of the eyes and the control of attention has wide implications for every ministry role. People working with youth do not allow themselves to gaze at a young woman's breasts, for example, even if they think she would not notice. Sexualizing anyone in the congregational community is a role violation, because it objectifies the other person and uses them for one's own gratification. In all church functions, to take our attention away from the matters at hand, even briefly, disrupts the effectiveness of the event.

Why does this matter so much in ministry? While inattentive driving threatens the body, inattentive ministering impoverishes the soul. One of the key ways we demonstrate that someone is important to us is by giving them our undivided attention. A family meal without a TV or other electronic device is remarkably different from a meal that includes these. Without such distractions, attention can be fixed on those present (including one's own full presence) in order to know what to share. When the pastor or Stephen Minister[8] does not establish a mental boundary when visiting with someone and allows the mind to wander during the visit, even a very brief lapse can bring a complete collapse in understanding what the other person is talking about. You do not have as meaningful a visit with that person if you let your mind wander to other things. You damage the value of the encounter when you vacate your role and ask them a question whose purpose is to satisfy your personal curiosity.

7. Armstrong, *Through the Narrow Gate*, 79.

8. Stephen Ministries, founded in 1975, trains laypeople to minister in their congregations as one-to-one counselors and pastoral caregivers.

In times of need people notice when you switch out of your proper role with them by either talking about yourself or asking them questions out of personal rather than professional interest. Molly, for example, told Ellen (her Stephen Minister) about a painful experience at a recent family reunion in Colorado. Since Ellen was planning a reunion for her own family, she asked Molly where the reunion was held and about the accommodations. While Molly was gracious, she felt the loss of focused attention on her distress. People do notice. People know when you mentally vacate the room, even briefly. One can sense it. Consciousness creates a field that projects around us. When we are fully present, people perceive our presence; when we lapse, they feel our absence.

No role in ministry is too insignificant to warrant mindful presence. The custodian who pulls the bell rope and focuses on the sacred call to worship knows that faithful performance of this role means not just pulling the rope but praying for people to come to worship and celebrate the Sabbath. She recognizes the difference from those other times when she was focused merely on getting back to bed. It was not just a matter of pulling the rope. Because we have become so accustomed to split awareness, we do not always notice the difference until we are forced to do so. At first young people at camp or on a mission trip get out of sorts, when not allowed to use their electronic devices to distract themselves. After a few days, however, they experience the world around them more fully and settle more deeply into themselves and their relationships with others.

The committee chair who is fully mindful in leading a meeting will not only be able to manage the agenda but will also be aware of what is unspoken and unexpressed by those present at that meeting. The Sunday school teacher who is mindful is not just focused on the curriculum and discipline but can tune in to sense what is going on with each of the children in order to connect in a caring way, even briefly, with what they are experiencing.

Pastor Terry is no longer ministering to Chloe when he lets his attention wander out of his pastoral role with her. He needs to exercise custody of the eyes with Chloe as well as with others for whom he may experience sexual attraction. This is not just a matter for clergy; it also applies to parishioners to remain faithful in their roles. Women clergy in particular complain about people looking at them sexually while they are performing their role. Even worse is for someone to put it into words: "Pastor, you look so cute in your collar!" This is a boundary issue that begins with control of attention and custody of the eyes, based upon custody of thoughts and desires.

Those who serve in the helping professions recognize that personal feelings can interfere with adequately serving others, whether the feelings are attraction or repulsion.[9] When that happens, the responsibility of the professional is to get consultation to try to clear up the personal feelings in order to be faithful to the professional role. Pastors are under more pressure than other professionals to resolve and control their clouded and conflicted feelings since they cannot refer the parishioner to another church the way a counselor can refer a client to another counselor.

Pastors and parishioners are most at risk for violating the integrity of their roles when their personal needs are not adequately met.[10] If Terry allows relations with his wife to go sour, he is more at risk of becoming inappropriate with the Chloes in his congregation. If Chloe has done the same in her marriage, she is more at risk of being exploited by Pastor Terry. If Mavis is not spending enough time with her friends outside of church, she is more at risk of using church events to spend time only with them, instead of attending to her primary church role of promoting inclusive fellowship. If Wendy is not tending to her finances or her gambling problem, she is more at risk of "borrowing" money from the youth fundraiser. She may even put herself into the position of being asked to be the treasurer for that account.

The better we are at appropriately meeting our own needs, the less we are at risk of using our church roles to satisfy those needs and so violating role integrity in the process. In our personal lives, personal needs and interests take precedence. In our church roles, those specific roles take precedence over our personal interests. Many would like to believe that the church should take care of their personal needs, but that is a form of using the church, not serving Christ through the church. This is a matter of role integrity.

As Susan Nienaber observes, "The healthiest congregations have the lowest tolerance for inappropriate behavior. Unhealthy congregations tolerate the most outrageous behavior."[11] What do we do about bad behavior? Do we tolerate it or confront it? The optimal work of the church also encourages the ability to say no to others. When the pastor allows

9. Peterson, *At Personal Risk*, chap. 3.

10. Harbaugh et al., *Covenants and Care*, chap. 3.

11. Sevig and Watson, "Bullying the Pastor."

someone to take too much time, the pastor then have less time for other things. When the meeting leader allows people to come late, waiting for them before starting, or allows the discussion to become pointless, the chair is failing to protect the integrity of that role.

The point here is not to be rigid, since rigidity can be both inconsiderate and less adaptive than flexible discipline. Disciplines that are overly rigid tend to break down because they do not flex when circumstances are different than normal. But many people who argue for flexibility really want no discipline, standards, or accountability at all. They argue for unconditional acceptance, meaning tolerating everything. Discipline is more sustainable when it is clear and consistent, while also taking conditions into account. When road conditions hold people up, for example, you might well wait a bit to start a meeting, while under normal circumstances you would start precisely on time.

More significant and challenging issues of flexibility and adaptability of boundary keeping occur when we consider that some people are at risk of violating boundaries due to psychological or medical conditions that can damage social perception, judgment or impulse control. Head injuries can do all three. Cognitive limitations can interfere. Developmental disabilities such as Asperger's syndrome and other autism-spectrum disorders can interfere with a person's ability to interpret other's behavioral cues. They may also be quite rigid and unskillful in applying behavioral rules. Personality disorders also complicate interpersonal decision making. There are people without a conscience who are motivated solely by self-interest. ADHD makes it harder for a person to conform their behavior to boundaries and interpersonal agreements. With regard to such conditions, boundary setting while respecting the identity boundaries of these persons means not identifying them with their condition. The condition isn't who they are; it is a condition that they have. Setting boundaries with people having these conditions calls for both grace and skill. People with these conditions may also be challenged in setting boundaries with others.

Some personalities are built in such a way that saying no to others makes them very uncomfortable. In many communities, this can be fairly common. They would rather accommodate others than disappoint them. Or they can feel they have no viable alternative since they need to continue to live with the person they may wish to stand up to. Some people with weak boundaries take on the feelings of others and have difficulty not feeling bad themselves when the other person feels bad. These people have an innate tendency to minimize the importance of boundaries since boundary keeping makes them very uncomfortable. They can also twist the notion of "loving others" to mean always doing what others want. The result over time, however, may be resentment toward those who want things from them, or even burnout.[12]

Role clarity and mutual accountability are required for the high level of functioning, which the Great Commission demands. Churches often have an aversion to both. We hate job descriptions for various reasons: They are a lot of work to produce, and they tend to become outdated. We also do not particularly enjoy being held accountable or holding others accountable. However, churches, like secular organizations, function best when it is clear who is responsible for what. Job descriptions end up reducing stress, including the stress of pastors, insofar as pastors are being evaluated by people in any case. It is unavoidable. Is it really better not to have unrealistic or ill-defined expectations: "What are we paying the pastor to do anyway?"

Job descriptions protect people from being unfairly evaluated. In many cases, pastors are expected to do whatever someone else has not done, while many of the things left undone are not in anyone else's job description.[13] Or if they are, that person is not held accountable for them, because in the church we hate to hurt people's feelings. By contrast, the best functioning organizations normalize mutual accountability. Within a culture of mutual accountability, feelings need not be hurt, because holding another accountable for their behavior is not the same as attacking the person. The more routinely and lovingly it is done, the more accountability can evoke gratitude instead of hurt feelings from the one holding the job. Clear job descriptions also help us objectively evaluate our own work performance.

In the work of the kingdom, all roles are informed and infused by the Great Commission. Worshipers cannot fill their roles when they just passively show up for worship and are unprepared to participate. The role of worshiper, like all other roles, is either filled fully, partially, or minimally. Like worship leaders, worshipers have a vital role in helping to create the optimum conditions for worship. When ready to fully engage and contribute, to read and sing, when ready to hear the lessons and the sermon deeply, worshipers enhance the worship experience for all

12. Lehr, *Clergy Burnout*, chap. 2.

13. Cf. Bacher and Cooper-White, *Church Administration*, 148–49 and Appendix F.

involved. Outside of worship, members have a role to play in hospitality for new people and responsibility for fostering an inclusive fellowship for one other, including for those at the edges of the social system.

The role of the religious education teacher, when informed by the Great Commission, is not just to teach the curriculum with competence; this role also encompasses understanding each student's relationship with God in order to nurture it. The communion deacon is not just a distributor of the elements; the role also entails engaging the "communion of saints." The acolyte is not just about lighting candles at one point and snuffing them out at another: the acolyte helps to evoke reverence and awe.

When each person knows well their particular role, including how and where it fits with other roles, and when together we fully live into these roles with a sense of call, beautiful things begin to happen. It is like playing jazz, where rules, conventions, and shared expectations create the conditions for beautiful expression and improvisation. You can truly let your light shine in a collaborative way when you are willing to take your turn within the ensemble. Jazz requires courage and creativity, built on a foundation of self-discipline, careful listening, and communication with others.

Ours has been dubbed the information age. We have ready access to all kinds of information and opinions from virtually anywhere in the world. Access to information has been put to positive ends (such as influencing governments via Twitter to prevent violence and injustice) to criminal ends (such as stealing personal and confidential data) to other evil ends (such as cyberbullying, which leads to violence toward the self and others). When Arden decided to finally get a smartphone, his daughter, who had had a couple of years of experience with smartphones, informed him, "Dad, to have a smart phone you need to have the self-discipline to let questions go unanswered. Otherwise you will be on it all the time!"

Prior to the information age, there were boundary quandaries from the fishbowl effect. In many communities, it seemed, everyone knew everyone else's business for good or for ill. The good occurs when we watch out for and care for our neighbors, even beyond what they intentionally reveal to us. The ill occurs where we jump to faulty conclusions and in other ways do harm to our neighbors. It really never was everyone, however, who kept track of that was going on in the community. Some people meddled, pried, and stuck their noses where they do not belong. They were up to no good, just satisfying their curiosity and perhaps a need for power in gossip circles. By contrast, in traditional societies people designated as elders of the tribe are required to know what is going on with everyone in their charge, in order to care for the welfare of the individual and simultaneously the group. The welfare of individuals and the welfare of the community are intertwined. The elder needs to know people better even than they know themselves: for example, knowing who can marry whom based on family trees, without causing problems through inbreeding. So what is the difference between meddling and serving as an elder? An elder acts from a legitimate and agreed-upon role in the community and is doing so responsibly. An elder is not acting in secret.

It takes a village. It still does! Robert M. Franklin, with regard to restoring hope in African American communities, makes reference to "the central local institutions in villages as 'anchor institutions'—the institutions that have an enduring presence and operate to stabilize people amidst chaos and rapid transition."[14] He names the three primary anchor institutions as church, family, and school. Enduring institutions of the village are characterized by their effectiveness according to specific criteria: innovative capabilities, governance and leadership, information flow, culture and values, adaptive response, risk structure, and legitimacy.[15]

We might ask ourselves to what degree congregations are genuinely equipped to serve as enduring institutions for anchoring future generations to live out their calling as the body of Christ with integrity? Some use of social media by young people keeps track of and cares for members of their group who are in trouble. You do not let friends hurt themselves or others. You do not let brothers and sisters in the body of Christ venture into harm. The prevention of harm is one principle that trumps confidentiality and privacy. In our discussion of boundary keeping, we affirmed that in violating a boundary, there must be a principle that overrides keeping the boundary as one normally would. In this case the conflict is between confidentiality and assuming the role of one who cares for others in order to prevent harm. In this spirit, the parents who hear from others in the community that their daughter is using drugs would be appreciative. To say something could appear to be sticking one's nose in someone else's business, while not doing so would be to fail to fulfill the

14. Franklin, *Crisis in the Village*, 4.

15. Ibid., 12–13.

role of community or congregation member on behalf of others and on behalf of the whole.

Into the information age came HIPAA: the Health Insurance Portability and Accountability Act. HIPAA places controls on the transfer of medical information on the part of patients and on the part of those who have direct roles to care for them medically. No one else can have access to a patient's medical records without the patient's consent. Given their care role, medical professionals are allowed, unless prevented by state law, to exchange information about the patient among themselves, in order to assess and coordinate care on behalf of the patient. A person with power of attorney over medical decisions also has a legitimate role to access medical information about a patient. A person who is on the staff of the medical facility is only to access a patient's medical records if they are in a direct care role with that patient.

The computer system monitors who accesses what and for how long. A staff member who accesses the records of a friend or relative will be fired. Because of the temptation and potential consequences, the computer systems have an additional level of protection for records of alcohol and drug treatment and mental health treatment, and for the records of public figures. For the sake of the patient safety, emergency access can be had by an unauthorized staff member via a preset procedure referred to as "breaking the glass" (taken from the notion of having to break the glass to access a fire alarm or fire extinguisher).

Faith communities desire to be caring communities, but when someone joins a congregation, are such persons giving consent to others in the community to keep track of them beyond what they reveal? That certainly could be part of the covenant. If it were, however, accessing information about another person would have to be part of a caretaking role, not based on personal curiosity. Staying in role would require that the caretaker turn away from gossip, unless the caretaker needed to inform a person who was a victim of the gossip. Maintaining the caretaker role would mean refraining from looking up out of curiosity what the minister's family paid for their home, even though it is a matter of public record. By contrast, for a covenanted caretaker it would be in role—exercising due diligence—to look up the driving record of someone who would soon be driving a vehicle on a congregational outing.

Another measure for legitimately accessing information about a parishioner or staff member would be that you inform the person that you did so, just as the hospital monitors digitally the accessing of patient records. If you feel the need to keep your access secret, it would not be legitimate. This also applies to doing a Google search on someone or poking into social media about them. The fact that information is publicly available does not mean that it is morally correct to access it. If you need such information to fulfill your agreed-upon role toward the person and the congregation, and if you are willing to inform them of it, it may be sound boundary keeping.

Accessing electronic information can take on a compelling quality that interferes with good self-care boundaries. Keeping your finger on the pulse of late-breaking news can become a way of life. Many teens want to keep their cellphones on all night so they can keep connected with friends at all times. This is simply not healthy. If a friend is at risk in the middle of the night, parents should be informed. Some people monitor emergency radio communications as a hobby. They want to be in the know about such things, while it has no bearing on any agreed-upon role that they have in the community. While this is legal, it is not ethical to do whatever they want with that information. The temptation to misuse information is great. An important act of self-discipline and spiritual discipline in the information age is knowing when not to use information, when to turn away from a screen, and when to turn off your device or go offline in order to do other important things uninterruptedly.

FOSTERING MUTUAL ACCOUNTABILITY

Just as many other professional organizations have standards of accreditation, and just as professions have periodic reviews to maintain certification, so churches do well to develop clear structures of accountability,. Annual audits and personnel reviews, while appearing to be an additional burden, actually secure the integrity of the church's identity and mission. Building a climate of accountability creates the conditions for synergy in an organization. The members of a band have to be able to hear each other in order to play together and create something new. In an organization this begins with mutual accountability and communication, asking the question about who is doing what with their time, talents, and resources (financial and otherwise). Keeping track of such information allows congregational leaders conscientiously to budget the use of available resources and to identify the additional resources that are needed.

Many pastors, however, object to accountability as itself a kind of boundary violation, holding that competent and responsible professionals should not have to answer to others, especially to laypeople. To the contrary, most professionals are answerable to others, and it is good that they are held accountable, though professionals may not like being evaluated any more than anyone else. Physicians, for example, have their work reviewed by accrediting bodies. Would you want to visit a surgeon whose work was not reviewed by anyone, or who was not accountable to anyone? Although no one likes it and many balk, without accountability standards of practice tend to decrease. When we believe others should "just trust us," what are we asking them to trust? What is our realistic appraisal of human nature?

Mutual accountability means that everyone is called to account for their own areas of responsibility, not just the paid staff. Shared accountability is different from micromanaging or excessive monitoring, which most often is driven by anxiety or control issues rather than inspired by the Great Commission. It is imperative that each member understands both their own role and the roles of others. But who should define roles in the church: (a) the pastor or lead pastor, (b) the church's lay leadership, (c) the congregation itself, (d) the clergy as guild, (e) the denomination, (f) the person occupying each role, (g) the Bible, or (h) all of the above? In practice, congregational roles are social contracts fashioned by all stakeholders. This is why formally defined roles eventually tend to give way to informal definitions. They are shaped by external and internal pressures over time. Congregational members and staff judge each other based on what they think they should be doing, whether or not it is in the formal description. Roles are agreements among people.

Unrealistic expectations are a major source of failure in relationships. A pastor cannot live up to everyone's expectations.[16] The running joke is that pastors are expected to do a long list of things at any time of day or night, inclding interrupting their vacation to do these things; and on top of all, the pastor must "walk on water." However, when roles are defined by a select group without everyone having input, expectations likely will not correspond with what those in power have decided. Expectations become coherent when all stakeholders help shape role descriptions. Through the crucible of such input, expectations become more realistic. But it also needs to be acknowledged that in some cases

16. Everist and Nessan, *Transforming Leadership*, 59–60.

the unrealistic expectations come from the occupant of the role—for example, from the pastor him- or herself.

Fidelity to the congregational role is similar to fidelity to the role of a spouse. It is not just defined by one's self, but it is relationally defined. One test of fidelity to the role of spouse can be measured by this question: if one's partner were able to view one's interactions with others, would they feel betrayed or not? Is one having an emotional affair or just a friendship? We can delude ourselves if we only stay in touch with our own point of view. One of the measures of accountability is to raise questions about the common tendency toward self-justification and self-delusion.

As with the role of spouse or parent, congregational roles may include a list of tasks or functions. But they are more than that! Informed by the Great Commandment, all roles are about love: expressing love for God and neighbor. The pastor's first responsibility is to love the people with God's own love, and it is the congregant's first responsibility to love one another, including the pastor, with this same love. Role descriptions, if reduced to a list of tasks, do not capture the spirit of a role any more than you can create a task list for being someone's spouse. Complex relationships require more than just breaking them down into tasks and assigning the tasks to people. While task definition may be important, it is merely the skeleton around which sinew needs to grow so that a fuller synergy can emerge.

Roles constitute the functional units of the congregation. Respecting role boundaries makes for better fulfillment of the congregation's mission. To simply ask more often, whose role is this? Whose decision is this? can itself contribute to better functioning. For example, a group of Sunday school teachers take it upon themselves to clean up the storage room where educational materials are kept. They come across some obviously used materials that they had not seen before. They figure no one would be using them again and throw them out. The question, whose is this? would have revealed that these teachers did not get to decide the fate of those materials. If they had asked, they would have discovered that the materials were being kept for vacation Bible school. Would it have been their role to take it upon themselves to throw out materials owned by the church? Communication is a two-way street. The vacation Bible school staff had not communicated to anyone that they had intentions for the used materials.

When flowers were ordered for Easter, someone had to ask, whose role is it to water them and care for them? No one had been assigned that role. Two-way communication allows the body of Christ to become not just a collection of roles or organs but an organism that is greater than the sum of its parts.

Some insects and other crustaceans have compound eyes composed of up to thirty thousand separate lenses pointed in slightly different directions, an arrangement that is especially good at detecting movement. The brain of such creatures takes the information from each lens and puts together a composite, a mosaic, in order to construct a complete view of the world. Single-lens eyes such the human eye also gather bits of data. Inside the eyeball thousands of photosensitive cells send their information to the brain, each by its own nerve. Every part must communicate what it is sensing in order to have healthy vision.

The early Christians constructed their worldview and view of Christ by valuing personal witness: "What did you see?" "What did you hear Jesus say?" "What did you experience?" "What healing have you received?" Hearing each one's point of view creates a more complete picture. This is another aspect of the primary role we have as a Christian—to bear witness to what we have seen and heard so that others may be transformed by it. We also have the responsibility to create a culture of respect and safety so that each and every person's witness is valued. Where this climate is fostered, Christian community can move to a new level. In the next three chapters we turn our attention to the implications of healthy boundaries for the life of the Christian community.

PART 2

Integrity of Community

4

Integrity in Worship

SCENARIO FOUR: PRIVATE WORSHIP WAR

Driving to church, Martin and Barbara expressed their dread of another Sunday at St. Paul's. Pastor Hulteen had driven them to the edge of dropping out. "I just can't stand how he leads the service," Martin complained. "And his sermons are unbearable," Barbara added. It was just not the way they liked it. They were used to having things done a certain way. After all, they were charter members of the church. The last pastor had conformed to their expectations in nearly every way. But Pastor Hulteen did not listen. He had told the congregation that when they entered the church, they should be quiet and pray. The tradition at St. Paul's had always been that this was a time for fellowship and getting caught up with your friends. He had also told them that worship was not a spectator sport, so they should not applaud for any reason, even for the children's choir. How impudent! How would the children and other performers receive recognition for sharing their gifts? They would not be surprised to see members stop participating.

During the entire worship service, Martin and Barbara silently seethed. What awful hymns! They could barely even listen to the pastor's voice, let alone pay attention to what he said. When it came time for the passing of the peace, they made sure to turn in the other direction when he came down the aisle. At communion, they were especially glad that they sat on the side of the lay communion assistant, so they did not have to receive the bread from him or look him in the eyes. As they went through the line after the service, Martin said, "Nice sermon, Pastor." Barbara just smiled and nodded her head. Then they made a bee line for their friends, most of whom were also charter members. "What are we going to do?" asked Barbara. "Maybe all of us should boycott until he changes his ways," added Martin. "It just doesn't feel like church anymore," replied one of their closest friends. They all agreed that something had to be done to demonstrate their frustration and discontent. "I am going to stop going up for communion," Martin declared. "And we are going to stop giving our offering to the general fund," Barbara chimed in. The group of friends agreed that they too were going to send a message to the pastor.

As soon as they got in their car, Barbara breathed in deeply and sighed, "That was a good Sunday morning." "Finally we are getting somewhere," Martin agreed. Both were glad to have such good friends at church, who would see to it that things got back to normal again. The sermon on this Sunday had been titled "Speaking the Truth in Love." The prayers had focussed on the theme of reconciliation. The congregation had celebrated Holy Communion in the name of Jesus for the forgiveness of sins. The closing hymn had been "Blessed Be the Tie that Binds." "How much should we reduce our offering?" asked Martin. "Let's give it all to the building fund," proposed Barbara, not missing a beat.

INTEGRITY OF WORSHIP: DELINEATING THE ULTIMATE BOUNDARY

After receiving the Ten Commandments for the second time, Moses came down from the mountain transformed. Everyone could tell. His countenance had changed. He was glowing (Exod 34:29–35). He had encountered God and had done so on God's terms. But this was not Moses's first transformation. Much earlier in his life, before Moses began to lead the Israelites, God called Moses to his special mission. At the burning bush, God told Moses he was standing on sacred ground and to take off his sandals out of respect. Moses took off his sandals. God reminded Moses that God was God and he was not. Moses respected that boundary. And so, he was transformed (Exod 3).

The most sacred of all boundaries is the distinction between God and creatures. God is God and we are not. The first commandment given by Moses was "I am the LORD your God, who brought you out of the land of Egypt, out of the house of slavery; you shall have no other gods before me" (Exod 20:2–3). As an observant Jew, Jesus gave his disciples the Great Commandment in this form: "You shall love the Lord your God with all your heart, and with all your soul, and with all your mind. This is the greatest and first commandment. And a second is like it: 'You shall love your neighbor as yourself'" (Matt 22:37–39).

Whenever and wherever human beings attempt to transcend the primordial boundary established by their creatureliness, they fall into sin and idolatry. The power of sin, taking over our lives in manifold ways, deceives us into believing that the self is god. Thereby I place myself at the center of all existence and assert that my own will accords with the divine intention for the world. There is no end to the mischief and evil of which human beings are capable as soon as they seek to defy this original boundary by claiming their own divinity.

Only God gives life. When human beings strive to express their transcendence over creation, inevitably they transgress the limit that God has established as the fundamental boundary between heaven and earth. Believing that I myself am the center of the universe, I seek to order the world self-centeredly and at the expense of others, a state of affairs that inexorably leads to death, not life. If I am god, then all others should bow to my will and obey my commands. In a world where many view themselves as distinct centers of divine power there emerge intractable conflicts among these gods, each one thinking the ego's own views deserve universal acclaim and acknowledgement.

Feminist theologians such as Rosemary Radford Ruether have criticized such an analysis of the human condition as reflecting male bias.[1] While the original sin of men may be selfishness, feminist theologians contend that the original sin of women is submissiveness. If men tend to assert themselves at the expense of others in hubris, women tend to denigrate themselves through the inability to accept and claim their full status as human beings. Only by affirming their created goodness as those created in God's own image can women overcome the socialization process that attributes to them second-class human status. The sin of pride in men finds its converse in the sense of humiliation in women. Therefore feminist scholar Carol Lakey Hess calls for intentional "conversational education" to counteract and transcend entrenched patriarchal patterns by recovering "(1) the thread of recovering women's experience of caring

---

1. Vaughn, *Sociality, Ethics, and Social Change*, 193.

and connection and (2) the thread of promoting women's capacity for voice and differentiation."[2]

In both pride and humiliation there is a fundamental transgression of the goodness of the creation. For many men, this entails claiming too much for the self; for many women, too little. If men are tempted to transcend the qualitative difference between God and humans by thinking themselves divine, women are tempted to deny the goodness of what God has created in them. In both cases the distinction between God and the creature is distorted in destructive ways. The first distortion leads to the exploitation of creation on the part of humans; the second leads to the loss of self-respect and abdication of one's worth as a valued member among those created in God's image. Both distortions disrupt the intended relationship between God and human beings in demonic ways.

Worship is the human activity that most reorients human beings to live according to God's original creative purpose.[3] The very act of worshiping God reestablishes human beings in the role afforded them from the creation of the world. Human beings are neither gods unto themselves nor humiliated creatures unworthy of being. At worship those who think too highly of themselves are instructed to let God be God and are set free from all presumption. At worship those who claim too little for themselves receive the affirmation of their created goodness and are restored as those made in God's own image. Worship of the One who is truly God grants to humans their status as creatures—nothing less and nothing more. We were created to serve as stewards of God's creation, responsible for tilling and keeping the garden (Gen 2:15) in which God graciously placed us for nourishment, enjoyment, and life.

Observing the boundary between God and created humanity establishes the fundamental limit for acknowledging and honoring all other boundaries. When we recognize the ultimate boundary between God and human creatureliness, we receive the perspective by which we may acknowledge the boundaries that must be respected in our relations with other creatures, including other human persons. The practices of worship assist us in honoring the infinite qualitative distinction between God and creatures, free us from distorting our created role, and teach us to observe

2. Lakey Hess, *Caretakers of Our Common House*, 182.

3. Lathrop, *Holy Things*, 2–4.

the primordial boundary without which we as humans will violate God's purposes.[4]

BECOMING TRANSFORMED BY THE PRACTICES OF WORSHIP

Worship involves many distinct elements designed to connect us with essential truths and states of being important for our relationship with God, including our capacity to do God's work. We might think of the elements of worship as being comparable to the Stations of the Cross, in that each has its own meaning and integrity. We are challenged to enter fully into each element of worship and then transition, sometimes very quickly, into the next worship element that builds upon the previous. The worship leader has the responsibility to work with others in designing the worship service and presiding in such a way that facilitates the full participation of those who gather in the pattern of worship toward soul-restoring and reorienting states of being.

Before worship, worship leaders must carefully transition from the matters of personal life into the right attitude for worship—into the right mind, the right heart, and the right energy. After the service they have occasion to connect with those who were engaged in worship as deeply as possible, even though brief encounters. These postworship relationships also require the right mind, heart, and energy. Worship leaders must seek to discern what is going on with each soul present at worship, be they known members or guests, in terms of their current pastoral needs. If there are multiple services, worship leaders must then set previous experiences aside, in order once again to be in the right state of soul to effectively lead worship each time. Psychologists call this *state shifting*. It involves the important skill of shifting from one state of consciousness to another at will. State shifting is an essential skill in pastoral ministry. Also essential is controlling one's attention during worship to keep focus on worship. The worship leader is challenged to both lead worship and to participate personally as an engaged worshiper as fully and meaningfully as possible.[5] The spouse and family of the pastor are also challenged to enter into worship mode and not be evaluating.

4. Cf. Kierkegaard, *Concluding Unscientific Postscript*, 313.
5. Schmit, *Sent and Gathered*, 114.

Worshipers must also engage in state shifting if they are to engage worship in the most meaningful way possible. Without state shifting, worshipers tend to keep the mental state and mood in which they entered worship, or something close to it. Pastor Hulteen as worship leader, although perhaps clumsily, was trying to help St. Paul's worshipers more fully engage the integrity of each element of worship. He was trying to help parishioners experience worship as something different from secular performance that calls for applause as a show of approval. When worshipers interrupt the silence after a musical piece with applause, for example, they effectively undermine the function of worship music (which is to lead worshipers into deeper communion with God and one another); applause turns the focus away from worship and toward the performers themselves.

Musicians themselves recognize that music needs to linger to reach its full effect, especially when challenging lyrics are involved. As the musician knows, rests and silences before, during, and after the music are major factors in enhancing music's effectiveness as means of state shifting. The silence after the music provides a moment of liminality, a thin space, when many worshipers can more easily enter into the Spirit's presence and guidance through the musical offering. Those who applaud deprive themselves and others of such experiences of liminality. Worshipers who applaud after a section of worship are also switching roles from worshipers to audience members—two entirely different stances.[6]

Pastor Hulteen also desired that the children in the children's choir experience their singing as a contribution to worship, something different from the performances they may do in school. Some parents even want to treat their child's participation in worship as a photo opportunity. When they do so, they are not in worship mode; instead they undermine their child's emerging understanding of worship, as well as distract others who are themselves hopefully in worship mode. There also may be instances where other lay leaders in worship may succumb to the inordinate temptation to draw attention to themselves and their own performance. Such *hijacking* of worship out of one's personal need for recognition also undermines the integrity of worship by shifting the focus away from the relationship between God and the assembly.

Worshipers can more fully engage worship from the very beginning by making a transition from fellowship to worship at least a few

6. Cf. ibid., 117–25.

minutes before the formal call to worship. The musical prelude is meant to ready the mind and heart for worship. It can only do so if one enters into worship by listening to the prelude or to the silence, not treating it as background music or as the occasion for conversation, as one would at a bar or nightclub. The worshiper also finds that one can go deeper into the music and lessons of the service when one reads and contemplates them before the start of worship.

Worship begins with the invocation of God's presence in the midst of the worshipping congregation. The assembly and each participant enter worship in the presence of the Living God.[7] This shifts us into recognition of our identity as those who were created by God, gathering now in the presence of the One who created us. This fundamental relation is underscored through the rite of confession of sin and absolution. We confess before God that we have sinned in thought, word, and deed, by what we have done and by what we have left undone. We are creatures begging mercy and pardon from the only One with the power to forgive us. The divine-human relation is nowhere more starkly portrayed as when we tell the truth about our existence by admitting we are sinners in need of God's forgiveness in Christ. Our identity is defined as those who are forgiven sinners and who therefore owe God gratitude by extending the same generous forgiveness to those who have offended us.

But these are mere words that we mouth when our minds and hearts are elsewhere. They become meaningful when we have spent time before and during worship in self-examination, comparing our thoughts, words, and actions of the previous week to what Jesus calls us to be and do. It is very challenging for us to acknowledge, for example, that we routinely engage in unjust practices at work, in our relationships, and as part of God's creation, when these practices are in fact more in line with conventional wisdom reinforced daily by the society around us. Worship juxtaposes such conventional reality and the countercultural coordinates of God's own kingdom.[8] In this regard Rebecca S. Chopp summons the church to become a "community of emancipatory transformation."[9] After we realize how implicated we are in violating the way of Jesus by our acquiescence to conventional social expectations, we can put meaningful

7. Lathrop, *Holy Things*, 113–15.

8. For the following, Nessan, *Beyond Maintenance to Mission*, 42–49.

9. Chopp, *Power to Speak*, 71–74.

content to our confession and experience deep gratitude in response to the worship leader's proclamation of God's forgiveness.

Many of us must also prepare our hearts to fully accept the precious gift of forgiveness. When we engage worship with our whole being, it becomes transformative for the choices we make about our thoughts, words, and deeds in the days ahead, including in our choices to hold others accountable and extend forgiveness toward them. When confession and forgiveness are offered in a mindless way, we publicly purport to confess our sins and accept God's grace when this is not really the case. So we lull ourselves into believing we are doing something when really we are not entering into and trusting God's promises.

In the passing of the peace, we are challenged to act as God's agents of love and grace to all who are assembled, regardless of how we might have felt about them before worship. To do so requires that we see each worshipper as equal in the presence of God, not selecting out some for special treatment because of who they are to us outside of worship— friend, family member, lover, or coworker. We may want to ignore or avoid others because of how we feel about them. Our inner state in relationship to God during the passing of the peace shows us how far we have come, or have yet to go, in living the kingdom.[10] During worship (and in the Christian fellowship that precedes and follows worship), not only are we called to outwardly and visibly treat each person as someone precious to God, but we are called to bear each person in our hearts with divine care as we extend God's peace to them. Undoubtedly, this practice requires a deliberate transition.

Dietrich Bonhoeffer in *Life Together* proposes that it takes the spiritual discipline of seeing the other through the eyes of Jesus Christ rather than through our human eyes: "Now other people, in the freedom with which they were created, become an occasion for me to rejoice, whereas before they were only a nuisance and trouble for me."[11] These disciplines of integrity in worship expand our capacity to live lives of love well beyond our human limitations.

At worship we sing praises to God. God is worthy of our praises as the Author and Sustainer of our lives. We learn at worship that we were created to praise God; we exercise this praise through our hymns until our entire lives become songs of praise. Many of us can grow by

10. Nessan, *Shalom Church*, 79.

11. Bonhoeffer, *Life Together*, 95.

increasing our capacity for praise and celebration, becoming less self-conscious and concerned for how we look to others, in order to let loose the joy that passes understanding. We attend to God's Word at worship through readings from Scripture and the preaching of the pastor. Thereby we acknowledge that it is the Word of God that lends orientation and direction to our lives as we navigate the challenges and dilemmas we face every day.

Protecting the integrity of the sermon is a challenge for all concerned, from the preacher's preparation and delivery to the hearing of the sermon by those assembled. In preparing the sermon, the preacher protects the integrity of the sermon by maintaining good boundaries. Preachers must set aside a host of private agendas that can contaminate the process, from the desire to impress people or win their loyalty to the impulse to lecture or scold those who oppose them. The question about whether the preacher should set aside political agendas is worthy of reflection. Does the addressing of political issues violate the integrity of the sermon, or is it a necessary aspect of prophetic preaching? While the preacher does well to avoid partisanship regarding political parties, addressing the urgent social issues of our time corresponds to the Scripture's own engagement with such questions.

Respecting the integrity of each sermon requires that the preacher spend prayerful time in study and reflection in order to discover what the Spirit is speaking to this people through these texts, even when they may have preached them many times before.[12] Even more challenging may be texts that preachers find personally disturbing or baffling. The point is to bring the reading of God's Word alive for worshipers to hear in a way that has integrity for the congregation as a whole and for each person assembled.

Those hearing the sermon must, in worship mode, set aside their conventional likes and dislikes.[13] They are called to set aside cultural and educational trappings to hear God in the thoughts and speech of the preacher, as mediated by the Holy Spirit. Not only the Bible readings but also the words of the preacher become for us the Word of God in the act of preaching. Self-control begins with control of attention. Keeping attention on the sermon, with openness to the Spirit, may help amplify what the preacher says, bringing awareness of thoughts, images, and

12. Lathrop, *Pastor*, chap. 2.

13. Samuel D. Giere has provided a useful resource for the hearers of sermons: *With Ears to Hear*: http://www.withearstohear.org/.

memories associated with our personal hearing of the Word. Some of the thoughts we bring to the sermon enhance our understanding, while other thoughts must be let go as mere distractions. Barbara and Martin have fallen prey to putting their attention on their own likes and dislikes about Pastor Hulteen and his style of preaching, giving it more importance than the biblical text and how God is speaking to them through this Word. Sermons, like worship music, are not performances, and we degrade them when we treat them as such.

We confess a creed at worship, using ancient forms that have guided the people of God over the generations. These creeds are affirmations of core beliefs, things for which we stand and for which the martyrs died. Each successive rehearsal of worship further elaborates the boundary between God and our lives, establishing our accountability to God in all things. Each element requires that we be fully present to it. Thus we enter into prayer to God at worship, presenting intercessions for God's care and concern. These, however, are not just petitions we hand over to God. If these are the things for which we dare pray, then they serve also as a mission statement for ourselves and the church in its outreach and ministry. In this way the prayers of the church are a commitment on the part of those who pray to give their lives to exactly those things for which they pray. This only happens when we enter into prayer with our whole, conscious being. The offering of the church also clearly defines the relationship between God and creature. God has provided everything we are and have. As creatures we owe to God only thanksgiving for every gift we have received. Therefore the basic posture of the creature is one of gratitude to God, demonstrated by generosity toward the world of neighbors God has given us to serve.

In the meal, the Lord's Supper, the church gathers at the table to remember and receive the presence of Jesus Christ in bread and wine. This is the banquet of the kingdom of God. At this meal we receive the gifts of Christ's forgiveness, deliverance from evil, and the reality of eternal salvation. Here all are welcome, calling upon those communing to subordinate our everyday tensions and differences with others to our unity in the presence of Christ. At this meal there is enough for all. There is no shortage of either food or grace in the economy of God.[14] The body and blood of Christ are given and shed for you! Each person receives from Christ sustenance for living and hope in the face of dying. We are

14. Nessan, *Shalom Church*, 93.

precious, although sinful, recipients of God's mercy in Christ. Nowhere do we find our lives defined more clearly and profoundly by what has been accomplished for us by Christ Jesus than in the sharing of the Lord's Supper.

PASSING FROM THE BOUNDARY ZONE OF WORSHIP INTO SERVING IN DAILY LIFE

Worship concludes with a benediction and the sending. We receive the blessing of the triune God—grace, love, and hope. The face of the Lord shines upon our way. Moreover, we are sent to live as creatures defined by all the practices of worship. We are sent to serve the Lord, share the good news, and be generous to the poor. Christ himself is with us. Thanks be to God!

Worship easily can be faked. But then it is not really worship. We can sit through the whole thing and say all the right words without engaging our hearts, minds, or souls. It is tempting to do so, since engaging worship with our full being can take us out of our comfort zone, translating us out of conventional reality into the presence of Holy God. We may like to keep our emotions in a narrow range of control, while worship calls us to surrender control to the Spirit. We are called to transcend our conventional sense of ourselves. While we may feel timid, we are called to sing boldly. Make a joyful noise! While we may be shy, we are called to engage in the passing of the peace. While we may be loud and domineering, we are asked to be silent and yield to God's presence.

Worship involves making ourselves vulnerable—vulnerable to God and before others. As essential as vulnerability might be to the life of faith, our humanness does not like it. We do not like having our lives engaged so fully or our feelings affected so deeply as they are when we fully engage in each element of worship. We may cry with tears of immense joy and gratitude or with tears of great pain and disappointment. We may sing out of tune. We are certain to become emotionally uncomfortable—guaranteed! We may embarrass ourselves. Therefore the worship space must be a safe place, safe from our own self-criticism and safe from the judgment of others. It is to be sanctuary. And we must help make it a sanctuary for others. We are invited to stretch our awareness vertically to engage the transcendent presence of God and horizontally to engage in community with others. Worship fully engaged is thereby the most psychospiritually challenging activity of the week.

The sanctuary is a sacred space for worship and for the protection of what is sacred to us. We take off our shoes and enter with respect. Boundaries are kept by what is allowed at worship and what is not. Nothing is to be located in a sanctuary that summons our allegiance to anything other than God. No symbols are allowed that serve private interests or are promotional in nature, even those of nonprofit or fraternal organizations. The sanctuary is protected from anything that might distract us from the worship of God alone.

Within the practice of worship, keeping the integrity of each part means recognizing the boundaries within the elements of worship and making successful transitions between them in order that we participate fully and mindfully with our whole being. At worship our lives are oriented by the primordial boundary that defines our existence: the relationship between Creator and creatures, Savior and sinners, Spirit and those in need of the life only God can give. The boundary between the life-giving God and our finite lives provides the fundamental orientation for how we are to live in relationship to other persons. The God who created us, forgave our sins in Christ, and gives us life by the power of the Holy Spirit is the One who holds us accountable for observing life-giving boundaries in relation to all the persons we encounter in our daily affairs.

Since God is the source of life for us, as experienced in every practice of worship, we are to be conduits of life for the people who are entrusted to us in all arenas of our lives: family, daily work, local community, and global connections. The boundary between God and humans, established at the creation of the world and exercised through the practices of worship, undergirds all the boundaries we must respect in our dealings with other people every day of our lives and with the creation itself. God holds us accountable to relate to others honorably and to be concerned about their welfare and life, just as we are creatures who owe everything to God. We are not gods. Worship, in all its diversity of elements, reinforces that God is God, the One who in Jesus Christ finally comes again to judge the living and the dead. Our core identity and mission are clarified by what we do at worship. We are to fear, love, and trust in God above all things. And we are to love our neighbor as our self. This overarching truth, as established at worship, grounds and safeguards every boundary with which we are entrusted in our lives as creatures in God's world!

5

Bearing Witness: Integrity in Interaction and Communication

SCENARIO FIVE: BEARING FALSE WITNESS?

Maria: "I'm thinking Steven would be a good person to work with our youth group. He is such a nice guy."

Megan: "But haven't your heard? He is a sexual abuse survivor, and sexual abuse survivors are more at risk of abusing others. We shouldn't take the chance.

Claire: "How do you know he is a sexual abuse survivor?"

Megan: "Evelyn, the church secretary, told me."

Beth: "Isn't it odd that Steven and Fey don't have any children? They've been married eight years."

Joanne: "I heard Fey doesn't want to have children."

Megan: "Maybe she doesn't trust him with children?"

Claire: "Is it really true that sexual abuse survivors are more at risk of abusing others?

Megan: "That's what I heard on *Oprah*."

Joanne: "Well, my husband, Jim, was molested by his older brother for a couple of years, and you can't tell me he isn't safe with kids. That's ridiculous!"

Megan: "Well let's ask Pastor about it!"

RELATIONAL PERSONHOOD

What does it mean to be a human being? A foundational understanding about who we are as human beings is indispensable for clearly naming, analyzing, and honoring the boundaries necessary for flourishing human communities, including faith communities. Theologically speaking, our understanding of human beings derives consequently from our concept of God as the One who created us. Although after the Enlightenment human beings have been increasingly conceptualized as individuals, especially as individuals who have capacity for intellectual reasoning, a Trinitarian understanding of God—and of human beings as those created by this triune God—gives a qualitatively different shape to our interpretation of human being.

In modernity the human being has been depicted primarily as an individual, as one who has unprecedented capacity for reasoning.[1] This definition of the human has contributed to expanded human understanding and the discovery of vast knowledge, based especially on the fruitfulness of scientific method for formulating and testing hypotheses. Such knowledge is reliable and sure insofar as scientific findings can be quantified with mathematical precision. Thereby modernity has tended toward reductionism in its view of the human, stressing the achievements of atomistic, reasoning individuals as the drivers of history. In our contemporary, postmodern world, one of the chief characteristics affecting human life is the transforming of individualism into "hyper-individualism."[2]

In multiple ways, contemporary society takes the autonomy of the individual as the presupposition for every form of technological innovation—in electronic communications, information systems, transportation, education, health care, and virtually every other arena of contemporary life. Our lifestyles have become extremely individualized. Consumerism caters to the desires of the individual and the affinity groups into which individual desires may lead us to congregate. How much we see ourselves as individuals is revealed by how we make decisions. Who do we consider when we make decisions? How much do we act from self-interest? How much focuses on, what's best for my family? How much is based on my personal affiliations, my tribe? How much

---

1. Cf. Borgmann, *Crossing the Postmodern Divide*, 37–47, on "ambiguous individualism."

2. Beck. *God of One's Own*, chaps. 7 and 8. For a description of what he names "monadic relativism," Jameson, *Postmodernism*, 412–13.

relates to, what's best for others affected by my decision? Or what's best for God's work in the world? Hyperindividualism locates the self in a position of inflated importance at the expense of other considerations in all the decisions that we make, large and small.

In contrast to the hyperindividualist tendencies of the postmodern world in which we are immersed and by which we are often overwhelmed, theological anthropology, following belief in the triune God, views human beings not as individuals but as *persons*. Just as the One God is constituted through the dynamic interrelationships among the three persons of the Trinity in life-giving mutuality (*perichoresis*), so human beings find their fulfillment not in the pursuit of individualizing agendas but through relationships of mutual consideration and mutual accountability.[3] Catherine Mowry LaCugna writes: "Everything comes from God, and everything returns to God, through Christ in the Spirit. This *exitus* and *reditus* is the choreography of the divine dance that takes place from all eternity and is manifest at every moment in creation."[4] One imaginative depiction of the relational character of the Trinitarian persons is the icon of the Trinity by Andrei Rublev (ca. 1360–ca 1430). The Holy Trinity is portrayed as three remarkably identical persons seated at table around a common vessel, in full communion with one another and inviting the viewer(s) to join their communion.

The Latin word *persona* refers to the "masks" we wear as human beings always in relation to other persons. As those created in the very image of God (Gen 1:26), we are made for life-giving relationships with God, other human beings, and all of God's creation. In the words of Dwight N. Hopkins, "the *imago dei* unfolds outward into the *missio dei*. We are called to exhibit healthy humanity by recognizing this divine image and sharing liberating evangelism with others."[5] We exist as persons, donning masks, always in relationship to others, which relationships provide fulfillment and meaning for our lives. Social-scientific research has demonstrated that it is not wealth, status, or even health that ultimately makes people happy. Rather, human happiness is grounded in the quality of the relationships we have with others. The quality of our relationships with other people is the crucial factor whether we experience joy in living. Is it not providential that the Christian church engages exactly in the "relationship business," with love as the guiding principle?

3. LaCugna, *God for Us*, chap. 8.

4. Ibid., 274.

5. Hopkins, *Being Human*, 185.

Jesus Christ reveals and re-presents true human being. Jesus existed in life-giving relationship with God through worship and prayer, the intimacy of which was indicated by his naming God as *Abba*, Daddy, in relation to his own Sonship. Moreover, Jesus instructed his followers to address God as *Abba* in prayer, reminding us of our shared lineage, that we are sisters and brothers. Jesus welcomed all people to live in communion with God, inviting us to share table fellowship with one another in his presence (Mark 14:22–25). Following in the way of Jesus, the early church "devoted themselves to the apostles' teaching and fellowship, to the breaking of bread and the prayers" (Acts 2:42). Jesus revealed his way to his followers both by the witness of his life in ministry and by teaching what it means for us to live in relation to others.

Family-systems theory provides a constructive framework for reinterpreting how the Christian understanding of justification by grace through faith contributes to self-differentiation, in contrast to the hyper-individualism of contemporary society. In systems theory "self-differentiation" and "nonanxious presence" derive from two human capacities: (1) the ability to constitute a centered self and (2) the ability to relate to others in life-giving ways.[6] The distortion of either of these capacities leads to disfunction: an inadequate sense of self undermines one's ability to relate to others, resulting in either inability to enter into and maintain life-giving relationships with others ("cut offs") or overidentifying oneself with particular others (enmeshment). In systems theory the way toward self-differentiation involves close examination of one's family of origin and family dynamics, especially as schematized through a genogram. Through insight into established patterns of emotional reactivity, one is able to attain a greater measure of self-differentiation and nonanxious presence.

The doctrine of justification by grace through faith in Jesus Christ provides a theological grounding for self-differentiation and nonanxious presence that both respects the insights of systems theory and transcends them.[7] While it is imperative that church leaders come to understand the emotional patterns that inform how they relate to others based on the patterns from their family of origin, there is an ultimate source for self-differentiation and nonanxious presence that comes to us as a gift of God in Jesus Christ. Trusting in God's grace serves both as a spiritual

6. For an accessible summary related to self-differentiation, see Richardson, *Becoming a Healthier Pastor*, chap. 5.

7. Nessan, "Surviving Congregational Leadership," 390–99.

foundation for self-acceptance and as a source of freedom to relate to other persons, which is created at worship (through Word and sacrament) and fed by spiritual practices. One's relationship with God, based on the gift of justification by grace through faith in Jesus Christ, grounds self-differentiation in God's acceptance of us for Christ's sake and provides a source of nonanxiety and peace deeper than the world gives (John 14:27). This is why the practices of Sabbath discussed in the next chapter are so crucial to the well-being of church leaders and members.

God's creation of human beings, we know today, took place through a long evolutionary process. Although the Genesis creation stories capture lasting truth about who we are as persons created in the very image of God and about the power of sin over human life as a consequence of "the fall," it is vital today that we attend to the insights of evolutionary science regarding human nature in order to fathom the dilemmas we face in following the teachings of Jesus—especially the radical imperatives of the Sermon on the Mount. Through our evolutionary inheritance we share many basic instincts, drives, and tendencies with our relatives in the animal kingdom. These include not only regulating the body (as with respiration or blinking) or satisfying bodily appetites (by gathering or hunting for food) but also engaging in behaviors instrumental to social relations. For example, human beings have an unprecedented capacity for face recognition, an ability that assisted humans to interpret social relations with acuity amid the complexities of human relationships, some of which might have threatened our very survival.[8]

Similarly, human beings inherited from our animal ancestors many primal instincts and drives in relation to behaviors such as aggression, social hierarchy, sex, and the avoidance of pain. When threatened by others, human beings are hardwired to respond aggressively, through emotional intensity, facial expressions, bodily posture, verbal warnings, and physical readiness to (defend from) attack.[9] As other species do, human beings also participate in symbolic displays and ritualized behavior to establish social hierarchy, especially among their sexual rivals of their own gender. One attains a sense of security in life by dominating and subduing one's rivals.

8. Cf. Bates and Cleese, *Human Face.*
9. Nessan, "Sex, Aggression, and Pain."

In terms of human sexuality, men and women have distinctive strategies for "success" according to our evolutionary inheritance.[10] Males of the species are genetically most successful through sexual behaviors that propagate sperm promiscuously, impregnating as many females as possible. Females of the species are most successful through the selection of genetically "strong" sexual partners and through mating strategies that will protect offspring from danger into adulthood (the age when they can themselves begin to propagate). Regarding the function of experiencing pain in evolutionary perspective, human beings share with other animals both the perception of pain and well-developed behaviors linked to pain avoidance.

Much human behavior is fruitfully explained in terms of how we relate to others based on such primal instincts and drives. Commonly, the reports we hear or read about in the news can be interpreted insightfully according to the instincts and drives we share with other animals. What complicates these impulses, however, is the evolution of the human mind. With the emergence of the neocortex and the human mind's unprecedented capacity for reflective self-consciousness, what once was natural for other animal species has become a moral and religious problem for the human being.[11] Because of human awareness about how, for example, our aggression or sexual behaviors can do harm to others (and have ramifications for our own well-being), human beings face moral and religious dilemmas based on our peculiarly human cognizance about how what we do affects others, either negatively or positively. This human mindfulness unveils the dislocation of the human animal. Whereas other creatures do what comes naturally without violating conscience or accruing blame for their aggressiveness or sexual behaviors, human beings are morally culpable for their actions. The human condition entails accountability for living responsibly with behaviors that are innate and natural in other species.

The evolution of the human mind also has opened the path to the development of human culture as one of the most powerful influences upon human behavior. Whereas other species, especially the higher primates, have rudimentary cultural practices, human beings have developed complex symbol systems to shape and direct human history. Kathryn Tanner comments: "to a particular group of people, *culture*

10. Cf. Ridley, *Red Queen*, chaps. 6 and 7.
11. Nessan, "Sex, Aggression, and Pain," 452–53.

tends to be conceived as their entire way of life, everything about the group that distinguishes it from others, including social habits and institutions, ritual, artifacts, categorical schemes, beliefs, and values."[12] Socialization into a particular culture or subculture significantly shapes what we consider normative human behavior. One of the functions of human culture is either to endorse or resist the primal instincts and drives that motivate human action. This means that cultural elements (such as stories, rituals, or values) can work upon the human person to either accentuate or resist the evolutionary impulses that are deeply embedded in our human psyche. For example, culture can either endorse expressions of human aggression against enemies in a time of war, or culture can promote nonviolent means of conflict resolution. Culture can titillate innate human sexual drives through advertising images in the marketing of products, or culture can set limits on the sexualizing of human persons as objects to motivate consumption.

Religions, with their warrants about what we are to regard as ultimate in life, are powerful shapers of cultural values. For this reason, as Musimbi Kanyoro argues, we need a vital "cultural hermeneutics" for interpreting particular cultural phenomena.[13] Religious beliefs and practices, as elements of human culture, can either endorse or curb innate human impulses regarding aggression, hierarchy, sex, or pain. Appeals to religious traditions can provide warrants for either just war or principled nonviolence, dictatorship or participatory democracy, polygamy or celibacy, corporal punishment or restorative justice. In relation to Christian beliefs and practices, the Bible too can function to shape human culture variously, depending on one's interpretive lens. Christian leaders appeal to the Bible to pray for the victory of "our" nation over its enemies, to authorize varied forms of ecclesial government, to combat or allow committed same-gender sexual partnerships, or to support or oppose the death penalty. In each of these instances, it is useful to consider how the innate instincts and drives that condition human behavior are either authorized or resisted by religious teachings.

Further, religion can either reinforce the cultural values within which it exists, or religion can contrast and conflict with them. When it does contrast, its adherents need clear direction from the religion in order to not be overly influenced by the dominant culture. The boundary

---

12. Tanner, *Theories of Culture*, 27.

13. Kanyoro, *Introducing Feminist Cultural Hermeneutics*, chap. 5.

practices we are exploring in this book are in most cases not in line with the practices of the dominant culture in which we find ourselves: this contrast gives us all the more reason to be clear about them, to teach about them, and to refer to them explicitly. Without such clarity, behavior will inevitably drift toward the norms of the dominant culture rather than toward what is spiritually derived.

The teachings of Jesus make strenuous demands on human beings to live not according to the norms of our animal ancestors but according to those potentialities that belong to the evolution of the human mind and culture in fostering life-giving relationships with God, other persons, and God's creation. We find especially in the Sermon on the Mount the most radical of Jesus's teachings about what it means for the church to be a "contrast community" to both our animal nature and the dominant culture.[14] With regard to striving for power in a social hierarchy, Jesus teaches that those who are great must become as a child (Matt 18:1–5). This is how love works; it makes us subservient to it and gives us the desire to elevate others. With regard to sex, Jesus teaches his disciples that they not only are to avoid adultery but also are not to look with lust at other persons (Matt 5:27–28), which would be to objectify them. Regarding avoidance of pain, Jesus instructs his disciples to take up the cross and follow him (Matt 16:24–26). The goals of love must become stronger than the urge to avoid pain and loss.

Regarding aggression and retaliation—the taking of an eye for an eye or a tooth for a tooth—Jesus teaches his followers to turn the other cheek, to love our enemies, and to pray for those who persecute us. (Matt 5:38–47). Being oppressed and mistreated does not excuse one from the command to love. Those who use and abuse others remain themselves in need of love and generosity. However, as we show love and generosity, we must always insist that those who have been harmed remain safe. To experience compassion in response to aggression can open the perpetrator to life-changing transformation. The oppressed and mistreated can serve on the front lines of the campaign of love and compassion, provided that they have been involved in a process of truth and reconciliation with the perpetrator about what has occurred. It is important that we reframe reconciliation from a matter of individual forgiveness to a process of communal reconciliation in the form of restoring right relationships and justice.[15]

---

14. Bailey, *Contrast Community*, chap. 1.
15. Cooper-White, *Cry of Tamar*, 253–62.

Human beings are best understood not as individuals but as persons! Individuals pursue self-interest while persons are made for life-giving relationships with others and with creation in the presence of the triune God. Following Jesus means following his way in the things that make for life, peace, and shalom. According to Randy S. Woodley: "Shalom is always tested on the margins of society and revealed by how the poor, oppressed, disempowered, and needy are treated."[16] This way of discipleship places us in tension with many values endorsed by our culture and even by many conventional religious beliefs and practices. It pits Christian community against the dominant culture that competes in shaping our thoughts, beliefs, and behaviors. The moral assumptions we make based on our innate instincts and drives, even as these may be endorsed by culture and religion, often mislead us about the higher righteousness to which we are called as Christians (Matt 5:17–20). Only comprehensive attention to boundaries in all areas of life—in thought, word, and deed—can grant us life—true life, eternal life.

THOUGHT, WORD, AND DEED

We are relational beings called to love with our whole beings in relation to God, others, and self. Hopkins underscores the relational character of human persons:

> Relationality names the living presence of others in the self and the self in others . . . Each self, in this regard, internalizes prior human experiences from a massive span and scale of time and place. Likewise, each day during the self's sleeping and non-sleeping, conscious and subconscious moments, the individual takes in, through reason, intuition, the five senses, and spiritual avenues, a flood of information from others.[17]

The Great Commandment to love everyone and to do so unconditionally engages us in caring for the relational integrity and effectiveness of ourselves and others. This begins with our basic posture toward others, which Jesus addresses with the command to love. He did not just say to act according to love outwardly. Universal and unconditional love is a posture of the whole being, an inner and outer state of welcoming openness to all others, an eager invitation to know and be known. Good

16. Woodley, *Shalom and the Community of Creation*, 15.

17. Hopkins, *Being Human*, 99.

boundary practices cultivate this holistic posture of love in ourselves and in others. By necessity, it includes what we do within our hearts and minds, not just what we do overtly.

How we think about others can either strengthen or weaken our capacity to love them. What we say to another person can either strengthen or weaken their capacity to love themselves. What we say about someone to another person can either strengthen or weaken that person's capacity to love the other. How we think about ourselves, and the nature of our self-talk, can either strengthen or weaken our capacity to love ourselves. The same is true of our capacity to love God.

The mission of "doing no harm" in relationship to others involves keeping various types of boundaries. To apprehend self and others accurately in our mind and heart, with no false images, requires the absence of bias from preconceived ideas. Sloth (that is, laziness) loves bias. It wants hasty conclusions and generalizations, because taking each person at each moment in an open manner requires effort. Laziness would rather speculate than abide in a state of not knowing. It would rather judge than be uncertain. The stressed mind has the same tendency, since it wants to expend as little energy as possible. It wants to categorize people and secure them in those categories, rather than to go through the trouble of getting to know people as they are. The Christian directive against making false images as "impression building" pits this tendency of the human brain against secular culture, which promotes and reinforces impression building. The spiritual discipline of tolerating and even embracing "not knowing" is well described in the fourteenth-century Christian text *The Cloud of Unknowing*.[18]

What we experience in life involves an interaction between what happens objectively and what we bring to it subjectively. Fundamentally, when I encounter a person, what category do I put them in—the ingroup or the outgroup? Are they one of us, or not? The human brain wants to know, while Jesus tells us to treat everyone as being within the ingroup. Jesus instructs us to consider all people our neighbors and, even more fundamentally, our sisters and brothers. Everyone is in the ingroup; no one is in the outgroup. Jesus says as much in the Lord's Prayer. The word *Abba* implies that we are all in the same family. When we hold on to this truth and are filled with love, there is no bias; there is only charity.

18. Walsh, ed., *Cloud of Unknowing*.

Because we cannot know the extent of our subjective distortions in perceiving the other, some people advise that we operate with the *principle of charity*. The principle of charity operates according to the values not only of truth and honesty but also of helpfulness and kindness. The principle of charity conflicts with the wiring of the human brain to keep us safe. The safest thing is to assume the worst about someone else, not to assume the best. Martin Luther, for example, encouraged us to interpret another person's actions "in the best possible light."[19] But is this not naive charity at the expense of the truth? When we put our own behavior in the best possible light, for example, the result can be unhealthy denial of our genuine intentions and actions. With others, it can lead to allowing someone to persist in taking advantage of us or of others, because we do not want to think ill of them. It can lead to our turning a deaf ear to a complaint against someone whom we want to trust rather than investigating the matter out of concern for someone else's well-being. It could lead to irresponsible trust rather than due diligence—for example, in congregational youth protection policies.

An alternative is the *principle of truth in love.* Unconditional love toward the self creates safety so that we can see ourselves realistically, as we really are. It does not provoke defensive denial in us. It does not provoke shame but rather compassion for our human and animal natures. Unconditional love and acceptance does not hide from unpleasant truths but rather increases our capacity to apprehend the truth, which strengthens and protects our relational nature. In contrast, denial puts a person at undue risk of misbehavior while shame evokes the urge to withdraw from others. In shame we may well turn on ourselves with abusive self-talk and hurtful overt behavior justified by our negative attitude. In both cases life-giving relationships are damaged rather than enhanced, thus failing the test of love.

A healthy use of the principle of charity allows for accurate and truthful representation so that each person can contribute maximally, including ourselves. Each person legitimately has a different point of view and a different set of abilities and skills. The more points of view that contribute, the more fully we can apprehend the full truth. This view is consistent with the research, which shows that decisions tend to be better when more people contribute to them rather than fewer people. Truth is

19. See Luther, *Small Catechism*, "Explanation of the Eighth Commandment," 1160–67.

beyond the comprehension of any single mind, so we need the benefit of as many points of view as possible.

The spreading of the good news and therefore our very understanding of Christ depended upon the willingness of those who had encountered the risen Christ to bear witness to what they had directly seen and heard for themselves. To know what was going on, the disciples needed to hear from the women who saw the empty tomb and the angel who spoke to them. They needed to hear from those who encountered Christ on the road to Emmaus. A person's willingness to bear witness is enhanced when they know they will be met by a caring, listening ear. Sadly, surveys show that a vast majority of Americans have had meaningful spiritual experiences that they have not shared with others. We lose out from that reluctance. Unfortunately, it is common that when one does share such experiences, the listener does not respond with charity but rather puts their own spin on the other person's experience. To have the enormous benefit of another's experience, an attitude of open, nonjudgmental listening is needed. This respects boundaries. As Paul Tillich famously observed, the first duty of love is to listen.[20]

Listening requires mental, emotional, and even theological discipline.[21] We must set aside the filter of our own beliefs and experience in order to understand the other. If we approach others with the presumption that they are wrong because their beliefs are different from our own, we are incapable of understanding them. Philosopher Donald Davidson suggests that understanding requires applying the principle of charity, by which we assume the truth of what the other is saying.[22] Without that assumption, we are unable to understand the person, as we remain constricted by our own point of view and thus misrepresent the ideas of the other. Similarly, psychiatrist David Burns has found that it works best to first agree with someone who is upset with us.[23] When we subsequently are able to explain their point of view and perhaps even amplify it, the person feels understood and relaxes, thereby being more able to hear a different point of view from their own. Burns, who has widely taught this technique, also finds (as Davidson too would predict) that this act

20. These quotable words are widely attributed to Tillich, but they look like a composite: "In order to know what is just in a person-to-person encounter, love listens. It is its first task to listen" (*Love, Power, and Justice*, 84).

21. Hedahl, *Listening Ministry*, chap. 9.

22. Davidson, *Essential Davidson*, 234–35.

23. Burns, *Feeling Good Handbook*, chap. 21.

of agreement helps us enter into the mindset of the upset person. While students may initially object that they cannot agree to what they do not think is true, Burns advises that this objection falls away with repeated use of the technique. People learn from their own experience that the commitment to finding truth in another's viewpoint leads to just that. There invariably is truth in what the other is saying, while initially it might not appear to be so. Application of the principles of charity and seeking the truth in love can result in more people feeling safe enough to share what they have seen and heard, so all can benefit from it. In short, good boundary keeping helps us perceive the truth.

While this approach is not easy, it is also not easy to apprehend the truth of our own experiences. What we experience is the product of the interaction between what has happened externally and what we bring to events subjectively. This interaction constitutes our perception and experience. In order not to misinterpret events or create false images of others, we must approach each situation and person free from bias, free from hasty conclusions about the present, and free from faulty conclusions about the past. The subjective state we bring to experience is our inner world, the psyche, which we compose from the raw materials of the thoughts, feelings, memories, impulses, desires, urges, and images that impress us. We select from the vast array of inner experiences available to us those to which we give importance and priority, those on which we choose to dwell, and those which we choose to let go. This often unconscious selection process creates our disposition and predispositions. Our thoughts, feelings, and predisposition either help or hinder our being able to see the truth. What we do in our inner world matters. Good internal boundary keeping helps.

Thoughts that increase stress simultaneously reduce awareness, including awareness of the feeling states of others, thereby reducing the capacity for empathy and related empathic responses. Such thoughts make the situation in which one finds oneself seem worse than it really is (thinking, for example, "This will never work!"). Negative thoughts can make our own capacity seem less than it really is (for example, "I'm an idiot; what am I doing?"). We may also misperceive what others are doing and ascribe to them negative motives that are not actually present.

Enhancing and protecting our relational capacity takes into account how we relate to others in the privacy of our own minds and imaginations. Every thought about another person is an opportunity to love or not to love. Being loving enhances relatedness, while unloving thoughts and feelings damage our capacity to love. Love is a subjective state of heart, mind, and soul that regards and treats all others as part of one's ingroup. All are to be regarded as neighbors, not as aliens. Every thought is an opportunity to objectify and exploit, or to resist doing so. Lust provides one example of using another for our own pleasure, even if only in our imaginations.

In the other direction, jealousy and resentment cast us into the outgroup by our failure to participate in the joy of a sister or brother. Shame likewise casts us out from shared community. For a follower of Christ, the litmus test of our inner state is similar to the test for our actions: do we show love and the capacity for inclusiveness in relation to community with others?

While it belongs to our human-animal nature to have objectifying thoughts and feelings toward others, we are given the capacity to control where we put our attention. With each thought we can decide to dwell on it or not. We can either keep our attention on it or turn away. Spiritual practices like *centering prayer* and *welcoming prayer* exercise and strengthen our capacity to control our own attention; thereby we protect and enhance the capacity for relatedness in our own minds and hearts. As we gain control of the environments we create and inhabit, certain kinds of thoughts are more likely to occur in our minds. An important part of self-control is monitoring the environments into which we imagine ourselves. It is like controlling an appetite by not going to an all-you-can-eat buffet.

Jesus gives us a concrete way to assess our love: how we treat the least important person. Jesus said that how we treat "the least of these" is how we treat him (Matt 25:40). We perhaps care least about those we perceive as harming us. Since love is meant to bring us together, those most in need of my love may be exactly those who inflict harm on others and exploit others for their own gain. Thus, without perpetuating their own harm, victims are called upon by Jesus to love those who harm them. This advances love, adds love where it is missing. When perpetrators experience love, they may be transformed. In contrast, when we hate or harm them in return, we do nothing to increase their capacity for love. Further, when we harm them, we harm those who care about them—everyone in their family. As one who regarded himself as the brother of all, Jesus is harmed when we harm others. Likewise, Jesus is given joy when we give joy to others. Some have even taken this in a metaphysical sense—that Christ dwells in each of us: The Christ in us honors the Christ in others.

In this way, we do not favor those for whom we have personal affinity over those for whom we do not. This is the discipline of *love equality*. To see the other person through the eyes of Christ is to see them through the eyes of love. This is the Christian standard. To love is to bear witness to Christ, especially when it is most difficult to do so. We recall the opportunity for witness that was afforded to an Amish community. The community immediately extended forgiveness to a man who killed their schoolchildren, even as they also extended compassion to his family. They immediately recognized that his was the act of a troubled soul.[24]

Another test of whether a thought enhances life-giving relationships or not involves asking whether it meets the following four criteria:

1. Is it honest? Many in our culture believe that if a thought is honest, then it is healthy to think it and perfectly fine to say it to someone else. But that is not enough when our concern is for also for the other person.

2. Is it true? How certain are we that it is true? If we are not certain, then holding the thought and sharing it with others is being careless with the welfare of the other person about whom we are speaking. The same applies to thoughts about ourselves. As we stated above, speculation or predisposed interpretations about behavior do not meet the standard of certainty of truth. In our opening scenario, Megan passed along a rumor that Steven had been sexually abused and did so by labeling him ("a sexual abuse survivor"). She also speculated to herself about his trustworthiness and passed along that speculation to others. None of this passes the test of truth in thought or word.

3. Is it kind? The principle of compassion toward self and others precludes unkind thoughts, feelings, and actions as unworthy of our time and energy. Unkind thoughts damage our subjective relationship with a person. To verbalize them to others is to potentially damage another's relationship with that person and so to harm that person.

4. Is it helpful? Some thoughts and words may meet the above criteria but are simply not helpful in a situation. In those cases, the loving thing is to let them go.

24. See Doblemeier, dir. *Power of Forgiveness*.

Prayer and meditation are practices that help condition our hearts and minds to be loving. In the Lord's Prayer Jesus taught us to regard all others as part of the ingroup to which we all belong.[25] When someone asked Jesus how they should pray, his instruction was to pray not as an individual but rather as a "we" praying on behalf of an "us." He addressed the prayer to the One who created us all, our common "parent" or *Abba*, as in the voice of a small child. In this prayer, we pray for love and compassion to reign on earth. We pray that all persons will have their basic needs met. Compassion comes from a shared sense of vulnerability, with which this prayer connects us. In that regard, it is interesting to note that when Jesus was asked, "Who is our neighbor?" in effect the answer was that our neighbor is anyone and everyone (Luke 10:36–37). We are all from the same neighborhood. In the parable of the Good Samaritan, the person in the story who stopped to help the man who was beaten and robbed was someone who was himself highly vulnerable to being attacked on that road. The man he helped was from a group of people who treated him as an enemy. When we lose our sense of shared vulnerability, we lose our capacity for empathy. And so this prayer reminds us of the utter dependency on God that we all share in common. In this prayer, we pray for healing in broken relationships through acts of forgiveness. We are in this together, and together we shall remain. There are no outsiders.

Another spiritual practice that enhances life-giving relationships is the blessing of others. When we consider who is suffering in the world and extend our blessing toward them in our prayer life, we enhance our relatedness with each other. Since we are also encouraged to "bless the LORD, O my soul" (Psalm 103), we get the amazing reminder that blessing can even come from us to the Lord. This is one expression of our love of the Lord. We are not relegated merely to request that the Lord bless us or someone else. We are the agents. Even more sobering in this regard is Jesus's statement that if we do not forgive someone, they are also not forgiven in heaven. We act on behalf of the whole by how we relate to others, so this is both a huge responsibility and a vast opportunity.

We have been through an era in North America when people have wanted to believe that our inner lives do not matter: for example, that it is fine for someone during sex to fantasize about being with someone other than their partner, if doing so gives them more pleasure. Some have wanted to believe that infidelity does not hurt anyone if the partner never finds out about it. Some have wanted to believe that taking what does not

25. Cf. Bailey, *Contrast Community*, chap. 10.

belong to us does not matter if the other party can afford to lose it and never finds out who took it. What makes something wrong is "getting caught." But attitudes and secret actions do matter. This is why Jesus's Sermon on the Mount and Luther's Explanation of the Ten Commandments include our thoughts and feelings in the same moral category as outward actions. There are boundaries to be respected in both arenas.

To summarize, here are seven types of individual boundaries to be respected in our covert (internal) actions:

a. *Identity boundaries.* We respect a person's identity boundaries when we internally and externally regard them according to their core identity as a distinct and unique person, a child of God, and as someone for whom Christ died. We do not simply view people as objects for our use or according to what they can do for us. We do not create false images of others either in our own minds or in the way we communicate about them to others. We think of them and refer to them with the name they wish us to use, not using labels or nicknames they do not offer. We do not generalize about them, which leads to misinterpreting their behavior. We do not speculate about them; instead we stick to what we know for sure.

b. *Physical boundaries.* We do not imagine exploiting the person by sexualizing them in our mind or fantasizing about them in ways that turn them into objects for our own ends.

c. *Will boundaries.* We do not mentally consider how we can dominate or control another person. When we make a request of another person, we inwardly and outwardly respect no as an answer without demanding explanations or judging their reasons.

d. *Emotional Boundaries.* We inwardly and outwardly allow others to have their own feelings and thoughts without invalidating them or deciding for them what they should think or feel.

e. *Mental Boundaries.* We appreciate the importance of other people's thoughts as an important expression of their identity. We do not criticize others inwardly or outwardly for what they think or believe, but rather seek to understand and learn from them.

f. *Resource boundaries.* We do not covet the resources others have or lay claim to them in any way, including their physical resources, money, time, and talents. We do not impose guilt or manipulate others to use their resources in the way we desire.

g. *Spiritual Boundaries*. We do not judge another's relationship with God or interpret another's spiritual experiences. We do not invoke God's action toward the other person without their consent. We do not decide for others what they should believe or practice spiritually. We do not use God to manipulate, correct, or condemn others even in our own minds.

Speaking is a form of action. All of the above apply also to how we speak to another and what we say about them to others. Jesus taught his followers to discipline what they say. For example, Jesus tells his disciples not to swear using oaths but rather to simply let "your word be 'Yes, Yes' or 'No, No'!" (Matt. 5:37). Moreover, Luther taught us not to "tell lies about our neighbors, betray or slander them, or destroy their reputations. Instead we are to come to their defense, speak well of them, and interpret everything they do in the best possible light."[26]

Returning to our opening scenario, we see many kinds of boundary violations. Megan "reports" to others that Steven is a sexual abuse survivor, which, if true, is not her information to share. But she does not really know it to be true; she is simply passing along what she has heard from the church secretary, which is unfair to Steven (and might well put the church secretary at risk of losing her job for violating this boundary). Megan then generalizes about sexual abuse survivors being more at risk for abusing others. Even if her generalization were valid, which it is not, it would be prejudicial and unfair to Steven. Beth and Joanne then talk about Steven and Fey not having children and engage in speculation about it, imposing false images of them.

BEARING WITNESS, TESTIMONY, GOSSIP

The dominant culture values power and influence. Every opportunity to speak is an opportunity to gain power and influence. We are advised by business consultants that if we wish to be successful, we should treat ourselves as we would a commercial object, because in fact we are a commercial object. We need to sell ourselves in order to have others desire us socially and vocationally. If we are not successful, we need to "rebrand" ourselves according to what would be more successful, look the part, and act the part. To get a job, you need to figure out what the employer wants and then shape your resume and yourself to fit it. Once in the job,

26. Luther, *Small Catechism*, "Explanation of the Eighth Commandment," 1161.

the project of shaping and selling one's self continues by our performing the actions the employer desires. In this course of action, while material success may be forthcoming, demoralization occurs internally. Moral injury may occur if one violates one's deepest values, which includes the spiritually derived value about doing good in the world rather than the culturally assumed value of making money.

In order to prevent ourselves from feeling bad, we learn from the dominant mental health community the art of *reframing*. Reframing, when applied without integrity or moral guidance, easily becomes the practice of thinking about what we are doing in a way that prevents us from feeling guilty, rather than finding words that reflect the truth of the situation. Thus there may be ways that reframing is "helpful" in keeping us going, but really not true. Similarly, a manipulative person will put a spin on another person's words, in order to create the appearance of support, when in fact it is a stealthy ploy to alter what the other person has said. Another example of this is telling others what they think about something in order to appear to have their approval of your own idea: "I know you'll agree with me that . . ." This is pure manipulation.

The standard in court is to tell the truth and nothing but the truth. As Sargent Friday famously said, "Just the facts, ma'am; just the facts." To tell the truth and only the truth takes the spin out of things, because spin is a form of manipulation and deception. It is an interpretation. Manipulation damages life-giving relationships by treating others as objects to get what one wants. It also damages life-giving relationships by risking loss of trust on the part of the other. Self-deceptive reframing even damages our relationship with ourselves, making ourselves less trustworthy in our own eyes.

To not interpret what we perceive in order to keep to the facts requires a deliberate sustained campaign. It is well worth the effort. It is hard enough to accurately report what you see and hear in an auto accident, let alone the extraordinary events reported in one's spiritual experience. In bearing witness and testifying to what we have seen and heard that has spiritual and religious import, we again have enormous responsibility and enormous opportunity. Take, for example, the story of the empty tomb reported in John 20. Mary visited the tomb where Jesus was buried and saw that the entrance was no longer covered by the stone that had enclosed it. She interpreted that it had been "rolled away" and that someone had "taken" the body of Jesus. This was all misleading interpretation. It would have been factual to state simply that she found the tomb empty and did not know what had happened. To remain factual requires a willingness to not know and to say that one does not know. Comfort with not knowing is essential to the ability to know the truth and report it accurately.

"God came to me in a dream last night and told me the pastor has to go. He is destroying the church." But when Ed's friend asked him to say exactly what happened in the dream, it became clear that Ed had distorted the actual dream material into the interpretation he wanted and was giving it authority from beyond. We can distort our dreams instantaneously. In recalling them, thinking about them, writing them down, and telling them to others, they filter through lenses constructed from our own perceptions of reality based on assumptions, fears, and desires. Sticking to the facts is hugely important.

When we listen to another's testimony, we are also challenged not to interpret. To assert "Oh, that is a God moment!" or "There are no coincidences" is to tell other people what they should believe about their own experiences. In doing so, we make it our own and impose it on the other person, a boundary violation. The sad result is that people do not feel safe in sharing spiritual experiences with others. Neither do we want others to distort it, nor do we want others to think we are crazy, because we had an extraordinary experience. On the other hand, respecting our own boundaries can mean, at least temporarily, keeping extraordinary experiences to ourselves. Mary told no one about the message that she was pregnant with Jesus but kept it safe in her heart where she could come to understand it free from the contamination of other points of view. This was wise.

When we communicate with others, we are carefully attuned to how they are reacting and tend to adjust what we are saying in order to get approval. Without those visual and auditory cues, social media have trained users get their entries "liked" in order to get "friended." We are constantly being judged "thumbs up" or "thumbs down." This setup works against integrity. It easily results in a sense of self that is shaped by the dubious interpretations of others regarding our actions online. In no way does this enhance life-giving relationships, because the object presented to ourselves and others is a constructed self, not who we really are. It is a deliberate fabrication. It appears, however, to give us power about what we want in life, except, of course, the deep desire to be known and loved just as we are. When churches use social media, this should only be on the terms of the gospel, not involving "liking" and "friending." "Thumbs up" and "thumbs down" was a Roman practice, not a Christian one. The sanctity of the psyche must be respected for God's unconditional love to prevail.

Some clergy rationalize their speaking ill of others as healthy "venting." Many people still feel that venting, which involves complaining about others, is helpful psychologically in order that things "do not build up." Clergy groups support and may even encourage this. The mental health field has long since abandoned this approach, however, as it neither matches current understandings of how the psyche works nor accords with the research. Research instead verifies that venting negative feelings toward others simply reinforces those feelings, which is what behavior theory predicts. Venting is deceptive, because initially we may feel better after doing so. But as we know, many unhealthy behaviors initially bring pleasant feelings.

When we want to express our feelings, it is best to always follow the same rules that we would if we were expressing those feelings directly to the person (or persons) who evoked those feelings. Even when they are not in the room, using "I" statements to express own our feelings is far healthier in every respect than making "they" statements about others. The latter lead to cynicism. Venting with "they" statements can also be attractive because it leads to a sense of intimacy and support with the people to whom we are talking. But this is false intimacy whenever the subject is "they" instead of "I." Internally, the same principles and considerations apply. When in the privacy of our own thoughts we think in terms of "you" or "they," we create false intimacy even within ourselves. We feel like we are being honest with our own feelings, when we are actually avoiding self-reflection by endorsing our own projections upon others. Venting also issues from a selfish motive, an ego motive, rather than the motive of bringing out the best in ourselves and others. Whatever the activity, the final criterion is, does this make us more loving, more able to serve, or less so? You will know them by their fruits.

This chapter has examined theological foundations, anthropological evidence, and best practices of boundary keeping in order to guide us in preserving the church's integrity both through our internal processing and through our interactions with others. As we have indicated, the practice of Sabbath is crucial for the centering of our lives necessary for maintaining wise boundaries in thought, word, and deed. The next chapter focusses on the meaning of Sabbath shalom for the sake of preserving the integrity of the body of Christ as a shared responsibility.

6

Sabbath Shalom: A Day in the Kingdom

SCENARIO SIX: SUNDAY CHURCH MEETINGS

RENALDO WAS RELATIVELY NEW to Lord of Life but was well liked and quickly voted into leadership positions. He had a very busy business and family life, as did many other members of the leadership team. For this reason he initiated having meetings after the first service on Sunday mornings, so people would not have to make an extra trip to the church for another meeting. The initial response was very positive and they encouraged other congregational committees to follow suit.

THE NATURE OF SABBATH

Sabbath is in many ways the crown jewel of all boundary keeping. It belongs to the first of the Ten Commandments. In the first Genesis creation story, Sabbath is the goal of creation, coming after the creation of everything else, as the very crown of all creation. But the meaning of Sabbath's value has been elusive. Most obviously and conventionally, it is about the need of the body and soul for rest. Sabbath is, in part, the antidote to "the cares and riches and pleasures of life that choke the spirit" (cf. Luke 8:14) As Michael Kerper notes, "Without a generous amount of leisure, the spirit dies." Further, he says, "And when this happens, faith communities become lifeless museums used for 'holy days.'"[1]

1. Kerper, "Loss of Leisure Time, Loss of Faith."

Less apparent, especially to the busy mind preoccupied with the things of this earth, Sabbath (as itself a product of creation) is the threshold to a dimension of creation that is not readily accessible. Sabbath, fully engaged in by us, demonstrates that good boundaries not only prevent bad things from happening through the choking of the spirit but help create the conditions for wonderful things to happen that would not otherwise be possible, when the spirit is fully functioning. Walter Brueggemann believes that the first table of the Ten Commandments clarified for the Israelites that Pharaoh was not their god.[2] They no longer needed to serve Pharaoh; now they were to serve God. The commandment to keep the Sabbath naturally follows as a reminder to worship God above all things. After the Sabbath commandment comes the basics of what it means to care for God's people rather than to exploit them.

Every person, every place, and every time reveal aspects of the Divine. Without this awareness, we know less about God. Sabbath, when entered into deeply, helps us connect with the Divine in all persons, places, and times because it allows us to look past the blinders imposed by our usual preoccupation with "function": What do I need from you? What can I get from you? What can you do for me? What do you want from me? What do I need or what can I get from this place I am in? All these considerations are suspended in the practice of radical Sabbath, allowing us to see and appreciate everything that is. It is a time to relate to others, to our own true selves, and to the living God according to the values of the kingdom.

Sabbath turns off the usual sense of purposefulness we normally bring to our work and to the other tasks that we need to do to survive. We refrain from "using" what others do or say. When we suspend viewing others as objects for our own use, we are better able to see their genuine identity, the "who" of the person and not just their "what for." In Sabbath we also relate differently to ourselves. We put aside the ways we tend to objectify ourselves by "branding" ourselves. When we are in our conventional mode of relating to ourselves and others, our awareness is constricted to functional value. We are focused on task, which excludes awareness of other dimensions.

Stress further constricts our awareness, especially time pressure. Under time pressure, we are more likely to walk past someone in need than stop to help them.[3] This is our usual state of mind. In this mode, those

---

2. Brueggemann, *Covenanted Self*, 49–51.

3. Cf. Darley and Batson, "From Jerusalem to Jericho," 100–108.

who can contribute something to us get more of our positive attention, because of their advantage to us. People who are neutral to us do not count, and those who are in our way often get treated poorly. This approach is light-years away from loving our neighbor and treating the least of these as we would treat Jesus. Other natural objects are also thought of in terms of their potential usefulness to us, not as ends in themselves. A tree is not at thing of beauty; it is potential lumber. The world of nature becomes occupied with things we can possess, because we are operating with a "production and acquisition" frame of mind. We entirely squelch true mindfulness as we strive merely to get by functionally in the world. Thereby the spirit becomes choked and thereby the work of the kingdom.

The intent of Sabbath is easily co-opted to simply serve the cares, riches, and pleasures of life. To remain effective, the body and the brain need rest. The anxieties of our cares and "urgent" priorities both serve to keep us from taking Sabbath breaks or, if we do, motivate us to compromise Sabbath. We keep working the treadmill instead of engaging in something that might threaten to be disruptive of our established way of life. Our behavior may appear like Sabbath as a kind of rest from work, but in actuality there is little or no sense of the Divine in our rest. Brueggemann describes this as going "through the motions of Sabbath."[4] Renaldo wanted to use Sabbath time to get church business done, during which he and the other leaders would principally relate to each other in terms of their congregational functions, not according to their true personhood. Sabbath is elegant in design.

Sabbath instruction tells only what not to do, not what to do. We are to keep the time holy, which is a matter of quality, not content per se. Without resting in God, rest can merely serve to support the status quo. We are commanded simply to rest from our work and to grant that rest to others as well. Why is this so hard?

If you have ever been to Cloquet, Minnesota, you have probably had the odd pleasure of seeing the only gas station in the world designed by the famous architect Frank Lloyd Wright. Mr. Wright, as they called him, was a utopian. He did not design buildings to accommodate how people live and work; he designed them purposely to shape how people live and work in accordance with certain ideals. In the homes he designed, for example, the bedrooms are very small, really just sleeping chambers, because he did not want people to isolate themselves from others. You are not allured to want to hang out in one of his bedrooms but rather are

---

4. Brueggemann, *Sabbath as Resistance*, 62.

attracted to the great room with its welcoming large hearth, where you will be in the company of the rest of the family.

Cloquet was to be the site for an entire utopian community that Mr. Wright envisioned. But the only building that was ever constructed was the gas station. He designed it with a second-floor lounge where weary travelers could rest. As with deep Sabbath, however, rest was not the only goal for the lounge: it was to provide a place of rest so that relaxed folks could notice and enjoy the beautiful view of the forests of northern Minnesota. What do you suppose the travelers' lounge is used for now? Storage! Travelers today do not want to stop and rest; they want to stop and go. They scarcely care about beauty; they want to get to their destination as quickly as possible. Similarly, God's rest stop at Sabbath is largely going unobserved.

To a large degree we are afraid to stop due to our attachment to "the cares and riches and pleasures of life." We fear that we will lose something, not accomplishing what we think needs to be completed. We become anxious that our families will lack for something. All boundary keeping involves loss, or the risk of loss, of the good for the sake of the best. Our occupations, which are meant to serve us, instead actually enslave us when we are afraid of losing them. Our possessions do the same when we are unwilling to risk losing them. We do not understand how we can slow down or stop for any significant period of time. It just does not seem practical or even possible, at least to the anxious mind. The anxious mind, like that of Pharaoh, always expects something more, demands more and more work from us. In fact, we increasingly feel we must always be multitasking in order to get everything done that is important to us.

But suppose we do stop, then what? Here is the elusive part. For those who are adept at setting the boundaries to enter deeply into Sabbath, there is beauty, awe, wonder, and joy to connect with aspects of God and God's creation that normally are obscured by our busyness and preoccupation with the practical, utilitarian concerns of the material world. Why do some people, however, who try to stop and to rest quickly become bored and restless for their usual preoccupations and sources of stimulation? Rest can seem tedious, even depressing. Rob Bell, in his book *Velvet Elvis*, describes his own early attempts at keeping Sabbath.[5] He initially became depressed. Rather than turning back, Bell persisted and broke through the fog of depression to experience the joys of Sabbath. Bell's experience is not unusual.

5. Bell, *Velvet Elvis*, 116.

In the early 1900s a psychiatrist recognized that some of his patients became depressed on Sundays. He called it Sunday Neurosis.[6] Others also struggle with Leisure Sickness, the phenomenon that some people feel less happy during vacations.[7] Typically, however, these are transitory phases of adjustment that open a path to the benefits of actual Sabbath keeping, when we learn to set aside our usual concerns and recover from the toll they take on us. Many of us experience that the first few days of vacation are spent catching up on sleep. There may be a period of less mental clarity or even sluggishness until we emerge on the other side, at last able to experience things we would not experience otherwise.

Camp counselors report that when campers, particularly youth, are deprived of their electronic devices, for the first couple days they get bored and restless. They grumble and complain. They must go through withdrawal from artificial stimulation. Then after a couple days, other dimensions of the natural world open up to them. They are able to appreciate the stillness of the woods, the scent in the air, the amazing flight of the birds, the aliveness of the clouds, and the depth and grandeur of the night sky—none of which were previously accessible to their awareness, given the state of their preoccupations.

The dimension of reality Jesus named the kingdom of God, which some now refer to as the shalom of God, requires a certain state of consciousness in order to perceive and enter. In the shalom of God, unconditional love is shared in life-giving relationships with all—with neighbors, with self, with the Lord God, and with all God's creation. The lens of unconditional love suddenly makes all reality clearly accessible. It provides the "eyes to see and ears to hear." It is an awareness of everything around us and in us, which is difficult to maintain all the time. Normally, the mind gives value and priority to certain things over others in terms of our attentiveness, thereby distorting our perception through the exercise of judgment. In contrast, nonselective compassion engages everything willingly.[8] In our everyday lives, priority is given to utilitarian matters. Realistically, except for the mystics, there is no way to be aware of the holiness of all reality and its glory apart from Sabbath. It rarely happens any other way.

When we look at what the most expansive states of awareness require, we find that our energy must be on the high side rather than the

6. Frankl, *Man's Search for Meaning*, 112.

7. Vingerhoets et al., "Leisure Sickness," 311–17.

8. Cf. Nussbaum, *Upheavals of Thought*, chap. 6.

low side—something that Sabbath helps to create. Awareness takes energy. It also takes energy to sustain a positive mood. Our energy must be calm rather than agitated in order for us to have fullest awareness. When water is clear and calm and the air is clear and calm, you can see deeply through both into the nighttime sky. Our consciousness must be clear rather than foggy, and our awareness must be broad rather than narrowed by utilitarian concerns. Both of these qualities of consciousness are more available in deep Sabbath and invite entry into loving awareness of the shalom of God. If we use Sabbath merely for recovery, in order to get ready to go back to work, we miss out on this most blessed gift, while possibly believing that we actually are keeping Sabbath. That is just scratching the surface of Sabbath. "Sabbath is not simply the pause that refreshes. It is the pause that transforms."[9]

Here is where we must add something to our typical understanding of Sabbath as merely resting from our work. Martin Luther wondered whether a man passed out on the floor on Sunday was keeping Sabbath. He was, after all, resting from his work. What was missing? He was not keeping the Sabbath holy. Holy intent involves neither becoming unconscious (in order to recover, numb out, "veg out," or forget), nor simply doing what feels good (for example, enjoying the benefits of our labor through consumption). Sabbath is not payday. A holy intent and focus can help carry us into awareness of God's shalom and assist us in avoiding lesser interests that do not have shalom qualities. This is possible, however, only if we are prepared.

Entering into the sacredness of time brings with it feelings of vulnerability, as it did for Rob Bell. Is that surprising? Do not all encounters with the holiness of the sacred involve vulnerability? Brené Brown's conclusion from studying vulnerability is that it is the doorway to many very special things, including intimacy.[10] We would add that vulnerability is the threshold to deep Sabbath. Of course, awareness of the sacred threatens the comfortable confines of the ego and the pursuit of ego interests. Becoming comfortable with our own vulnerability aids in the experience of Sabbath, just as it does with other forms of boundary keeping. If there is no zone of vulnerability, it is probably not deep Sabbath. In deep Sabbath, we invite others to enter as well by reducing their sense of risk through our own good boundary keeping. When we purposely refrain

9. Bruggemann, *Sabbath as Resistance*, 45.

10. Brown, *Daring Greatly*, 104.

from regarding what others say and do in terms of our own self-interest, they can feel safer to explore and share who they really are.

Left to our own devices, most of us respond to vulnerability and other forms of emotional discomfort by backing off rather than leaning into it. We turn on our smartphone, laptop, or TV to avoid the initial discomfort of silence and apparent aloneness. We say "apparent" because in the reality of God's shalom, there is no such thing as being alone. We are always surrounded by God's creation. When the ego is motivated to reduce its discomfort, we rationalize doing what brings us pleasure and enjoyment in the free time of Sabbath. Again, our relationship to our feelings is crucial for living a faithful life. When we let ego-based feelings control us, we deprive ourselves and others of what is possible, instead of riding the waves of the Spirit.

Sabbath is a state of being. Boundary keeping is fundamentally about love. When we love someone, we give them time and attention. In the case of Sabbath, it is about fully receiving God's love even with awareness of our unworthiness, realizing that God's unconditional love is beyond any sense of being worthy or unworthy. It can neither be earned, nor can it be lost. We are referring here to unconditional love as grounded in God and directed toward the Self, not love of ego and its trappings: loving God, loving our neighbors, and loving ourselves. Sabbath helps us increase our awareness in all dimensions—physical, emotional, mental, and spiritual—making us more able to love.

There is something paradoxical about Sabbath, which reflects the paradoxical nature of unconditional love itself. Sabbath is both a gift and a commandment, a delight and a duty. It is a gift of love, which we have a duty to receive. It is a gift for us and yet it belongs to God, because we belong to God. Our lives belong to God and our time belongs to God. When we refuse the gift of Sabbath, we steal from our relationship with God and thereby also intrinsically from our relationship with ourselves. When we encroach on another's Sabbath time, we steal from them as well as from God. Renaldo's practical considerations in doing the business of the congregation after worship, during what is Sabbath time, is a form of theft, no matter how well intentioned.

Like Sabbath, love is both a gift and a commandment: the greatest commandment. It is both grace and law. The ability to accept ambiguity and apparent contradiction comfortably is also required of those living God's shalom. Deep Sabbath and unconditional love change our likes and dislikes. Like and dislike considerations are subordinated to holiness.

All self-discipline involves the subordination of likes and dislikes to something of greater value. Self-discipline is, after all, the ability to get ourselves to do what we do not feel like doing and, conversely, to get ourselves to do things that we do not feel like doing. With what we might call "God-discipline" rather than self-discipline, we yield to holiness and the commands of love.

Complete awareness requires holding all things together, including contradictory things, instead of excluding some for the sake of others. Reality is not an either/or. The ability to hold together conflicting things is essential to living and working in a way fully informed by Christian values (rather than, for example, isolating business decisions from those values). It is also critical to our ability to recognize the truth. Researchers have discovered that our willingness to believe their findings is based on whether or not we like the implications of the data, a phenomenon called "solution aversion."[11] In order to acknowledge the truth, we must recognize and be able to suspend our personal likes and dislikes.

There are two versions of the Sabbath commandment in the Bible. In Exodus 20:3, Sabbath is referred to as a reality to be remembered, harkening back to the first Genesis creation story, according to which the seventh and final day of creation was a day of rest for God. Sabbath is the goal of creation. The ostensible reason for us to keep Sabbath is as a remembrance of God's original ordering of creation. In Deut 5:15, the reason given for keeping Sabbath is for the Israelites to remember their freedom, that the Lord delivered them from slavery. Now they were free to serve God, not Pharaoh. These reasons—God's ordering of creation, gratitude, and the celebration of freedom—inform deeper levels of Sabbath keeping.

The Sabbath commandment is brilliant in that it only tells us what not to do with it; it does not tell us what to do with it. We are to not work. People of faith over the centuries have put great effort ("great work") into defining both what work is and what it is not. For our purposes, we will understand work to be anything that carries a sense of obligation to the things of this earth, anything that is on a to-do list, anything we are not free not to do, or anything that advances such obligations. Thinking about work, for example, is work. The mind can engage in work even while the body is resting. While we cannot stop ourselves from having such thoughts, we do control how we relate to such thoughts once they

---

11. Cf. Campbell and Kay, "Solution Aversion."

occur. We can simply turn away from thoughts of work during Sabbath time. No, it is not easy, but with practice it can be done.

As people seeking to honor Sabbath, we have a tendency to "bargain" with it and interpret this as freedom to pursue our likes and dislikes. Doing this, however, only strengthens the part of the self that attends to likes and dislikes. Hence the value of considering holiness. A soaring eagle is free only by having rapport with the air current, sensing and responding to air's subtle movements. One of the lessons of Sabbath is that the greatest freedom comes with the consideration of holiness: "Since I enjoy mowing the lawn, it isn't a chore; it is a pleasure. Doesn't that count for Sabbath time?" By the criterion of freedom alone, the answer would have to be that it could only be considered a Sabbath activity if you are free never to mow the lawn, not just today but ever again. Given our attachment to the cares of the world and our anxiety about there being more things to do than there is time for us to do them, it is understandable that we want to bargain for counting things on the to-do list as Sabbath. Getting tasks done is one strategy for reducing stress. Renaldo and the others liked the time savings from killing two birds with one stone on Sunday mornings. The stressed mind, as we have mentioned, becomes short-term in its thinking. The secularization of Sabbath wants to turn it into a mere self-care practice to serve the purpose of sustaining the status quo with its narrow interests, instead of challenging the status quo with an awareness of the awe and wonder of things and people beyond their usefulness.

We can enter into sacred places as tourists or as pilgrims. If you have ever been to any of the great cathedrals, you may have noticed this difference. You also can see this difference in awesome natural spaces like a redwood forest. Some people enter these spaces in a preoccupied state of mind, still talking about the last thing they saw on their itinerary or about where they want to go to lunch. They may take a few pictures and barely notice where they are. Just like a stone skipping over the water, the faster we go, the more we just glance across the surface of things. Others may see the money to be made if only they could cut down the trees or sell things to the tourists. By contrast, others enter sacred spaces as a destination, not just an attraction along the way. These are the pilgrims. They are interested in forming a meaningful relationship with the space itself and what inhabits that space. They are able to engage the Divine presence. They have prepared their minds and hearts to be fully present, fully receptive, and fully prepared to engage what is there with their entire being.

Awe, wonder, and beauty are open to them, as is the subtle movement of the Spirit. In Sabbath we can enter the sacredness of time either as tourists or as pilgrims. What we experience depends on our approach. We prepare for entering into the depths of Sabbath by slowing down, resting, and opening up before entering into it—not just using Sabbath to recover from our tiring endeavors.

Sabbath contrasts with other uses of time in that it is not utilitarian. Utilitarian interests have an extrinsic objective. They aim to go from point A to point B. In Sabbath time, there is no point B. An example is the archetypal Sunday drive. How can you distinguish a Sunday driver? They drive like they have all the time in the world and as though they do not know where they are going. Both are true. Sunday drivers are actually interested, as Mr. Wright hoped, in the beautiful scenery around them. And it is true that they do not know where they are going. Arden's mother used to say, "Let's just get in the car and see where it takes us." On a Sabbath drive, at any given intersection you could choose any option, not just continuing in the direction you were headed. Sabbath is antihabit, anti-inertia, counter–status quo. In this state of openness, you explore. Even when you go nowhere and stay put, you become aware of more and more aspects and dimensions of the place where you happen to be.

All kinds of activities can have this Sabbath quality. In a Sabbath walk, for example, you also do not know where you are going. You are exploring, engaging, and interested in relating to whatever is encountered. It differs from purposeful walking, in that it has no point B. It differs from an exercise walk in that it has no objective. While an exercise walk may be refreshing and healthy, it is purposeful and therefore lacking this Sabbath quality of nonutility. Holy freedom is a characteristic of everything related to Sabbath. It does not need to have anything to show for it.

BOUNDARIES AND SABBATH

In Sabbath, good boundaries open up new possibilities. Another great example is Sabbath talk. In utilitarian communication, one aims to transfer information from one mind to another mind. The goal is to do so as efficiently and effectively as possible. This is useful and even feels great when one is understood correctly. In Sabbath conversation, however, when the sacredness of time is respected, there is no time pressure.

When two people both are freed from the usefulness of what is said, whether now or later, there is safety to disclose freely. Sabbath conversation can wander without feeling like anything important was lost. This is precisely the kind of conversation that can lead to intimacy through vulnerability. It is the kind of talking some people can do in a car, while driving a long distance with a trusted companion. It starts and stops. It goes hither and yon. Campfires invite Sabbath conversation. In one such talk, after sharing an idea, Arden remembers his son saying, "I didn't know you felt that way." Arden replied, "I didn't know either. I've never had that thought before just now." Much of our talking is merely reporting rather than mutual exploration and discovery. This joy of discovery is made possible by the conditions of deep Sabbath: freedom from the distractions of one's usual concerns, holy intent, freedom to explore, and freedom from possessing or using what we encounter.

In our exploration of the different types of boundaries, we began with identity. Sabbath appeals to claiming our ultimate identity: who we are separate from our functions in the world. By remembering and engaging with God, we remember who we really are on the most fundamental level: we recall an identity that can never be lost. All other identities can be lost. Furthermore, we connect with our inherent freedom. When we grant Sabbath to others, we rest from relating to them according to their functional identities. If someone asks Arden on Sunday morning, "Aren't you Dr. Mahlberg?" he is likely to say, "Not today." Sabbath is broken by relating to others in their functional roles and is kept when we relate to others as wholly other than that, in the spirit of Buber's I-Thou relation.[12]

More challenging for many clergy is to separate who they are as persons from their identities as pastors or ministers, since those are thought to involve the whole person. Far from it! This belief is an excuse for not delving more deeply into the self and justifies the belief that clergy are somehow different from other people. Many clergy deeply long to be known as persons in distinction from their role and the stereotypes and assumptions that may go along with the role. Clergy spouses do also.

To rest from our work and engage otherwise, all part of the Self must disengage from work. Take the example of clergy. One part of disengaging is mentally resting from our work. Comedian Bob Newhart once observed that comedians are never really on vacation. No matter where they are, they are looking for material. This is as much an occupational hazard for preachers and teachers as it is also for writers—to be constantly looking for insights and material. One is always "on duty." Without an explicit Sabbath discipline all prayer, meditation, and devotional time, as well as

12. Cf. Buber, *I and Thou.*

other personal and family recreational time, can be spent mining for material, insights, or life lessons to use in sermons, Bible studies, or counseling. When one tries to mine Sabbath experience for work purposes, it is a violation of the integrity of Sabbath. It requires discipline to differentiate and safeguard personal time with God from its professional use, no matter how brilliant the insights.

Part of the preparation for going into Sabbath time is the reminder not to put to use any insights or material that comes up. There is precedent for relating to God differently during Sabbath. In the Jewish tradition, some distinguish between Sabbath prayer and non-Sabbath prayer. Sabbath prayer does not include petitioning God or asking God for anything, which would treat God in a utilitarian manner as someone from whom you want something. Sabbath prayers are prayers of thanksgiving. Similarly, clergy may find it helpful to distinguish relating to God in their work mode from encountering God in Sabbath, which is to be protected from professional use. Likewise, Sabbath can be a time to refrain from speaking for God.

Beyond physically resting from work and mentally resting from work (and from other areas of responsibility), one also needs to learn how to rest from work emotionally, to put down what we carry in our hearts. Resting from ministry emotionally means, in part, giving over the sense of responsibility that is usually carried. We simply must take significant rest breaks from the caring that is part of the job, as well as breaks from the trauma and suffering with which we have to deal. Some cannot go home and watch more suffering on TV. A good practice is to look back and debrief the past work period to see if there are feelings that remain undigested and, if so, to deal with them intentionally. If we do not do so, the result will be compassion fatigue, an inability to care. Instead of caring, we become cynical, resentful, and bitter toward those we are called to serve. This is true for any caregiver, professional or otherwise. It would seem odd that Sabbath time would be a time to stop caring. Jesus, after all, did heal on the Sabbath. But here it makes good sense for helping professionals to discover rest from their work by giving their caring concerns over to God for the duration of their Sabbath time. This frees you to have energy and time to care about other things and other people in personal rather than professional ways. Emotionally resting from our work and from other burdens of caring opens us to experience emotional states not as available when we are in work mode, for example, delight. Isaiah says to "call my Sabbath a delight" (Isa 53:13). Emotionally resting from caring work, we are more capable of engaging a broader range of feeling states, like delight, love, joy, and playfulness.

Spiritually resting from our work involves putting aside our primary call. We are in receiving mode. In doing so, we are not only refreshed, but we have time and energy to discover and engage in the other things we are called to do, in other roles that have importance for God's presence in our lives. Parent, friend, lover, writer, inventor, gardener, artist, naturalist, photographer, woodworker—God created us to be so complex and multifaceted that no earthly role, however important, can contain all of us. Sabbath is a time for exploring all the rest of what God calls us to be, the rest of who we are. When we are not getting enough time away from our daily work mindset, we lose track of the fact that we have other calls. Many pastors complain that they feel called to get involved in something that their congregation has no interest in, like justice work. When the pastor decides to do it anyway, even on their own time, they become more fully alive. Also, having a date with one's significant other in a committed relationship is a time to set aside other issues and just enjoy each other's company. Sabbath is a time to set aside one's issues with God and just enjoy God's company.

One of the occupational hazards of professional ministry is the objectification of God. We know that worship can be harder for clergy when they are worship leaders, because they must keep tracking in a work mode. They cannot just lose themselves in the experience. Even when clergy are worshipers in the pew, it can be similar to the difference between a nonmusician at a concert and a professional musician. The nonmusician listens with the emotional or experiential part of the brain, letting the music move them in a receptive mode. By contrast, the professional musician listens with the analytical part of the brain. The professional musician may even be "playing" the music, or "conducting" it with micromovements of the muscles. They are in active "work" mode, not receptive "being" mode. So when clergy and other worship leaders are in the pew, the challenge for them is to switch off the work mode and switch on the experiential. One's professional relationship with God can become devoid of an experienced faith component, given the constant pressure of speaking for God, speaking about God, and representing God in some responsible way. The professional minister can begin to encounter Holy Scripture exclusively in an analytic and utilititarian manner, not as an experience to ponder for the feeding of one's own soul.

In the novel *A New Kind of Christian*, Brian McLaren has his character Neo observe that "Talking about God for pay always threatens to
work against really loving God . . . The people who talk the most about
God are the ones most in danger of taking [God] for granted, of letting
God become just a comfortable word in their lexicon, a piece of furniture,
rather than a reality, a friend, a constant surprise."[13] This is strong stuff. In
Buber's I-Thou relationship, we stay with and savor the vastness and inex-
plicability of the Other, reaching well beyond what we have experienced
or have yet understood about the Other. We respect the inexpressible
nature of the Other that cannot be reduced to the categories of language.
Sabbath rest from the work of ministry includes the soul's being with
God in ineffable mystery, not trying to reduce this mystery to words or
to use it in any way.

Dual relationships are always complicating. To lend money to
a friend can risk the friendship. Working for or with family members
can risk the integrity either of the family role or the business role. Many
a farm boy has grown up feeling that they only had working relationships with their fathers, not personal relationships. What happens in the
boss-employee relationship during the day can be hard to set aside after
work is done in order to pick up a father-son relationship. Sometimes
after work you would rather not spend any more time with each other.
Spouses who work together are challenged to learn to set the boundaries
necessary to keep the roles separated so that each can adequately flourish.
Many clergy couples who work together, for example, go to bed and talk
shop. Rarely do they have set staff meetings with each other, like they
would if they were not married to each other. They do not see the need
for it, since they can always talk shop. On their days off, they may wish
to go their separate ways. Their personal relationship becomes weakened
by poor boundaries.

Like the farm family, some clergy would rather not spend their free
time with the same people they work with. Some clergy admit to not
wanting to spend Sabbath time with God. In their meditation practice,
some clergy prefer to have a nonspiritual focus rather than a spiritual
one. Beyond that, many clergy contend with the desire to spend nonwork time in secular—and possibly even unholy—pursuits, to get as
far away from work mode as possible. Some refer to this as "carnalling
out," pursuing carnal interests as a break from "the holy life." We can get
tired of being good, especially when there is a sharp contrast between

13. McLaren, *New Kind of Christian*, 167.

how we would like to act and the constraints of the role we occupy. In this circumstance, switching from religious or spiritual work mode to Sabbath mode can feel unfulfilling, too much like more of the same, too much "not me." This is a barrier to Sabbath keeping, not only for spiritual workers but for others in the helping professions. We get tired of being good. We long to engage in "conduct unbecoming" our professions. This involves splitting off parts of ourselves for the sake of indulging our appetites, impulses, urges, and desires. Usually this involves numbing our consciousness rather than fostering clear and heightened awareness. This is a serious condition calling for the kind of disciplined attention professional consultation can provide.

The answer is not to degrade Sabbath. There can be much fulfillment within Sabbath when all parts of us are integrated within holy intent. In some Jewish traditions, for example, the strong recommendation is for married couples to make love on the Sabbath. When we consider that the Sabbath way of doing things is to savor them, unhurried and not goal-directed, Sabbath lovemaking can be the best of all, because of the greater awareness and integration of relating the body with our deepest values. Likewise Sabbath eating can be the best of all. Sabbath conversation becomes a delightful discovery process about the self and the other. On Sabbath we do fast from some things, things related to work, in order to feast on others. It can be a time of holy indulgence, with the whole of us involved, in contrast to the habitual multitasking and halfheartedness whereby a part of us is dissociated or split off so that many experiences are less than satisfying.

The examined life allows us to be more fully integrated within the clarifying awareness of the Spirit. Within the safety of God's unconditional love, we can see more fully how our actions relate to core values of the kingdom. Retreats tend to serve that purpose, allowing people to see what they cannot see when they have their nose too close to the page. Most people's experience is that they are better able to connect with the big picture when they "get out of the office," so to speak. We must find the conditions that will short-circuit habitual ways of thinking, feeling, and acting in order to attain greater awareness.

There are whales that periodically stop swimming, raise their heads up vertically out of the water as far as they can, and then slowly turn 360 degrees before lowering themselves back down into the water. They may then change their course or direction. Though they live in the water, they are apparently orienting themselves to landmarks above the water. One instruction for the Christian life is to be in the world but not of the world. This means, like the whales, that we take our bearings from a different element than the one we usually inhabit, the one we might think of as conventional reality, the lowest common denominator. Unfortunately, the church inevitably absorbs and even emulates aspects of the dominant culture. Part of the value of a Sabbath-modeled sabbatical, in contrast to an approach patterned after academia, is to get some distance from the usual mindset and worldview of one's work in order to return with new eyes to see and new ears to hear on the other side of habituation. Weekly Sabbath subverts the kind of habituation that results in no longer recognizing the incursion of the dominant culture into the church, most notably the secular business model or entertainment worship model. Regular Sabbath keeping accentuates the contrast community, also between the shalom of God and dominant church culture.

It might actually be harder for pastors to recognize the value of a radical reorientation than it is for laypeople. Church members often know how they compromise their Christian values in their work by either simply giving in to temptation or feeling powerless to do otherwise. All of us conspire to remain oblivious to the ways we work and live in violation of the kingdom. And so we keep our heads in the water and try to reduce the dissonance between the kingdom and how we live, masking our awareness of the contrast by overworking, numbing ourselves with TV or computer games, consuming, or dulling our awareness with alcohol or drugs. Taking intentional Sabbath breaks to reorient to God and to one's soul can be very unsettling to our comfortable lives.

The 2002 *Time* magazine "Person of the Year" was shared by three people who blew the whistle, exposing misconduct in the organizations for which they worked: the FBI, Enron, and WorldCom. Others knew of the problems these employees encountered but chose to go along with them. The *Lutheran* commented on the article that two of the three were Lutherans, who credited their faith with guiding them to do the right thing and giving them the courage to deal with the consequences. The motto of whistle-blowing is "Commit the Truth." Regarding the 2014 revelations of dangerous, dishonest appointment practices at the Veteran Affairs hospitals, Representative Jeff Miller remarked, "At great risk to themselves and their families, whistleblowers dare to speak truth to power."[14] Jesus said the truth shall set us free. By contrast, the slogan of

14. Mockenhaupt, "Confessions of a Whistleblower." Unlike Rep. Miller, we are not using the label "whistle-blower" as it brands the person, rather we use the term

secular society is, "Go along to get along," which often entails participating in dishonesty and greed for the sake of self-interest. The only way to gain the perspective that what we normally are doing is inconsistent with our core values is to fully step out of that context and set it aside for a period of time, entering into the holy and noticing the contrast when we come back. It helps to "go away" as far as possible from the usual world we inhabit. The routine of weekly Sabbath can help us avoid getting too far off course so that we do not have to confess that we made a lot of money but lost our soul. For others it may be, "I helped a lot of people, but I lost myself." "I had a good career, but I was a stranger to my children." And so on . . . This is an obvious challenge for most church members. Many of our people suffer from moral injury or soul injury, incurred from doing things in their work that violate their core values. Clergy are also significantly at risk for not stepping far enough away from church culture in order to recognize how off course we may have strayed.

As deep Sabbath strengthens our compassionate relationship with all that is, we become more courageous to follow the way that compassion inspires. Courage is another quality that is required for living shalom. Jesus said we must be willing to lose much, even our own lives, to advance the cause of love. The people who rescued Jews during the Nazi domination of Europe risked their own lives and the lives of their spouses and children. They did so for the sake of love. People risk losing their lifestyles by being truly generous. Many risk losing their jobs when they refuse to "go along to get along" at work. People lose friends and social support when they act contrary to the status quo. The courage that it takes to break through one's vulnerability and enter into deep Sabbath can carry over into the rest of one's life. In fact, it is our conviction that deep Sabbath fuels the desire and hones the ability to keep good boundaries in general.

Careers that are meant to serve us become our masters. Legitimate priorities, such as care for our families become distorted by anxiety and social comparisons. This is what Jesus warned us about. As Jesus was tempted by the devil to use his powers for personal and earthly gain, so are we tempted to use our talents and abilities for the things of this earth that we will ultimately lose anyway. With Sabbath reorientation, it can feel like we risk losing them already now.

Perhaps Sabbath is a commandment instead of a recommendation, because God knows that we will lose our bearings when engaged in the

---

"whistle-blowing" to characterize the action.

things of this earth. We need regular interruptions of the Spirit to break the world's spell over us: the spell of fear and insecurity; the spell that we have no choice but to adopt the values of Wall Street; the spell of greed that businesses must keep expanding, that more is better and bigger is better; the spell that there are winners and losers in life, as measured by material possessions and earthly power; the spell that if you are not the best, you are a loser; the spell that sacrificing your health and happiness for success (playing hurt) is admirable; the spell that sacrificing integrity for success is necessary; the spell that social approval is more important than God's approval.[15] Yes, this spell, as promoted in our work culture, the media, and our mass-marketed entertainment seduces us to put other things before God and God's universal love. To not lose our way, and to keep our spirits free, we desperately need Sabbath breaks from these sources of persuasion so that we can examine the assumptions and beliefs that actually shape our thoughts and actions. How else will we be reminded that we are here to do God's work, the work of love for everyone and everything? How else can we keep track of what that work might entail as our lives unfold?

Sabbath reminds us about the true nature of time and its purpose. Time is precious because it is sacred, not because it is limited in quantity, which is what our anxiety tells us. The word "time" has the same root, *tempus*, as the word "temple." Time is a meeting place for us to be with God, and for God to be with us. There is no need for time to make us anxious. Clocks were not invented by employers or unions; they were invented by Christian monks to keep track of the times for them to stop working and pray together. Clockmaking was motivated by faithfulness. Clocks and calendars need not enslave us or stress us; they can help liberate us by reminding us to set everything else aside and spend time with God at designated times and on designated days.

John Calvin said, "On Sabbath we cease our work so that God can do God's work in us."[16] A big part of that work is for God to reorient our bearings, and for us to pay attention. Since Christianity is the majority religion in our society, we can easily forget that our culture is not driven by spiritual values. We easily lose sight of how strongly we are influenced by the values and worldview of the dominant culture, in which we live, work, shop, and play. It is easy, even most natural, to spend our nonwork

15. Anderson, *Just a Little Bit More*, chap. 5.
16. Quoted in Thomas, *Even God Rested*, 162.

or "Sabbath time" as consumers. We merely switch from being produc-
ers (at work) to consumers (in our free time). If we spend our Sundays
watching TV, reading the paper, or going to a movie, we continue to be
submerged in the culture that sees people as consumable objects to be
used, exploited, dominated, or ridiculed. And we may even begin to see
ourselves as products to be sold to them.

What finally makes people happy? A significant body of research
into the source of human happiness contradicts our most basic assumptions. Contrary to everything we have been socialized to believe and to
pursue, the things we think make us happy may not really deliver.[17] From
the time of watching our first advertisement, we are immersed in a force
field that persuades us that the ability to buy things and purchase services will make us happy. While it is true that having a certain minimum
income is necessary for survival, accumulating excess does not appear to
increase happiness. In fact many people with very high incomes suffer
inordinately from high rates of depression and suicide.

Does status then make us happy? Consider people in high-status
positions—CEOs, managers, movie stars, senior pastors, university pres-
idents, and those in high political offices. Are such people happier than
others? Is the president, likely occupying the most powerful and pres-
tigious position in the world, a happy person? With high status comes
enormous responsibility and tremendous stress to perform and not fail:
this is not a formula for happiness! Then perhaps it is one's health that
makes you happy? You would think this would be the case. However,
those of us enjoying good health seem to take it for granted until we face
a health crisis of some magnitude. Only those who have suffered serious
illness may be truly in a position to see good health as a prerequisite to
human happiness.

What finally makes people happy are relationships: what we have
called life-giving relationships. Life-giving relationships begin with our
relationship to God, the Maker and Giver of all life, the source of shalom.
Happiness also derives from life-giving relationships with others—the
kind of gratuitous, serendipitous relationships fostered by Sabbath time
with others. And it is especially urgent in our time of environmental
crises to recognize that human happiness depends on our developing a
new life-giving relationship to God's creation, a relationship based on the
intrinsic value of the natural world, not based on our instrumental use of
nature. Wonder, amazement, and awe typify such life-giving encounters

17. See Ched, prod., with Engel, dir., *Human Spark*.

with creation. These are the contours of shalom: life-giving relationships with God, other persons, and creation itself. This is what we were finally made for and these quality relationships, the essence of Sabbath, are what make us happy.

In Sabbath mode we can more easily relate to everyone, including God, according to an I-Thou relationship, instead of in an I-It manner, treating people merely as objects or as functions. A trucker who stopped regularly at the same diner had the waitress come over, recognize him, and say, "Oh, you're the corned beef." If she were to have one foot in the kingdom of God and the other in work, she might have said, "Joe, you're late today. Is everything going okay?" Likewise, the lives of children have become strongly oriented away from enjoying life-giving relationships to building resumes for future success. We see the parental task as building up children's market value instead of helping them to find God's calling. The inculcation of these values is so insidious that we do not recognize that we have lost our way. Or we believe we have no choice.

A nutritional therapist who is sensitive to Sabbath values was at a conference of professionals where the focus was the "war against fat." She was disturbed by the way people were talked about. Fat is the enemy; the patient was characterized as the adversary against whom the professional wages the war based on the fat in another person's body. In all of our work, it is too easy for people to become objects or functions and stop being to us children of God or citizens of the kingdom of God. The same thing can happen with objects. A Sabbath-sensitive young man had worked for a couple of independent bookstores, where the employees love books and know about them. For them and the store owners, the goal was to help customers get just the right book for their needs or interests. Then this same young man got a job for a multinational bookstore chain, where books are not even referred to as books but instead as "products." Books became exchangeable products, and the goal was to "move product." It is not surprising that young adults refer to such jobs as "soul-sucking."

A Sabbath perspective also may reveal to employers that they have become like Pharaoh, demanding more and more productivity while re-ducing the resources workers have to meet those goals. Corporate leaders may become morally unsettled by the practice of keeping for themselves the profits from increased productivity rather than sharing them with the employees through commensurate increases in compensation. Employ-ers may find themselves realizing that they could in fact hire more people in order to benefit their fellow citizens of the kingdom who are without employment. Supervisors may cringe that they are forcing employees to train others, here or abroad, to do their jobs at lower pay and then terminating that trainer-employee. People may come to question their participation in practices that are deceptive, dishonest, or exploitative of other people. Some may realize they work for corporations that engage in predatory practices. How can our economy become informed by Sabbath values, transforming human labor into a more life-giving environment, providing sufficient, sustainable livelihood for all?[18]

TRANSITIONING OUT OF SABBATH

Good boundary keeping is essential to entering into meaningful, deep Sabbath. Specifically, it takes the ability and willingness to set aside our ego-based concerns and identities. Learning how effectively to make that transition determines the depth of the Sabbath relationship. As Barbara Brown Taylor has observed, in Sabbath we do not rest because our work is done, we rest "as if" our work is done.[19] The transition out of Sabbath is also important. As Oscar Romero noted, "The spiritual life does not remove us from the world, but leads us deeper into it."[20]

Just as worship culminates in a sending, deep Sabbath inspires a kind of "sending forth" with the intention and desire to continue what has been experienced and transformed by the Sabbath. Since Sabbath is not work, one does not need to have something to show for it in terms of a product. Partaking of the shalom of God connects us with unconditional compassion, inspiring and motivating certain ways of living, as Jesus described in his parables. As we leave behind our tendency to objectify others, we discover we care about people who once were seen only as the means to an end when we are in work mode. Sabbath, as worship does, helps us access states of being that serve as a reservoir to inform and reshape whatever comes next. Therefore, healthy transitioning out of Sabbath helps us integrate the resources of Sabbath into the rest of our lives.

We draw attention to three themes: retain, inform, and inspire. Living in the shalom of God, we retain what we have gained to inform our thoughts and to inspire loving actions. Preachers decry the fact that

18. Evangelical Lutheran Church in America, A Social Statement on "Sufficient, Sustainable Livelihood for All."

19. Taylor, *Leaving Church*, 228.

20. Nouwen, *Making All Things New*, 55.

great sermons on Sunday do not necessarily carry over into making a difference on Monday. One reason for this involves the limitations of the human mind. The phenomenon is called "state-specific learning," which is part of a larger pattern of the mind that connects things by association. What we learn in one external context may not transfer in our minds to another setting, because the same associations are not present in the new setting. What is learned in the classroom may need to be relearned in the field, because it may not automatically occur to the student on their own.

State-specific learning carries the risk of compartmentalization. When compartmentalized, "what we experience in Sabbath stays in Sabbath" and does not interact with the rest of our lives. The transfer value needs to be carried out intentionally and deliberately. Resources such as Mary Gentile's *Giving Voice to Values* increase the likelihood of addressing value clashes at work by a process of rehearsing behavior outside of that setting.[21] It primes the mind to recognize ethical problems at work that would otherwise go unnoticed. Whether or not we use this specific program, ending Sabbath prayerfully and mentally by exploring how to apply Sabbath values to the rest of the week helps to prime the pump. Becoming more comfortable with vulnerability can help us to be more willing to be indicted and transformed by the gospel. Deliberate spiritual practices throughout the week can keep this alive.

One such practice is care for "the least of these." Jesus said that how we treat the least important person is how we treat him (Matt 25:40). Under stress and busyness, we lose track of whom we regard as least important. Psychologist Robert Levine has studied our "pace of life" and found overall that in the cities with the fastest pace (like New York City) people are less helpful to others than in slower-paced cities.[22] In a frequently cited experiment with seminary students, some of whom had just prepared to give a talk on the Good Samaritan story, the only predictor of who would stop and help someone in need was how much time pressure they felt.[23] When we claim paying attention to those who are the least important as a spiritual practice, that intention and awareness can guide our choices and behavior. Usually our decisions are based on who is most important, not on who is least important. Yet as we increasingly realize from the practices of deep Sabbath, unimportant people are much affected by our actions.

21. Gentile, *Giving Voice to Values*.
22. Levine, *Geography of Time*, 162–63.
23. Cf. Darley and Batson, "From Jerusalem to Jericho," 100–108.

To keep track of how we are doing, we can use an adaptation of the Prayer of Examen. Since we are more able to be aware of things through the lens of unconditional love and compassion, we begin by focusing on the realization that God loves us unconditionally. We are accepted by God just as we are. Unconditional acceptance does not mean liking everything about oneself or approving of all of your behavior. It is unconditional. To whatever degree you can, trust in that promise and savor it. Enjoy how good it feels to be understood and accepted just the way you are. You are neither worthy nor unworthy of unconditional acceptance. You cannot earn it, nor can you lose it. Enjoy how good that feels. Now from this viewpoint, look over the last 24 hours. Notice which people you were most loving and open toward, including yourself, and how that felt. Now notice which people, including yourself, you were least loving toward. Who did you most disregard? Imagine what it would have been like to give more consideration to that person, and be more compassionate.

Many people are now using the concept of mini-Sabbath to set aside brief times throughout the day to serve as Sabbath breaks. These can be both planned ahead of time or practiced as circumstances allow, such as when one is stopped in traffic or forced to wait for some other reason. Rather than using such time "productively," one can receive this interruption as the gift of a mini-Sabbath, time for reconnecting us with the values of the kingdom and helping us see how to live Sabbath more fully each day. Breathe out the stresses and conventional ways of relating to persons and things in your everyday life! Breathe in deeply the shalom of God that makes all things new!

In part 2 of this book, we have examined in detail indispensable boundary themes related to the advancement of the foundational identity and mission of the Christian community: the integrity of worship, the integrity of interactions and communication, and integrity in the practices of Sabbath. In part 3 we turn our attention to topics that focus directly on the integrity of persons: the pastor as person, boundaries as a shared responsibility of church members, and a concluding chapter on best practices in preserving boundaries for the sake of preserving the core identity and mission of the church.

PART 3

Integrity of Persons

7

The Pastor as Person

WHEN PASTOR JON CAME to Lord of Life five years ago, the congregation was struggling. While the challenges were great, he was confident because the situation called for just his set of talents, experiences, and passions. His last call had gone badly due to disgruntlement on the part of a small group of parishioners, which left him baffled and hurt. Lord of Life was welcome relief. He developed and identified new leaders and created new programs in the community. Due to his leadership, membership grew and giving increased.

The denominational leadership was so impressed and wanted to help inspire other pastors to greatness, so that they decided to inaugurate a Pastor-of-the-Year award to be given at their annual meeting. The denominational magazine decided to write a story on it as well and asked to interview Pastor Jon's wife and sixteen-year-old son. After a painful discussion, they agreed to the interview but also to be truthful with the reporter. "There's not much I can say about my dad," his son told the reporter. "I don't see him very much." His wife commented, "Frankly, I have been living the life of a single parent, except I don't get to date. I wish I could." After the interviews with his wife and son, the denominational magazine decided not to run the story and the district leadership was left in a quandary.

PROTECTING THE PASTOR'S IDENTITY
AND ROLES

Like every Christian, a pastor has received a core identity from God in Christ through the gift of baptism. At baptism God made the person, who later in life assumed the role of pastor, the recipient of all baptismal gifts in Christ: forgiveness of sins, deliverance from evil, and eternal life. At baptism by the power of the Holy Spirit, the person who later was ordained to ministry of Word and sacrament received unconditional belovedness as God's child for Christ's sake.[1] The gospel of Jesus Christ grounds all the baptized, including pastors, in their core identity as persons in relationship with God. One of the most difficult challenges facing those who serve in ordained ministry is keeping their lives primarily oriented to this baptismal identity rather than confusing this core affirmation with their "working" role as a pastor of the church. Much confusion and dis-ease in the lives of pastors is a consequence of allowing one's role as pastor to displace one's identity as a baptized child of God.[2]

When pastoral identity takes priority over all one's other roles in life, tending one's own baptismal identity in Jesus Christ through involvement in the practices of Sabbath, as articulated in the last chapter, often becomes neglected. While pastors know the importance of Sabbath and advocate to others commitment to Sabbath, often they find themselves failing to practice what they preach. The lure of pastoral ministry as a source of self-fulfillment and the emotional "need to be needed" lead to unhealthy patterns that undermine one's relationship with God, relationships to one's primary community of family, and even one's own health.

The call to pastoral ministry is a call to a particular role within the life of a faith community and the wider church. This role is specific, not all-inclusive of the person, and it is not to be confused with one's baptismal identity. Moreover, it is only one of several roles in which the pastor as person is called to serve in life. Other crucial roles include as a family member (in various capacities, depending on the particular relation—as son or daughter, as a spouse, as a parent, as an aunt or uncle, as a cousin, and so forth) as a friend, as a hobbyist, as a club member, as a neighbor, or as a citizen. Among these others roles is the one assumes by virtue of one's work: the role as pastor. While this role is important for the sake of the identity and mission of the church, the pastor not only

1. Nouwen, *Life of the Beloved*, chap. 3.
2. Cf. Harbaugh, *Pastor as Person*, chap. 1.

must acknowledge the responsibilities belonging to this call but also must place limits on this role. As comprehensive and far-reaching as the role of parish pastor is, it does not contain the whole person. As a pastor, one assumes the duties belonging to the pastoral office—the ministry of Word and sacrament, at the call of a particular congregation or agency of the church. Pastoral ministry is a leadership role within the life of the church among the people of God, who themselves are also called to Christian service by their own baptisms in the various roles they assume in their lives.

Each pastor brings unique personal characteristics to service as a church leader: parents, birthdate, place of birth, gender, ethnicity, appearance, height, weight, personality type, multiple intelligences, life experiences, education, and a host of other factors. These are the biological and biographical features that make each of us the unique persons that God has created us to be. These are also the factors that God employs whenever a distinctive person, with particular experiences and character, assumes the pastoral role.[3] It is vital for well-being in ministry that the pastor can affirm the unique features of personhood in assuming the pastoral role. There is no single way that every pastor is supposed to function. Different persons embody the pastoral role differently according to their God-given circumstances, abilities, and experiences. There is freedom in being able to claim and affirm one's own uniqueness without falling into debilitating comparisons with other pastors, who are simply different from each other in so many ways. Such differences are to be celebrated as belonging to the variety of gifts in the body of Christ.

At the same time there are professional and institutional expectations that belong to the pastoral office. To the pastor is delegated authority for serving as a public representative of God and the church; the pastor is someone held accountable to a letter of call and the standards of conduct belonging to a church body.[4] The pastoral authority that one exercises is finally above all accountable to God in Christ, whose Word one proclaims and whose sacraments of grace one shares with God's people. The call to the ministry of Word and sacrament orbits around some centering pastoral practices: *preaching the gospel*, especially at worship; *teaching and sharing God's Word*—not only in formal classes or Bible studies but whenever one speaks to others (for example, in church meetings, hall-

3. Everist and Nessan, *Transforming Leadership*, 56–57.
4. Ibid., 57–58.

way conversations, pastoral visitation; through church communications, e-mail, or social media); *presiding at worship and over the sacramental life of the congregation*; and in *the many forms of pastoral care*. While pastors are asked to get involved in many other aspects of church life and activities, these central things that most cohere with Word and sacrament ministry provide the plumb line for prioritizing the use of one's time as a pastor of the church. While the demands placed upon the pastor may seem endless and exhausting on the one hand and enticing on the other, setting clear boundaries about what is central and what is secondary is necessary for balanced life as a person, especially in order to fulfill the responsibilities belonging to one's many other vital roles and to lead a healthy, balanced life.[5]

Even as the pastor is called upon to fulfill these duties assigned by the church, well-being in life necessitates role clarity about what belongs to the pastoral office in relation to all the various other roles we assume in life. These encompass our connection to God, family members, friends, and other nonwork relationships. Baptismal identity means living out one's care for the neighbor not only by what one does in the work of pastoral ministry but by caring the members of your family, friends beyond the membership of the church, residents in your local community, and those to whom you are connected all over the world—all of whom are neighbors whom we are called to love according to the Great Commandment (Matt 22:37–40).[6] As we discussed in the last chapter, practicing Sabbath is crucial to a balanced life for all people, including pastors. Providing pastoral care and service to others is no substitute for engaging in spiritual practices that nourish the soul of the religious professional as person.

Perhaps the most neglected neighbors in the lives of pastors are the pastor's family members.[7] While we might understand theoretically that the primary community in which God has placed us is our own family, in practice it is easy for pastors to prioritize relationships to church members above one's family relationships. Family members are always at a disadvantage in competing for the pastor's time, insofar as time spent in relationship with church people can easily be rationalized as a "holier" or more urgent use of the pastor's time. As Thomas Merton commented: "Douglas Steere remarks very perceptively that there is a pervasive form

5. Trull and Carter, eds., *Ministerial Ethics*, chap. 3.

6. Brueggemann, *Sabbath as Resistance*, chap. 6.

7. Harbaugh et al. *Covenants and Care*, chap. 4.

of contemporary violence . . . activism and overwork. The rush and pressure of modern life are a form, perhaps the most common form, of it innate violence. To allow oneself to be carried away by a multitude of conflicting concerns, to surrender to too many demands, to commit oneself to too many projects, to want to help everyone in everything, is to succumb to violence. The frenzy of our activism neutralizes our work for peace. It destroys our own inner capacity for peace. It destroys the fruitfulness of our own work, because it kills the root of inner wisdom which makes work fruitful."[8] We must come to know the line between faithfully filling the pastoral role and foolishly exceeding it.

OUR MULTIPLE SELVES

Psychologists talk about an "Observer" part of the self that notices and observes without judgment or reactivity. It is this part of the self that allows us to consult with our deepest values before we act or respond to a situation. Roberto Assagioli refers to it as a "point of pure awareness."[9] It is without content, free and flexible. People learn to access the Observer self in meditation and types of prayer (for example, centering prayer). We also have other parts of ourselves that have substance and interests. I invite you to make a list. Take a piece of paper and list the numbers 1 through 20 in a column on the left side of the paper. Now on the top write "I am." Proceed to finish the sentence 20 different ways!

Typically from this exercise people will list affiliations that we identify with, such as, "I am a Christian." We name roles, like "I am a father," or "I am a good friend." We also name qualities, like "I am kind and considerate." We may also identify characteristics like "I am a musician" or "I am an avid reader." This and similar exercises can assist us to identify parts of ourselves that seek expression outside of our work roles. Free time for Sabbath also helps us notice these roles. When we value them, we want to create and protect time and energy for them.

It also behooves us to look for the history or motives behind some of the roles and qualities with which we strongly identify: "I am a helper," for example. Where does that come from? We must accept that we cannot and do not have completely healthy motives for doing many of the good things that we do; nor fortunately must we. But we do have to do our best

8. Merton, *Conjecture of a Guilty Bystander*, 81.

9. Cf. Assagioli, *Psychosynthesis*.

to be responsible for those motives. This requires that we be conscious of them. Only in this way can we keep track of the unhealthy motives so that we do not act based on them.

This is a challenge for everyone, not just pastors. A parishioner may wish to be council president in order to elevate his or her status in the community or to pad a resume. This person may also genuinely wish to serve God and to help the congregation be more faithful. This is not an either/or. But we do violate our church role when we put personal interest above the interests of the church or of God An example of placing personal interest above community interest would be organizing a trip to climb a mountain when you know no one else in your group will be fit enough to make it except for you. The pastor or group leader, however, gets a free trip out of the deal. A different trip would be more rewarding for everyone. Far better would be to discern what is needed in the congregation and find a trip to meet those goals.

There are several potentially unhealthy personal motives for going into the ministry that can lead to boundary issues:

Perpetuating certain things that were important for you as a child (such as filling helping role in an alcoholic family where parents did not provide adequate supervision). The child may have come to gain a sense of safety from being in control when it seemed no one else was in control. The "need to be needed" is another common reason for entering pastoral ministry. Some pastors found refuge in the church as children and felt acceptance there far more than anywhere else. The unhealthy motive is then to perpetuate that acceptance, which in the pastoral role becomes an unrealistic expectation.

Compensating for what was missing in childhood is also an unhealthy motive for ministry and a source of unrealistic expectations. Here are some possible forms of unhelpful compensating:

1. The need to be loved: the congregation is supposed to love you.

2. Difficulty making friends: with the congregation you have a ready social life.

3. Feeling unimportant: now you have people for whom you are important.

4. No one listens to me; now you have a captive audience.

5. A feeling powerlessness: now you have power.

6. A lack of status: now you have status, at least in some circles.

Recognizing our personal motives can help us keep them from having undue influence. When Henri Nouwen was writing *The Wounded Healer*, the Jungian analyst Güggenbühl-Craig was working on a similar book, *Power in the Helping Professions*.[10] He gives us an important warning for our well-being as helping professionals and for the well-being of those we help. We must not split archetypes. Healing and sickness are parts of one archetype. As many pastors know from clinical pastoral education, it is tempting for helpers to believe that if I am helping you and you are weak. I cannot be weak. I must be strong. If you are confused, I cannot be confused. I must be certain. If you are powerless, I must be powerful. Thus we deny the attributes in ourselves of those we help, believing that those qualities render us useless in being able to help. In the process of this splitting, we also deny the other person's strength, knowledge, and wisdom. And so we set up the dynamics for abusing our own power. Everyone in a position of congregational leadership would do well to discover their personal motives. One way to do so is to ask what you hope a particular role will do for you.

Dealing with contrast and conflict also requires the capacity to draw upon one's multiple selves. The individuals who compose congregations and those who work professionally with them can greatly benefit from expressions of individual differences in perceptions, priorities, values, beliefs, ideas and even preferences. When these are expressed unnecessarily as personal attacks, however, the person being attacked with criticism or contempt needs to protect his or her emotional boundaries. One constructive way to do this is not to identify oneself as the target but rather to sidestep the attack by adopting a neutral, third-party perspective on the matter. This promises a better outcome than either allowing oneself to be injured or counterattacking with defensiveness. While the parishioner may make the issue with the pastor personal by using critical "you" statements, the pastor may choose not to buy into that definition of the situation by taking it personally. Every criticism might instead be reframed as a request, which potentially reveals something important about the parishioner and potentially adds something of value to the community if the content can be identified and protected in the process.

The objective, third-party point of view is the stance a mediator must be able to adopt in order to arbitrate a disagreement. We can effectively mediate the disputes in which we are personally involved by

---

10. For the following, see Güggenbühl-Craig, *Power in the Helping Professions*.

intentionally positioning ourselves in that role, although it is inherently a dual role.[11] We must be able to understand and express not only our own point of view but also that of the person bringing the complaint. When and only when the other person has been heard and understood can that person also begin to understand the pastor's point of view. The steps are these: 1) sidestep the criticism so you do not identify yourself as the target; 2) adopt the posture of a mediator; 3) listen, inquire, and check to make sure that you understand the person correctly and that the person comes to believe that you do understand; and 4) only then express a contrasting point of view, if you have one. In order to know the best outcome to a conflict, the mediator must know from each party (1) what they want, (2) why they want it (the rationale), (3) how strongly they feel about it, and (4) why they feel as strongly as they do. The first two parts are usually concrete, factual, and framed rationally, while the last two are more emotionally based. If a person feels strongly about something, there is usually something in their past history that informs and shapes it. With enough safety, this can be discovered. For example, congregational conversations involving people's feelings about sexual orientation have had a peaceful and positive outcome, when people share their personal thoughts behind their own viewpoint in a safe and supportive context.

In any conflict situation, a person needs to decide which of the five basic options to adopt, as identified by Thomas and Killmann: avoiding, accommodating, competing, collaborating, and compromising.[12]

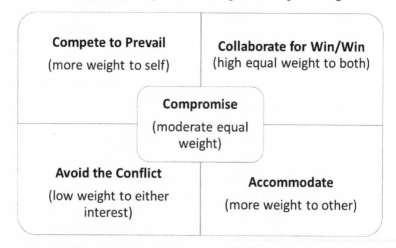

11. Cf. Everist, *Church Conflict*, chap. 5.

12. The table is adapted from Thomas and Killmann, Conflict Mode Instrument, http://www.kilmann.com/conflict.html/.

It is important to be comfortable and skillful at using all of the options according to which of them is most appropriate in a given situation. Our comfort level may depend on the context. For example, in the stereotypical abuse situation, a person may be overly accommodating at work and then become overly aggressive in getting one's own way at home. It can go the other direction as well. In the process of getting more comfortable with all the options, it is helpful to examine early life experiences from each person's family of origin as well as from other contexts, such as school. While some children learn to stay quiet and passive in family conflict out of fear of making things worse for themselves and others, other children learn that they can easily get their own way by insisting on what they want. However your family system responded to passivity or assertiveness on your part and whatever you may have learned about how to engage in conflict, it is important to recognize your own tendencies and patterns so you can increase your repertoire of responses to address various situations.[13]

When pastors talk about their comfort level with conflict, they usually think about unwelcome conflict initiated by someone else. They rarely think about the healthy need for they themselves to actually initiate contrast or conflict. Obviously, it is essential at times to do just that, not only to negotiate conflicted situations in ministry but also to think clearly and sustain meaningful time and energy for personal life. Many people attracted to the ministry are attuned to accommodating others rather than creating contrast or conflict. Because of this tendency, some pastors may either avoid raising conflict; and when they do create contrast or conflict, they do so with an edge or awkwardness that makes it less effective. Recall how Jesus supported saying no to others as the wise thing in the parable of the Wise and Foolish Virgins (Matt 25:1–13). For those with the habit of saying yes automatically in response to a request, it is recommended that the first response be one of buying time. For example, one can say something like, "Let me get back to you on that" so there is ample opportunity to make a good decision. If the request has merit but one already has a full schedule, the advised rule is only to say yes after you can identify what you would be able to give up to make time for it.

If you agree to talk to a church member in the grocery store, what are you giving up? For those with families, you are in essence making a decision for other family members to delay dinner and deprive them of

---

13. Halstead, *From Stuck to Unstuck*, chap. 6.

your presence. A practice to follow in tending boundaries is to ask, who does this belong to? In the case of time, one does well to ask, to whom or what does this time belong to? If your current time slot belongs to your family, you are imposing your decision on them by overstaying at the grocery store. It is useful to think this way about the different parts of oneself. Your pastor self is deciding to deprive your personal self of the allotted time by delaying dinner or some other involvement. Whoever the time belongs to deserves to have their needs and interests be your priority during that time. To think of your "personal self" as a separate self may seem strange, but it is useful. Since comfort comes with practice, look for opportunities to say no and set limits.

When a leader is willing and able comfortably to establish contrast and initiate conflict with another person, it assists others in the faith community to do the same.[14] Without this culture of honoring both the personal and the community, people will try to hide and withhold parts of themselves, to the detriment of themselves and the community. When they do initiate contrast or conflict, it may be carried out awkwardly or in an unhealthy way. It is actually fairly uncommon for people to be comfortable, graceful, and diplomatic in creating contrast. So we can learn to help each other out. One way to do so involves establishing and maintaining good identity and feeling boundaries. In constructively initiating contrast, one person informs the other person about something important to them and may make a request. These "I" statements are easy to hear. To fully inform the other person about what is relevant means telling them what you are wanting, why you are wanting it, how strongly you feel about it, and the reasons why you feel about it to that degree. Only with that information can the other party possibly know how much weight to give to what you are wanting in comparison to the weight given to what they themselves might want.

If equal weight is given to both parties, you know that it is important to work towards a compromise or a win/win outcome. If the information leaves you deciding that the other person's needs or wants are greater than your own, then you accommodate them. If you judge that what you need or want for some reason deserves the greatest weight, you initiate and hold your ground. It works best in the negotiation process if you proceed to share all of the relevant information about what you want, why you want it, how strongly you feel about it, and why you feel so strongly.

14. Cf. Menking, *When All Else Fails*, 68–70.

The first reason why is usually based on information or reason, while the last reason why is usually based more on personal experience. For example, the first reason why might be to avoid breaking a promise, and the final reason why might be to avoid harming the person to whom you made the promise.

In poorly executed conflict situations a person will employ "You" statements as accusations or complaints, making it about the other person—for example, the pastor. The pastor has the choice whether to accept being identified as the target or not. If you the pastor do choose to be identified as the target, you will become hurt or defensive. Those are about the only two options when one feels under attack. If, however, the pastor does not choose to be identified as the target, then the pastor can choose to take a more objective stance, essentially playing the role of mediator in the dispute. Even though the pastor may be personally involved in the conflict, choosing a mediating approach is the most desirable for all involved. Only from this vantage point, that of the Observer self, can one possibly know how much weight to give to the different aspects of the conflict. From this vantage point, one can advocate for one's own position with adequate emotional self-control, so as not to be careless about the feelings of others.

STEWARDING THE PASTOR'S LIFE

There are some advantages to a job where you punch in and punch out. You know when you are working and when you are not. It helps you not think about work when you are in bed, for example. It is also helpful to have a job with prescribed hours and a clear job description for everyone's benefit. That way you know when you are supposed to be working or not, and what your responsibility is or is not. How do you tell when someone is overfunctioning or underfunctioning without some demarcation in these areas? Certainly pastoral ministry can be like that. But should it be like that?

Pastor Jon's new call to Lord of Life was the perfect storm: falling prey to the temptation of overwork, John risked neglecting other important parts of his life. He felt he had something to prove. Lord of Life was his chance to prove it. There was an open slate for his creative talents. He had the vision to improve things beyond what anyone had seen before. He would get lost in these creative tasks and lose hours of time without realizing it. He enjoyed walking around the church late at night and seeing the improvements he had made—not just in the aesthetics and orderliness of the building but also in the programming that took place in each space. It was a source of joy and pride. He no longer felt like the failure as he had in his last call, where his efforts were resisted and not appreciated.

Our talents and passions desire an outlet. The parish ministry is great for that because there is such a variety of things to do—from preaching to teaching to interpersonal endeavors to artistic projects to music to organization, to much more. The list is endless. At Lord of Life, Pastor Jon had a large "sweet spot" between what he wanted to do and what the congregation wanted from him. While in many ways it is a desirable situation to have a large sweet spot, it also presents the temptation to overdo. When the sweet spot is smaller, it is clearer to the pastor that important parts of the self will need time and energy for expression outside the role. When the majority of interests can be met within the ministerial role, it takes more self-discipline to achieve healthy balance and awareness of who you are and who you should be outside that role.

Pastor Jon was also finally beginning to enjoy a sense of job security as his efforts got approval from the congregation and now even from the wider church. Always in his life he had felt the pressure of anxiety from unfinished tasks, which in many congregations are endless. While some people use avoidance to temporarily reduce stress, others like Pastor Jon use overworking, always working in order to check items off the to-do list. The healthy alternative is setting time limits on work. But this will result for some pastors in having to learn to tolerate the stress of unfinished tasks. The mental exercise of "one thing at a time" helps with this tendency, as does having a ritual of closure at the end of a work period: debriefing what was done, affirming it, and setting basic plans for the next work period. This helps reduce the anxiety of unfinished tasks. The consideration here is not about how much time it takes to complete all the tasks; it is what amount of work is fair and healthy. It is not the pastor's responsibility to compensate for the congregation being understaffed, as Lord of Life was when Pastor Jon arrived.

Many pastors come from a family system where some form of addiction or other dysfunction is evident.[15] This background puts one at

15. The following two paragraphs are adapted from personal correspondence between the authors and Robert H. Albers, who is contributing author of the clergy education curriculum called *Spiritual Caregiving to Help Addicted Persons and Families*, published by the Substance Abuse and Mental Health Services Association in

risk of falling into any of several unhealthy patterns: (1) making *heroic efforts* to make up for the dysfunction by accomplishing something to "redeem" the family and family name, or to make up for the dysfunction by engaging or overengaging in salvific ministry; (2) dealing with the dysfunction by *acting out* and getting into trouble, which can sometimes be helpful by bringing outside attention to the dysfunction in the family (The anxiety occasioned by the dysfunction can eventuate in such persons becoming addicted or getting in trouble with the law.); 3) *withdrawing* from the system, often engaging in fantasy thinking or becoming a loner: this behavior sometimes leads one to be deemed a social misfit or antisocial; and 4) *deflecting attention* from the stressful situation by being funny or cute, or in some other manner seeking a lot of attention and thereby drawing attention away from the addiction as the "elephant in the room."

While not precluding other patterns, many seminary students and pastors often have a high need for achievement. When such persons become pastors or lay professionals, they tend to see their task as "fixing" other people. This is not to judge them, for usually they are unaware of how the social matrix in which they have grown up has shaped them. Their investment in "fixing" prevents them from being able to establish appropriate boundaries, because they have adopted this role already in childhood as a way of coping with the dysfunction in the family. These people not only feel the need to fix things, but they claim responsibility for everything that occurs in the system, even if they are not responsible. Often they feel like failures if they cannot fix the dysfunction in their families or in their parishes. If parishioners assume that the pastor can "fix" them, then the members become hostile when the pastor is unable to accomplish that goal, and the dynamics of shame enter the picture. Almost invariably, these people, who some would say have a "messiah" complex, become disenchanted with ministry because a little voice inside them accuses them of being failures. They are also prime candidates for workaholism, which damages not only their health but their relationships as well. Theologically, such persons have little sense of grace and in essence have supplanted God in their lives by assuming that they can heal, when healing is entirely the province of God and not their responsibility. While a pastor can help to facilitate healing, they are not responsible for the healing.

2007. For a copy of the handbook, see http://www.nacoa.org/clergy.htm/.

Different types of backgrounds place us at risk of developing blind spots and habits that work against good boundary keeping beyond our self-awareness. One such background comes with growing up in a family with alcoholism—with the denial, secrecy, powerlessness, and lack of safety that is often involved. Research indicates that people with this background are not a homogeneous group; everyone with this background does not have the same tendencies.[16] This is important because otherwise we can be subject to stereotyping and profiling people based on this background, which would violate an individual's identity boundaries. Given that caution, it remains prudent for people who grew up with alcoholism in their families to evaluate themselves for the following tendencies, identified by Janet Geringer Woititz, which can interfere with healthy boundaries.[17]

1. Having to guess what normal is.

2. Having difficulty following a project through from beginning to end.

3. Tending to lie when it would be just as easy to tell the truth.

4. Judging oneself without mercy.

5. Experiencing difficulty with having fun.

6. Taking oneself too seriously.

7. Having difficulty with intimate relationships.

8. Overreacting to changes over which one has no control.

9. Constantly seeking approval and affirmation.

10. Feeling somehow different from other people.

11. Being either superresponsible or superirresponsible.

12. Showing extreme loyalty, even in the face of evidence that loyalty is undeserved.

13. Being impulsive and locking into a course of action without giving serious consideration to alternative behaviors or possible consequences. This impulsivity leads to confusion, self-loathing and loss of control over their environment. In addition, it can lead to an excessive amount of energy cleaning up the mess.

16. Hinrichs et al., "Personality Subtypes in Adolescent and Adult Children of Alcoholics."

17. Adapted from Woititz, *Adult Children of Alcoholics*, xxvi–xxvii.

Clearly such behaviors by pastors can lead to misunderstanding, conflict, and many boundary violations.

It is not emotionally easy to stop working when the pastor is feeling pressure of one sort or another. When there is the feeling of pressure, it is important to look for the source of that pressure in order to identify and solve the problem. This takes careful self-examination, which requires more objectivity than most of us have. This usually means it is essential to consult with an objective, outside person. Questions might be phrased as follows: Who is this for? In what way might this actually be self-serving? In many cases, the pressure is internal to the pastor (for example, a pattern learned in one's family of origin or an anxious posture toward the world). Overwork is then self-serving in the sense that it is a way to relieve pressure or anxiety. While congregations benefit in a codependent way, the result of pastoral overwork is inevitably unhealthy. Overfunctioning on the pastor's part begets underfunctioning on the parishioners' part. Ways to address this anxiety, other than overwork, can be found. Even when the pastor feels pressure to avoid criticism, and feels this as a realistic threat, it is still self-serving to try and reduce stress by overworking. The more comfortable a pastor gets with criticism, the less pressure one feels. If they keep trying to reduce the pressure by overworking, they will remain enslaved by the anxiety.

A similar internal motive is to avoid irrational guilt. Perfectionism is a source of internal pressure, though it may have originally been learned in order to protect the self from criticism by a parent. Perfection becomes a way to feel safe from criticism, and it may actually work, at least to some degree, with some people, though not all. The external circumstances can also provide pressure when, for example, a congregation is in decline and it seems like saving the situation can only be accomplished by overwork on the part of the pastor. While it is easy to say that it is not all the pastor's responsibility, the pastor's self-interest can get involved, since saving the congregation can mean saving one's own livelihood and career path. How stressful this seems depends on the perception of one's options.

An important principle for creating an environment conducive to healthy boundaries involves evaluating whether unmet personal needs are pressing to be met (inappropriately) within the pastoral role. Given the situation many ministers are in, it is much easier for them to meet their own social needs within the pastoral role with parishioners than outside the role with nonparishioners. As humans we tend to take the easy path, which leads to parishioner-based friendships that, as we mentioned earlier, end up depriving the parishioner of a pastor. The more church members are your friends, the less they will see you as their pastor. The pastor's responsibility is to protect the integrity and effectiveness of the pastoral role for others, not to pursue one's own self-interest. Being a friendly, sociable pastor is different from needing to become buddies with church members so that they forget you are the pastor. This is admittedly a challenging situation for pastors. It means meeting one's social needs outside the role in a way that does not compromise the effectiveness of the pastoral role. Often there is no easy solution.

In addition to the unhealthy long-term motives mentioned above (the desires to be loved, to be important, to have an audience, and to have power and status), unmet needs based on situational factors can also lead to boundary problems. A pastor's unmet needs for psychological, spiritual, and physical intimacy put him or her at risk of inappropriate thoughts, feelings, and actions toward parishioners, who might be able and even willing to meet those needs at the expense of the integrity of the pastoral role. Since our motives are often unconscious, it is best to rely on best practices to protect boundaries for the sake of preserving the church's identity and mission. Following best practices helps us detect when we are putting others or ourselves at risk. Many pastors who are not trained in counseling, for example, set a three-session limit on the number of counseling sessions they will have with a parishioner. If the situation calls for more than that, the pastor refers the parishioner to a mental health professional. When the pastor feels tempted to make an exception and go beyond three sessions for some reason, this is an indicator that it is time to consult with someone who can be objective about the situation.

Realistically, every area of personal need and interest, which could press to be met inappropriately or excessively within the pastoral role, needs a plan for addressing it in the pastor's personal life. This includes such things as planning regular dates with a spouse, setting aside time with one's children or ensuring time with the whole family. It includes intentional plans to stay in touch with friends and figuring out how to make new friends. Due to the lack of motivation that comes with fatigue, it is even necessary to plan time to discover, explore, and pursue hobbies and interests. Oddly, as we emphasized in the last chapter, we must make a plan for taking free time.

Pastors and other professionals might wish that they could be anonymous in their personal lives. Everywhere they go, however, people will recognize them. A pastor is not free to "be myself" in ways that might reflect poorly on the ministry. One might at least like to be able to go to the grocery store and not have others want to talk to them as their pastor. Protecting personal time from opportunities for spontaneous ministry means having comfort with diplomatic assertion. When a parishioner wants pastoral conversation in a grocery store or after a late meeting at church, it may well be an opportunity for good ministry, but it is even more a time to move along with one's personal life by continuing to shop or going home. Good boundary keeping on the part of pastors can help parishioners become more intentional about deciding to arrange for a pastoral appointment rather than following a spontaneous impulse to talk about a personal matter with their pastor as, for example, it might occur to them in the grocery store. The pastor can also learn to say, "This seems really important, so please call me in the morning at the office so we can set a time to talk." It does not have to be "now or never."

Some people who hoard are afraid if they throw something out, they may later find they need it. There is always the risk of loss in all good boundary keeping. We can learn to become comfortable with that possible loss rather than seeking to avoid it by overdoing.

Good boundary keeping between work and the rest of life, and between the self and one's roles, helps create and maintain time and energy for one's personal life. It helps to make clear transitions, intentionally making closure with work before leaving work, which also helps prepare the way for the next time one returns to work mode. An essential phase in this transition is to set everything else aside and connect for a few minutes, as best as possible, with the Observer self. Just before entering the home (or into whatever activity comes after work), you put your full self into what comes next, with the attitude and energy that belongs to this new time. When entering into relationship with a small child, for example, one wants to be able to fully concentrate on that person and match their enthusiasm about seeing you. The same is true for adults in our lives or even for pets. If one is returning to an empty home, then it is a matter of activating and engaging the other parts of the self by giving them priority. This requires that we quickly recover our energy (if it as depleted from work) or calm our energy (if it was agitated at work).

Paradoxically, the most effective ways to recover energy involve some expenditure of energy. As most of us experience, doing nothing and being passive (for example, by watching television) may be attractive to the stressed mind, such passive activities do not lead to recovery. Instead, mild to moderate exercise, even a walk around the block, will quickly reinvigorate. Talking with someone, listening to upbeat music, or doing some tasks around the house also can be helpful. While it may be great to listen to our feelings in shaping how we spend our free time, this does not work so well with the stressed mind, since it seeks short-term fixes that tend not to be satisfying in the long run. Because of that, most busy people find value in planning in advance how they will spend their time, including their personal time.

The integrity and health of one's personal life is also preserved by keeping personal matters out of work. Having one's personal life encroach at work results in getting behind at work, which then can increase pressure to violate personal time in order to catch up. Marital conflict that is not contained at home will distract the pastor from work. Texting or making phone calls can be a way to continue an argument or to try to resolve it. Often, however, letting the conflict wait for the next good time together actually helps resolve it. Some people have a lot of difficulty taking a break from conflict. If a person wants a good outcome to conflict, however, they must have the emotional self-control necessary to wait for that time. This may require changing one's own capacity for anxiety, so it has less control over us.

The transitioning process described above can help keep one's personal life from interfering with one's functioning at work. (To review, the transitioning process entails getting temporary closure with your home life, taking a brief mental rest break for refreshment, and then turning toward what you will be entering at work so you can fully engage with it.) While it is important that all parts of the self inform and enrich the other parts, not keeping them largely separate and distinct is like painting each stroke of a picture with the color that results from mixing together all the colors on the pallet. A painting is more beautiful when each color has its own distinctiveness. Having examined the integrity of the pastor as person in this chapter, especially focussing on the boundary between work and the rest of the pastor's life, we turn next to a discussion of boundaries as the shared responsibility of church members.

8

Boundaries as Shared Responsibility by Church Members

SCENARIO EIGHT: FRAN'S OVERINVOLVEMENT IN THE CHURCH

AFTER TWO YEARS AT St. Mark's, Pastor Christina made a home visit to the church's most active member, Fran. Fran was in her fifties, with very high energy. After her divorce at age thirty-five, Fran poured herself into St. Mark's. She was extremely generous with her time and was involved in virtually every aspect of the ministry. In each area she did great things and naturally assumed leadership to the gratitude of others. She was now in her final year of her second term on the Leadership Team. The Constitution only allowed two consecutive terms. They had been doing vision setting, and when it came her turn to speak, Fran said she wanted the church to continue to be a place where she could participate every day of her life. The contrast was striking; everyone else on the team had voiced a vision for the future of the congregation based on their sense of the needs of the community and had said nothing about themselves personally.

Pastor Christina came to the disturbing realization that the congregation and Fran at some point had developed an unhealthy relationship. She also realized that Fran's contributions in the church were largely motivated by self-interest, even while they also did benefit others. Fran had shaped church programs to fit her own interests, based on what she needed or wanted rather than discerning what the church needed from her that she could contribute. Pastor Christina raised her pastoral concerns with Fran and helped her see how she could benefit from having more of a life for herself outside the church. They agreed that Fran would take a six-month sabbatical from church involvement other than attending worship.

PROTECTING THE IDENTITY AND ROLES OF CHURCH MEMBERS

The sacrament of baptism is the entrance rite for membership into the church, the body of Christ.[1] Baptism grounds our identity in God's divine promise in Christ, a reality that is deeper than all the other characteristics by which human beings are judged: race, class, gender, age, or sexual orientation. As bell hooks comments, while these identifying characteristics indelibly contribute to who we are, affect how we understand ourselves in relationship to others, and condition how others treat us, we are summoned by God to existence in "beloved community" beyond all hierarchy.[2] Baptism serves as the primal "ordination" for all Christians. This is just as true for those who later are ordained into pastoral ministry as for those who are laypersons in the church. Laity and clergy both benefit from orienting the entirety of their lives in relation to the promises God made to them in Christ at baptism, claiming this sacrament as their rock and foundation through the chances and changes of life. The church would be enriched if all baptized Christians trusted and claimed baptism as the source of their own core identity for life, an identity that grounds and informs all the other roles they assume in all their arenas of life. At baptism the baptized person receives every gift that is freely bestowed by the grace of God in Jesus Christ. These gifts include the promises of forgiveness, deliverance from temptation, and the hope of eternal life. As a recipient of such amazing belovedness, every Christian grounds life in gratitude for the richness of God's blessings. One central purpose of the practicing of Sabbath through worship is to keep reclaiming these promises as the core of one's identity for all of life.

At the same time that church members as baptized persons are recipients of God's abundant gifts of forgiveness, life, and salvation in

1. Cf. Marty, *Baptism*.
2. hooks, *Killing Rage*, 263–65.

Jesus Christ, the baptized are given a commission about what it means to live out their baptismal vocation in the world. One liturgical articulation of this commission poses this question to the baptized: "Do you intend to continue in the covenant God made with you in holy baptism: to live among God's faithful people, to hear the word of God and share in the Lord's Supper, to proclaim the good news of God in Christ through word and deed, to serve all people, following the example of Jesus, and to strive for justice and peace in all the earth?"[3] Those affirming their baptism answer: "I do, and I ask God to help and guide me." This promise serves as the foundation for all church membership and Christian service to the world. Those thoughts, words, and behaviors that would lead us to compromise or deviate from these promises are the very matters from which boundaries are intended to protect us.

This baptismal commission sets forth the central provisions for the Christian life that guide the discussion of boundaries in this entire book. The true purpose of the congregation is to serve the mission of God by bringing the good news of Jesus Christ to the world and by sharing the love of Christ with others by our words and actions. Whenever church members are tempted to shift the purpose of the church toward some narrower or self-serving agenda, the integrity of the church's identity and mission is compromised, undermined, and even contradicted. We explore in this chapter how God's baptismal gifts to us and our baptismal promises to God must be preserved by church members through attention to boundaries in thought, word, and deed, in order that the God-given identity and mission of the church remain primary, not only for the relationships among those who belong to the Christian community, but also for the integrity of the church's witness to the world.

The churches of the Reformation committed themselves to what Martin Luther called the universal priesthood. This expression affirms that it is not only those ordained as pastors ("priests") who are accountable to standards of Christian practice; rather all Christians have inherent responsibility to live their lives in accordance with the teachings and way of Jesus Christ. Every Christian as a follower of Jesus is called to represent with integrity the good news of God's mercy and love by assuming the mind of Christ, speaking charitably, and living a life of service to others.[4] While captivity to sin inevitably also affects church members, nothing undermines the credibility of the Christian message more than hypoc-

3. "Affirmation of Baptism," *Evangelical Lutheran Worship*, 237
4. Wingren, *Luther on Vocation*, 28-37.

risy. God has given the law as a curb on human sinning in order both to prevent us from harming others and to help preserve the common good.[5]

Too often we operate in the church with a double standard. While clergy are rightly held to a high standard for living their lives according to the way of Jesus Christ, many church members fail to acknowledge how they themselves, like all church members, are to be held accountable to a comparable standard of behavior. The failure on the part of church members to maintain the integrity of the church's identity and mission as their own responsibility erodes the effectiveness of the church's life and integrity. If the universal priesthood accords to all Christians equal status before God by virtue of baptism, so also all Christians stand equally accountable in the presence of God in Christ for the conduct of their lives.

Not only does the Christian life encompass what happens within congregations, but it extends into all arenas of life. Christian freedom means not only that we have been freed by Jesus Christ *from* sin, death, and the power of the devil but that we have been freed *for* service to all the neighbors God gives us in our lives.[6] Jesus teaches, as in the parable of the Good Samaritan that all people are neighbors God has given us to serve—with no exceptions. Each person is made in God's own image. Each person is one for whom Jesus Christ died on the cross. Each person is one for whom Jesus Christ is risen from the dead. Each person we encounter is a neighbor. For Christ's sake the baptized are called to look upon, speak about, and act toward each and every person as a neighbor. The priesthood of all believers thus takes on the character of universal neighborliness, the neighborliness of all believers.

This means that we discover neighbors wherever we go, in every arena of life. One primary arena God has given us for serving neighbors is our own family. Too often we overlook that the members of our own family are as much neighbors, whom God has given us to serve, as those people we encounter in other life arenas. This is a particular hazard for church members, not only pastors, who may value what they do for the church more than they value what they do for the people in their own families. Grandparents, parents, aunts, uncles, siblings, cousins, spouses/partners, children, grandchildren, and all other relations are among those neighbors, whom God has given us as neighbors. God has put us in primary relationship with these family members for the sake of protecting them from harm and for preserving the common good. Only when we

5. Cf. Wingren, *Creation and Law*, pt. 2, chap. 2.
6. Cf. Luther, *Freedom of a Christian*.

are good stewards of the neighbors who are members of our own family can we be genuinely free to attend to neighbors in other arenas of life, including in church involvements.

God also gives us neighbors to serve in the arena of daily work. For young people this may mean serving neighbors in the daily work of attending school or college. For those who are employed, neighbors are all those persons who are affected by our labor. Formally, we serve neighbors through the fruit of what we do for a living—providing goods or services, or both, according to the purpose of one's employment. Whether one is employed in business, sales, medical care, construction, education, technology, government, food service, or any other job, we serve neighbors by the very goods and services provided through our work. We will not here explore the challenges many people today face in finding daily work that is both a good use of their own aptitudes and meaningful for the sake of others—let alone fairly compensated. These are ethical questions deserving their own careful consideration. Here we simply assert that what one does for a living is intended to be of service to others as a contribution to the public good.

Through the arena of one's daily work one also enters into interpersonal relationships with other people, who are also, each one, neighbors God gives us to serve. We come to know them not only as customers or clients but as human beings, who have the same gifts, challenges, and concerns universal to all. Through these relationships church members also have an opportunity to care for neighbors in need. By observant, active listening we attend not only to what is said by others but can invite them to share their deeper thoughts and feelings. As appropriate, such relationships become occasions for expressing and offering genuine care to people in their hour of need. Happiness in life derives above all from life-giving relationships with other people. The contacts we develop with others, fellow workers and the people we encounter at work, can become the opportunity for extending life-giving concern about their welfare and concrete expressions of help.[7]

One's local community is also an arena for Christian neighborliness. The erosion of community participation in recent decades has been cited by sociologists as one sign of societal decline.[8] Christians live out their baptismal vocations not only by through the social ministry of their congregations but by how they invest themselves in community

7. Cf. Kaptein, *Workplace Morality.*
8. Cf. Putnam, *Bowling Alone.*

service to neighbors through other involvements and activities.[9] Civic organizations, service clubs, scouting, and other forms of public engagement do genuine good for the sake of neighbors in need. Helping young people, the sick, the aged, the grieving, the hungry, the homeless, the imprisoned, the addicted, or those facing other life crises is a concrete expression of neighbor love. Moreover, these are situations that deserve not only our charitable service but also our active engagement in the responsibilities of citizenship. Willie James Jennings calls us to join a movement for "truly cosmopolitan citizenship": "Such a world citizenship imagines cultural transactions that signal the emergence of people whose sense of agency and belonging breaks open not only geopolitical and nationalist confines but also the strictures of ethnic and racial identities."[10] Christian people serve God by becoming active as cosmopolitan citizens by voting, becoming educated about social issues, and advocating for legislation and policies that preserve the common good for all people. Church denominations provide social statements and advocacy resources to assist church members in becoming thoughtfully involved in serving neighbors through responsible citizenship.

This chapter focuses on the boundaries most directly related to being a church member: it discusses those behaviors and practices that can protect and promote the congregation's genuine identity and mission. However, by observing best practices in church membership that guard against those things that distract from and undermine the way of Jesus Christ, we believe that the baptized will be empowered to serve their neighbors more effectively in all the other arenas of daily life as well—in family, daily work, local communities, and civic engagement. Through references to research about human nature and case material, we will explore issues such as motivation, communication, and conflict in congregational life on the way to recommending best practices for stewardship of the self and honoring boundaries for the sake of generative and faithful congregational mission.

9. Cf. Franklin, *Crisis in the Village*, 132–69.
10. Jennings, *Christian Imagination*, 10–11.

CHURCH MEMBERSHIP THAT PRESERVES GOD'S PURPOSES FOR THE CHURCH

As we saw in the last chapter, good boundary keeping for pastors involves a delicate balancing act among many integral factors involved in who they are as human beings. The same applies for parishioners. As with clergy, it is also the case for parishioners that their roles in the church are not intended to compensate for inadequacies in their personal lives, but rather to help inspire and strengthen members to live their lives in the world with love of God, love of neighbor, and love of self, and to do all of these in community together. The congregation is not necessarily to be an outlet for a person's specific interests and talents, except insofar as they serve the larger purpose. Otherwise, for example, a musician without adequate outlets will want to perform, or an artist will want the church to exhibit his or her artwork. While music and art are important parts of ministry to be sure, they can be offered in self-serving ways rather than in ways that really serve the community. Talents and interests seek outlets. When there are not adequate outlets other than the church, those interests will press until they are met, perhaps in unhealthy or inappropriate ways within the church. How do we tell the difference between healthy participation in congregational life and unhealthy use of the congregation for personal ends?

It is important to try to understand our motives, including those that might be unhealthy. However, experimental psychologists are not very impressed with our own ability to accurately perceive our personal motives.[11] We tend to think of ourselves as being more virtuous than we really are. Nevertheless, we can still come to greater self-awareness for the sake of the whole. Some motives will be conscious, as with a person who wants to become an executive or wants promotions at work and needs public service to fill out their resume. Such persons will want to position themselves to be on the leadership team, to become an officer, and to leave a record of their service. Some motives are less conscious. A person who felt unaccepted as a child except at church runs the risk as an adult of expecting excessive time and attention from church staff, instead of developing other social outlets. The same is true for involvement in other social activities, whenever a person comes to feel the church "owes them" something. Any time we feel the church "owes us something" should give

11. Cf. Sternberg and Fiske, eds., *Ethical Challenges in the Behavioral and Brain Sciences*, 219–26.

us pause for self-examination rather than engaging in the criticism of the church and its members.

A second way to detect whether our motives are healthy involves our response when we do not "get what we want," considering not only our outward behavior but also our inward attitude, thoughts, and feelings. As we have seen, we can violate boundaries by our thoughts, words, and deeds. Refusing to take no for an answer, even internally and without outward expression, is a boundary violation involving the will. Typically, however, when one cannot accept not getting one's way, this dissatisfaction finds outward expression by withdrawing or by withholding something, if not in outright hostility. According to 1 Cor 13:5, love does not insist on its own way. In Fran's case, getting her way was more a matter of opportunity and persistence than obvious self-assertion (combined with a lot of misplaced yielding on the part of others). One telltale sign is that Fran always would refer to St. Mark's as "my church," not "our church." As is often the case with clergy sabbaticals, during Fran's six months off, the congregation saw others step up in healthy ways to the benefit of both the congregation and Fran. While others previously had felt that their efforts were not as good as Fran's, what may have been lost in quality was more than made up for in improved esprit de corps.

Finding healthy levels and forms of member involvement within a congregation requires mutual trust and discernment both by the individuals involved and by others affected in the church. Such discernment takes seriously the needs of the congregation in preserving its identity and mission, as well as in perceiving what a particular person has to offer and is called to offer. This includes consideration of when it is one's turn to step up and meet a need. For the sake of the integrity of the church's identity and mission, congregation members are called to mutual discernment about when to listen, when to speak, when to act, when to not act, when to persist, when to yield, when to compromise, and when to search for a win/win outcome.

Individuals of many species, from humans to insects, differ greatly in their levels of being assertive, exploratory, aggressive, and in taking initiative toward others and their environment; there are also comparable differences in passivity, yielding, submissiveness, and receptivity. In some circumstances, assertiveness has more survival value, and in other situations passivity has more survival value. In any given social situation, the dynamics of dominance and submission come into play. At one extreme, people insist on getting their own way. At the other extreme, people let others take advantage of them and others. Both are boundary violations of different kinds. An example from driving in traffic shows us the value of both assertiveness and yielding. Driving in traffic is the largest scale cooperative activity, in which most of us routinely engage. Tempo, spacing, and flow are each factors involved in participating well in driving. Connecting with the flow of traffic takes good concentration and generalized awareness to know what each situation calls for at any given moment. Sometimes the context calls for us to be assertive, while other times to yield. The best thing for the sake of other drivers is to remain predictable. If we yield when it is our turn to go, we are disruptive. When we force our way unpredictably, we are disruptive. Likewise in the flow of congregational life, there are times to step up and be assertive and times to yield.

While dominance and submission as character traits may be natural to human beings, they are not simply to be perpetuated in Christian community because they can interfere with and undermine the core identity and mission of serving the way of Jesus Christ. In Christian community, even passive people must be willing to contribute their viewpoints in clear and direct ways for the sake of communal discernment, serving as the eyes and ears of the Spirit. As we have mentioned previously, just as insect eyes can have thousands of separate lenses whose inputs combine to create what the insect sees, so the congregation needs the input and influence of each person. Each person also needs to be willing to step up at the appropriate time. This approach can take us out of our personal comfort zones and require us to act uncharacteristically for the good of the whole. A domineering person chooses to remain silent based on discernment and requests the input of others. A passive person chooses to speak with authority about their point of view to the betterment of the common ministry. This is what it means to fulfill one's role as parishioner without squelching another's role. Initiative without receptivity is like a bull in a china shop. Receptivity without initiative withholds needful gifts, remaining passive and inert. In some congregations people with dominance in the community are deferred to by others who always wait for their opinion; they are given virtual veto power. While the council may deliberate without them, the final decision becomes, "Let's see how Ed feels about this. We can't do it without his support."

Accurate discernment about how much initiative to take requires an adequate exchange of information so that a member can know when they have something to contribute. Too often, if someone is informed at all, it is only after a leadership team or committee has already come to a decision. This then places the person who has a contrasting viewpoint into a disruptive role rather than into the constructive one they could have played if they had been consulted earlier in the deliberation process.

It is always disruptive, regardless of the stage in the process, when members wish to have anonymous input. Some congregations have the practice of not allowing any anonymous input or even input coming through a third party because of the disadvantage such input places on those who receive such input. First of all, we know that accuracy is lost whenever information is delivered secondhand. In such a case, there is no opportunity to get direct clarification so that others might be able to determine how much weight to give to such input.

In some cases individuals act more like consumers toward their congregation than like participants in its ministry. The stress of time pressures is one widespread reason for this. Another involves the needs of members not otherwise being met; this might happen in an aging congregation. Based on a consumer mentality, serving the human needs of the members becomes an end in itself; from a participant or discipleship viewpoint, meeting the needs of the members has the final purpose of equipping them for ministry to others.[12] The contest between the consumer and the discipleship attitudes sometimes comes to expression in relation to funerals, weddings, or confirmations. Through these celebrations self-interest rather than discipleship is too often promoted. At a wedding, for example, the church's mission involves having the couple's marriage grounded in the horizon of God's ministry in Christ, so that the marriage is a resource that benefits others, not just the couple. This calls for a different kind of worship service than simply complying with what the couple may want or like. Very often, however, the couple does not share, or sufficiently share, the mission of the church so that the requirements or wedding policies of the congregation come into conflict with what the couple wants.

Confirmation is another occasion where conflicts may ensue between member as consumer and member as participant in the larger ministry and mission of the congregation. In all honesty, some parents think they have an obligation to get basic religious instruction for their children and then "let them decide." Parents want children to receive such instruction with as little disruption as possible. Other parents

12. Foss, *From Members to Disciples*.

frankly just want to get their children a "diploma" to satisfy grandparents or other family members. For this same reason they may have gotten their children baptized in the first place, although parents also may be hedging their bets that the children need to be baptized in order to get into heaven. The consumer mentality is made even more difficult when you add to it a sense of entitlement. Because the parents are members, the congregation "owes them" what they want, which almost always comes into conflict with the integrity of a confirmation program. By analogy, consumers are free to shop around and get the best deal. When there is a conflict between the confirmation requirements and what the child or family wants according to their own interests, the better those particular members are able to deal with their own stress, the more easily they will see things from the viewpoint of the pastor and the congregation's mission, not remaining locked into their perception of their own needs. In contrast to such disgruntled consumers of confirmation, there are also many families, students, and parents, who do approach confirmation as an opportunity for participation in the church's ministry and mission.[13] The boundary question, whose is this? helps us realize that the confirmation program does not belong to the family. It belongs to the congregation, and the congregation has a right to set participation requirements for the program.

In a parallel manner, it is useful to examine carefully the question, whose wedding is this? It may seem obvious that the wedding "belongs to" the couple and their families. However, when it is being done as a religious service, a holy rite, the church is responsible for the mission integrity of the service and necessarily has considerations that parishioners (as consumers) unfortunately may not have adequately considered. The trained clergy, who are well educated about such matters, often take the heat for seeking to protect the integrity of the wedding's religious purpose. It is most useful for congregations to adopt clear policies that designate the expectations of for Christian wedding and to abide by those standards. It is helpful for church members to receive and learn about the congregation's requirements so that they can more fully understand and respect them, refraining from pressuring the pastor to violate the requirements or best practices in relation to all religious services, including baptisms, confirmations, weddings, or funerals.

13. Everist, *Church as Learning Community*, chap. 5.

When parishioners seek to disregard such requirements, they are violating the boundaries of the congregation itself and its ministry, not just the pastor's boundaries. Policies define the boundaries needed to preserve the integrity of the church's identity and mission. The same applies to the question of who is to preside at a wedding. In the consumer mindset, the couples want to choose. Some may even want a previous pastor, who has moved on, since they knew and liked that pastor and may not know the current pastor as well. But if the previous pastor does the wedding, it is in violation of the congregation's boundary. A former pastor has responsibility not to interfere with the ministry effectiveness of the current occupant of the pastoral role.[14] For the previous pastor to even ask the current pastor about it is unfairly putting pressure on the current pastor. In another variation, members may want a relative who is also a pastor to perform the ceremony, again making the function personal rather than respecting the mission of the church. Marriage in the church is a religious rite, not a personal ceremony. Many people do not understand that. If the couple wants a civil ceremony, the service could be performed by a justice of the peace. As a religious rite, it is performed by the pastor of the congregation, the person designated by the congregation for that role.

Similar reasoning applies to funerals. Funerals held in a church do not just belong to the family and friends of the deceased to conduct as they wish, or with whomever they want to preside. Perhaps even more than with weddings, the parishioner as person may want the funeral to be performed by a previous pastor who best knew their loved one. The family may also want the current pastor to come back from vacation instead of having the supply pastor, whom they may not know. Yet a funeral in church is a worship service, and so the church rightly has requirements to protect the integrity of that process. "Whose is this?" A worship service falls within the care of the church. That in no way sets limits on what else a family may wish to do as part of their remembrances, in order to make connections with one another outside the worship service.

Especially surrounding funeral services, parishioners may treat the church as a vending machine, expecting the church to compensate the family for the church's inadequate emotional self-care, desiring church involvement to reduce their stress and distress. Many people very easily want their church to be a place of refuge, solace, comfort, and reassurance.

---

14. Everist and Nessan, *Transforming Leadership*, 141–42.

"Come to me, all you that are weary and carrying heavy burdens," Jesus said, "and I will give you rest" (Matt 11:28). Yes, but it was also the case that Jesus challenged people, not just telling them what they wanted to hear. That is, after all, why they killed him. The very first day of his ministry, they wanted to throw him off a cliff, they were so upset by what he said (Luke 4:29).

Parishioner as consumer of a service from the church puts the congregation and its leaders in a bind: "Give me comfort"; "Don't disturb me"; "Don't challenge me"; "Don't call me out"; "Don't preach sermons that make me or others think you are talking about me." Clergy and laity unconsciously collude to avoid what it disturbing. Parishioners do not want to be upset, and pastors do not want to upset parishioners. After all, the members are the ones paying the pastor's salary! Should the pastor not always do what the members want? The ability to respond to the difficult challenge of loving Lord, neighbor, and self requires a high tolerance for becoming disturbed about the world as it is. Otherwise religion can begin to function as the opiate Karl Marx thought it was. Given the stress of our lives, we easily may not have the capacity to be aware of all the terrible things that could be addressed right in front of our eyes, let alone in faraway communities. We want to shut off our awareness in order to not become overloaded. An alternative is to come together in order to increase our tolerance for disturbing things, including disturbing realizations about ourselves.

When the parishioner's self-care is inadequate, they will look to the church to reduce their stress; they will look to the church to reduce their uncertainty. They will be intolerant of pastors and other church members who challenge them, because that increases their stress rather than decreases it. They will be intolerant of anything new, because adjustment involves the stress of the unknown. They will be intolerant of people holding them accountable, because self-reflection is hard work. By contrast, when we get our self-care needs met outside the church, we can accept, and even welcome, when the church challenges us to grow in our capacity to minister for the sake of others. Then we can welcome mutual accountability and the process of knowing and being known just as we are and just as we are becoming.

When parishioners join hands to face ugly realities through mission and ministry, it is a beautiful thing. When self-interest is set aside, as it is by observing the Sabbath, then emerges the needed mutual, unconditional support and trust that allows freedom to reign so that new dimensions of God's purposes can to be discovered and explored within community. Synergy can happen in unexpected and delightful ways. There is a paradoxical aspect to this. With the command to love God, love neighbor, and love oneself, and with the setting aside of self-interest, there is an increase in the love of God and love of neighbor. But there is also an increase in the love of self, when this means love of the self as a child of God, love of the self beyond all roles, beyond all stressors, beyond all likes and dislikes.

The spiritual discipline of setting aside self-interest in Christian community helps bring awareness to aspects of the true self that we ourselves benefit from exploring and that others benefit from when we do so. For example, many people who attend high school reunions notice that after a few years, people are willing and interested in talking to people who were outside their social circle in high school. When they do so, they are amazed to learn how interesting and wonderful these people really are. In relating to them now, they are not relating with their old selves but rather with their just-now-being-discovered selves. When at church we just congregate with those we already know and like, we likewise set limits on the true self who dwells deep within.[15] When we relate in Christian community equally, without playing favorites, something special can happen for all involved. The love of the Lord, love of neighbor, and love of self all converge into one celebration of life.

PRACTICING BOUNDARIES IN LOVING OTHERS AND OURSELVES

One way that we extend love to others is by protecting them from harm. Best practices, as described in this book, are ways of creating safety for all involved. Given the complexity of human existence, with all the unknowns of our shadow sides, it is more loving to set boundaries with others than to set before them open temptations. It is actually more caring toward children not to leave them alone in a candy shop. It is more caring toward those handling our money not to leave them alone with other people's money. It is careless toward all involved not to have safeguards in place. The part of the self that takes offense at not being trusted is the ego, not the soul.[16] Why give to the ego so much power? It is respectful to

15. Merton. *New Seeds of Contemplation*, chap. 4.
16. Ibid., chap. 7.

acknowledge everyone's weaknesses. Every day in the news we encounter yet another story about a person having done a horrible thing, which those who know the person would not have predicted. Every day, in the confidence of therapists' and pastors' offices and in confessional booths, ordinary people reveal how shocked they are by their own behavior, not having realized that they were capable of doing such harm. Every night countless girls discover that nice boys are capable of selfish aggression against them. Every day people are shocked to discover what their spouses and partners have done behind their backs.

Given all this, it seems more loving and caring toward the self not simply to trust the self but rather to draw upon best practices to protect some parts of the self from other parts of the self. It is an act of care to monitor the different parts of ourself. Many of us must set limits on how we allow parts of ourself to talk to other parts in the privacy of our own minds. Love of self means not being careless with ourself. Care for our future self means putting limits on destructive tendencies of our current behavior. The research on self-discipline and willpower is reinforcing the long-held tradition within the world's religions that self-control requires control of our environment, because willpower is weaker than the power of temptation.[17] The great religions agree that we cannot know what we are capable of until faced with the temptation. The well-known proverb states that "pride comes before the fall." Such pride is based on self-deceit, the self-deceit of recovering alcoholics, who boldly declare that you could place a bottle of whisky in front of them and they would not drink from it. This is careless talk. We do not want to believe our own vulnerability any more than we want to believe that our neighbor is capable of incest. But being faithful means facing up to reality. It is caring toward ourselves to say no if offered a free buffet. It is caring toward ourselves and others to not go to a "gentleman's club" for an outing with friends.

Currently, respect for our shared vulnerability is growing due to the work of Brené Brown.[18] It is careless to deny how vulnerable we are as human beings. It is also careless to be afraid of our vulnerability. The best way to respect our vulnerability and the vulnerability of others is to recognize and respect boundaries with ourselves, with others, and with God. An extremely helpful tool for doing so is the adoption of codes of ethics and best practices, to which we turn in the next chapter. Before doing so,

17. McGonigal. *Willpower Instinct*, chap. 3.
18. Brown, *Daring Greatly*.

we want to touch on the role of best practices in care for ourselves, that is, love toward ourselves.

Best practices in care for or stewardship of the self are well recognized. Here we point to the basic principles. The first is the motive of love and care—not only for our present self but especially for our future self. While not brushing our teeth today may not hurt us immediately, it takes a risk with our future health. We do not need to calculate the odds about getting cavities or gum disease in our particular case. We accept it as careless not to brush our teeth and as caring to do so. We do not need to think it through every day. It is a healthy habit. Just as driving can be a spiritual practice, when we recognize that we hold other people's well-being in our hands when we drive, so it is with many other aspects of our own lives. In many varied activities we hold our own well-being in our own hands. Valuing healthy practices comes more easily when we are in touch with God's unconditional love for us. When we are mindful of God's love for us, we more easily remember to care for others when we are driving. So we also remember more easily to care for ourselves. Daily spiritual practices that connect us with God's unconditional love help to motivate and reveal loving ways of relating to ourselves. Practices of caring for ourselves then are not a hassle. Rather they have importance, because we are important to God and our future selves are important to God. We choose to practice them, whether we feel like it or not, because it is the loving thing to do. It is at the same time also loving toward others, because reducing our own stress, for example, allows us to be more aware of the needs of others, more patient, more kind, and more able not to insist on our own way. We thereby also care for our congregations by caring for ourselves. This does not mean, however, that we withhold from pastors and congregations all awareness of our needs, as when we are hospitalized and decide not to inform the pastor about it. Sharing such information is not about placing a demand, but rather allowing the pastor and congregation to fulfill their God-given mission in offering pastoral care.

Following best practices and living by healthy habits assist us in recognizing that without them we fall prey to letting current feelings take control over us. In chapter 5 we identified several distinguishable types of boundaries: identity, physical, will, emotional, mental, resource, and spiritual boundaries. Each of these boundaries summons us to respect and protect others. However, they also apply to caring for ourselves.

Best practices with regard to our own *identity boundaries* are those that keep us in touch with our core identity as a child of God. We do not misrepresent ourselves toward others through dishonesty, nor do we misrepresent ourselves to ourselves. This is challenging, because we want to maintain a positive view of ourselves. Therefore we may tend to deny our faults rather than, with the help of God's unconditional compassion, see ourselves as we really are. We refrain from calling ourselves names: "You idiot! What were you thinking?" To engage in such derogatory self-talk is careless with our identity. We also avoid creating false or incomplete images of ourselves to ourselves. Love of self begins with accurate self-image. As in the case of Sabbath freedom, however, all we know about ourselves is our past, not what we are capable of in the future. The fact that we have not yet done something does not mean we never will. So, as one example of careful practice, we might drop the expression "I can't . . ." and replace it with "I have never . . ." or "I have yet to . . ." In relation to congregational life, we care for our identity boundaries by not allowing others to misrepresent us, or refer to us by names other than those of our own choosing. We also care for our identity boundaries by not using our professional, social, or psychological identities in congregational life—not doctor, not mayor, not incest survivor but rather child of God.

Caring for one's *physical self* includes maintaining healthy physical boundaries in relation to others, not letting our self be exploited or even touched in unwelcome ways. For some people with arthritis, this can mean not letting others grab their hands in a handshake, since it is painful. Caring for one's basic physical needs is an expression of love toward self. This includes protecting sleep from encroachment by such things as worry. The old image of a child saying prayers while kneeling beside the bed is instructive. Here one's cares are handed over to God even before getting into bed. Best practices of care toward self can be carried with us wherever we go. While traveling, for example, some people wisely continue their exercise routine regardless of where they are, as well as other aspects of their daily regimen. They tend to feel better and also function better with others because of this activity.

Physical body boundaries also include our appearance. Asking of our body the question, whose is this? can help us acquire freedom of self-expression in our physical appearance. The adolescent girl who spends two hours preparing her face and hair before she goes to school is giving others control over her appearance. As relational beings, it is caring to consider how others will react to our appearance, but that is only one consideration. The other is our own identity and ownership of our bodies.

Healthy *will boundaries* allow the will to assert itself appropriately without violating another's will. Assessment of the health of the will involves checking in with different arenas of one's life. People who feel powerless or jacked around at work can compensate by being overly aggressive at home, and vice versa. With regard to the will and congregational life, it is important that we use the will to contribute and participate as helpfully as possible, neither holding back (to the detriment of the congregation's mission) nor overextending the will to encroach on others or on congregational boundaries. Care for one's own will involves how we exercise it in different circumstances and different parts of our lives. To protect oneself from being controlled by another person, it is helpful to practice saying no. Best practice for a person who has trouble with this is to respond to another's request first by buying time, saying something like "Let me get back to you on that." And when saying no, it is helpful to not give a specific reason, since the other person may argue about it. "It doesn't work for me to do that" should be sufficient. The attitude here is that you are simply informing the other person of your decision. They do not get to vote on your decision. If a person continues to push, address that rather than the specifics, saying, "I would like you to respect my decision."

To protect ourselves from being controlled by inner forces—such as appetites, urges, desires, and emotions, best practices include avoiding certain tempting circumstances, especially when we are alone. Often our behavior is constrained by the possibility of being detected by others, so when we are alone our will is more at risk of being overpowered by temptation. Holding ourselves accountable both to ourselves and others, as with an accountability partner, is another way to care for the exercise of our own will. As with other aspects of our self, the will can be strengthened, so merely protecting its potential weakness is not the total answer. Deliberately choosing to do something different, as long as it is a realistic goal, is one way to strengthen the will. Lenten fasting is a way to strengthen the will, as can the practice of some kind of weekly fast. Daily spiritual practices also strengthen the will. Sustaining a good practice does not take as much willpower as starting a new one, even if the intent is for the new practice only to be done briefly. With a healthy, skillful will we strengthen and protect all dimensions of ourselves. We do not let our mental selves be controlled by unhealthy inner forces, including the urge to dominate others, and we do not let ourselves be dominated by what others think of us or want from us. We also respect the integrity of the other's will and the integrity of congregational boundaries and role boundaries.

With *emotional boundaries*, we protect the integrity of our own and others' feelings and emotional space. We pay enough attention to our feelings to find accurate ways to portray and describe them to ourselves and others. We do not jump to conclusions or speculate about what they might be, based on past experience. Excitement and anxiety can feel similar, for example, but to mistake excitement for anxiety is to hamper ourselves. We can deny our feelings also in order to protect our self-image: "I wouldn't want to think of myself as the kind of person who would be intimidated by the pastor." So then you might more easily believe that the pastor is bullying you.

It takes time and careful attention not to misrepresent our feelings, even to ourselves. Often, staying with one's own bodily sensations helps keep the mind from intruding with its own ideas of what must be happening or what it would like to believe is happening. To protect our feeling boundaries from intrusion by others can be difficult because we are such relational beings. It is very easy to simply to absorb the feelings of those around us, especially of people who are more dominant than we are. It is convenient to feel the same way they do, since then there is no conflict. But then there is also no contrast, and contrasts can enrich things for everyone.

As relational beings, we also easily pick up emotions related to alarm, fear, and anxiety. When one horse in a herd is spooked and runs, they will all get spooked and run. The same is true for birds in a flock. We can see how this might have some survival value, while there are also risks. The children's story about Chicken Little taught us not just to buy into another's anxious catastrophizing. This is an important life skill. Clergy are trained to be "a nonanxious presence" with people who are distraught.[19] All of us benefit from counteracting the tendency to pick up and adopt the feeling state of those around us, especially those feelings that sound an alarm, in order that we and the group can benefit from our own calm and maintain our own perspective on the situation. With our feelings separated and distinct from those around us, we can better

19. Richardson. *Becoming a Healthier Pastor*, chap. 5.

relate to others in a helpful manner when that is appropriate. Deliberate practice helps.

We similarly protect our *mental boundaries* when we allow ourselves to think differently from other people and even to think differently than we ever have thought before. The boundaries between thoughts and feelings are important, because one of these human functions can easily dominate the other. A common example involves how we tend to disbelieve research results when we do not like the implications of the findings. We also refuse to understand another person's point of view because we may not like the implications or we do not like the person. This is an instance of allowing our thinking to be dominated by our feelings.

With *resource boundaries* we protect our vital resources from misuse by ourselves and others. An old-fashioned but still useful way people protect their financial resources from their own misuse is by budgeting and designating certain amounts of money for certain needs. They maintain, in effect, compartments for different needs, each with their own boundaries. By doing so, for example, they can see how much money is left for food in their weekly budget. Budgeting time and energy has a similar benefit. When congregations set meetings without any established ending times, they are not keeping good resource boundaries for the participants. Members with good time boundaries will rightly insist on setting clear ending times for meetings. This practice tends to improve the discipline within the meetings themselves. Members with good financial boundaries will insist on best practices to protect their financial contributions to the congregation. All healthy relationships involve negotiating implicit if not explicit agreements about how much time and energy the interactions will take. In addition to financial, property, energy, and time resources, there are also relationship resources. When earlier we discussed stress, we mentioned that other people are a resource that can help reduce our stress. Protecting relationship resources means not overtaxing others, as well as not offering someone else's help without their consent nor allowing others to do so.

Congregation members also contribute much to their own spiritual vitality and to that of their congregations by keeping healthy *spiritual boundaries*. We will look at boundaries internal to the individual as well as at essential external boundaries. For an example of both types of spiritual boundaries, we will consider the case of Clayton, an elder of the Church of the Covenant. As Pastor Theo launched into his sermon, Clayton realized to his dismay that Pastor Theo was preaching about Jesus's pronouncement in Matt 5:21–22, which equates hatred toward one's brother with murder. Two prominent members of the congregation were brothers who had been feuding for decades. Everyone danced around the problem so as not to make an issue of it. Both were good men. No one seemed to know what had started it. Clayton tried to inconspicuously glance over to where Joshua, one of the brothers, always sat. He noticed that Joshua's face was red. After the service, Clayton rushed down to the pastor's study and was waiting there for him when he returned. Clayton asserted, "Pastor Theo, if you want to keep your position here, you will never preach on that subject again! Do I have your word on that?"

Pastor Theo later heard quietly from other members who were grateful that he had pointed out the elephant in the room. They realized how cowardly they had been and welcomed the opportunity to no longer collude in all the avoidance. Spiritually, we damage ourselves and others when we allow our ego-based feelings to dominate the spiritual part of ourselves. Part of healthy internal boundary keeping entails protecting our spiritual nature from such domination by internal forces and external forces. Likewise, we can question whether Clayton, as a lay leader, was not violating a boundary by trying to bully Pastor Theo over the content of his preaching.

Spiritual integrity may be the most important area needing our care and attention as congregation members. We too easily allow other areas of interest, such as feelings, to encroach on our spiritual well-being. We easily make the spirit subservient to other interests both individually and collectively. In the case of Covenant Church, important spiritual lessons were being avoided in order not to rock the boat and embarrass prominent members. Spiritual boundary keeping helps us not to let ego-based feelings like fear or anger violate spiritual integrity. We too easily structure our religious communities to avoid challenging issues. One device people commonly use is called "spiritual bypassing." Spiritual bypassing is the use of spiritual beliefs and practices to avoid issues rather than to deal with them. A common example is how we can use spiritual beliefs to reduce people's distress at the loss of a loved one, telling others what they want to hear rather than helping them to face the distress. Healthy spiritual boundaries can help us face directly what our feelings would have us avoid. They help us listen to the prophetic word without wanting to kill the messenger.

Healthy spiritual boundaries also help us differentiate our personal spiritual awareness from those around us. As some would say, these boundaries help us "not drink the poisoned Kool-Aid." We protect ourselves from spiritual abuse when we do not allow others to use God and Scripture against us or against others for their own selfish purposes. We also avoid employing spiritual reasoning to reinforce prejudices or to withhold deeper insights about God by attempting to control others. Who is in the driver's seat—ego-based feelings or the spirit? That is the boundary question.

With healthy spiritual boundaries we do not judge others' relationship with God or usurp their insights into their own spiritual experiences. We do not invoke God's action in relation to the other person without their consent. We do not decide for others what they should believe or practice spiritually. We do not use God to control others, such as the frustrated Vacation Bible School teacher did who demanded of a young girl, "What would Jesus think of your behavior? You should always ask yourself that!" God can be used to manipulate, correct, or condemn others, beginning with how we think about these things in our own minds. With healthy spiritual boundaries we endeavor to have the ears to hear what we do not want to hear and the eyes to see what we cannot comprehend, rather than letting habits and spiritual laziness dull our awareness. When asked what we believe about something, we answer for ourselves with integrity, even about our possible confusion, rather than deferring to some other source of authority. We can hear and respect the still, small voice within us and in others. As a consequence, with the benefit of discipline in our individual spiritual practices, we have much to contribute to the corporate spiritual practices of congregational life. We can maintain our spiritual boundaries rather than, as Clayton did, let our emotions limit and spiritually damage us and others.

Part 3 of this book has been devoted to boundary keeping in relation to the pastor as person and in relation to the shared responsibility of all church members to safeguard the church's identity and mission as together we steward the many boundaries affecting congregational life. We, all the members of the church, must give watchful attention to identity, physical, will, emotional, mental, resource, and spiritual boundaries. In our concluding chapter we gather our collective wisdom about preserving the integrity of the body of Christ in the form of best practices and try to articulate a vision for the church, which holds such practices in the highest regard.

9

Being Body of Christ with Integrity:
Toward Best Practices in Boundary Keeping

SCENARIO NINE: THE ANNUAL MEETING

The members and staff of First Church had come to dread the day of the annual congregational meeting. There were so many reasons for disregard: the meeting time was inconvenient, the agenda unclear, the preparation by the chair haphazard, the reports rambling, the business dull, the budget discussion contentious, and the elections pro forma. For years this pattern had repeated itself, to everyone's chagrin.

Two years ago a task force had been appointed to rethink and re-structure the annual meeting. A diverse group was recruited for this task, including people gifted in hospitality, worship, music, running meet-ings, finances, group dynamics, communications, and leadership. Their work began by analyzing what had gone wrong. The consensus was that the annual meeting was a prime instance of poor boundary keeping by the congregation in general. People did not respect one another's time. Many took disagreements personally. Reports often disguised problems, rather than promoting transparency. Gifts were not celebrated. People complained afterwards without making constructive suggestions. There was little sense that what they were doing had anything to do with the congregation's identity and mission as the body of Christ. The annual meeting was perfunctory and pointless. A bad time was had by all!

The task force decided to begin its work by developing a Behavior Covenant, which was adopted and implemented for all congregational gatherings, including business meetings. Today was the culmination of this project as the congregation gathered to hold its annual meeting. The results of the task force's labors were reflected in the following ways. Perhaps the biggest change was that the meeting had been moved to September, marking the beginning of the congregation's renewal of activities after the start of the school year. The meeting was now held on a Wednesday evening, starting at 6 p.m., along with a potluck supper. People of all ages were seated around tables in the fellowship hall and asked to sit with those whom they knew less well. Table conversation was to include sharing by each person about three questions: (1) How has the congregation challenged you to grow in your faith in the last year? (2) What was most effective last year in meeting the congregation's mission goals? (3) What goals should the congregation set for the coming year? One person at each table was asked to take notes on the responses, which would be collated and reviewed by the leadership team and made available to the entire congregation.

At the conclusion of the meal, forty-five minutes later, the gathered assembly sang two beloved hymns and was invited to rehearse the congregation's mission statement. The congregation was then asked to reflect on a theme Bible verse that had been selected for the coming year, Ephesians 4:15–16: "But speaking the truth in love, we must grow up in every way into him who is the head, into Christ, from whom the whole body, joined and knit together by every ligament with which it is equipped, as each part is working properly, promotes the body's growth in building itself up in love." The pastor was prepared to offer concise theological and practical reflections to the members about what this verse could mean for the next year of their life together as a church.

The congregation had received the agenda for the annual meeting at the beginning of August. Preparations had already begun in the spring for crafting a meeting that would be both energizing and efficient. The congregational president was prepared to preside according to Roberts Rules of Order and reminded the members that child care was now available for those desiring it, provided by those who were trained according to the congregation's child protection policy. The chair of the worship committee was asked to offer an opening prayer, which was taken from a resource provided by the denomination for this purpose. Written reports had been submitted in advance by all standing committees and each member of the church staff, and these had been distributed to the congregation with the agenda in early August. The reports focussed less on rehearsing past activities and more on imagining the shape of congregational life for the coming year. The chairpersons of the committees and the church staff were together invited to the front of the assembly in order to respond to comments and questions about their reports. At the conclusion of this discussion, the congregational president expressed the congregation's thanks to all those serving in leadership by offering a prayer and through the singing of a hymn of praise.

New business followed, beginning with the election of officers. Each position description was clearly presented, and at least two candidates had been nominated for each position. The candidates also had prepared brief statements in writing about their gifts and interest in serving in the prescribed role; these statements had been distributed with the other materials in advance. Elections took place by secret ballot, and all candidates were affirmed by applause after the results were announced.

For the budget presentation the finance committee now prepared a narrative budget, which both organized the line items into mission categories and provided a written explanation of how each category contributed to supporting the congregation's ministry and outreach. Special attention was given to the importance of the congregation's partnership in the work of the denomination. In this first year of the new congregational meeting format, a brief video depicted the effectiveness of the church's collective mission. (Next year instead of the video, a representative from the denomination was going to be invited to make a presentation by interactive video, in order to interpret the denomination's programs.) Congregational leaders framed discussion of the budget in terms of fulfilling the core identity and mission of the congregation as expressed in its mission statement. Other new business items had opportunities for hearings and discussion prior to the annual meeting and were presented concisely with the recommendation to approve coming from the congregation council and staff.

The highlight of the evening was a video that had been prepared by the youth group of the congregation. It consisted of video clips of interviews with many older members of the congregation sharing their best memories of their church. In the years that followed, the theme of the video changed, but it was always cross-generational and mission focussed. The meeting concluded promptly at 8:30 p.m. with the Lord's Prayer. Volunteers had signed up in advance not only for set-up and serving the meal but also for the job of cleaning up afterwards. It was understood that families with children would need to leave promptly. What had once been a meeting time filled with distaste had now been intentionally transformed into a participatory event renewing the vitality of the congregation's identity and mission. Through careful planning and implementation, this gathering was already one of the highlights of the year. These transformations occurred because the people at First Church were becoming more conscientious about good boundaries and learning to value them!

BEST PRACTICES IN PERSONAL BOUNDARY KEEPING

The tools for creating and the skills for maintaining healthy boundaries are not blunt instruments. They are more akin to dabs of color on an artist's pallet to create what is best for each particular situation. In this chapter we consolidate the best practices mentioned in earlier chapters as well as draw conclusions about other wise and ethical practices from topics we have discussed. Many of the practices we mention may seem obvious, the equivalent of "Do not text while driving" or "Look before backing up." Many of these insights are matters of due diligence that if not done constitute careless behavior toward others. If a problem occurs, the burden of proof is on the person who fails to follow such a good practice. Unfortunately, the response of many people tends to be "I was only doing what everyone else does." The purpose of this book is to raise the standard of boundary keeping in congregational life as a matter of routine practice by all members so that normal acceptable practice increases safety and well-being for all concerned.[1] Even more, such best practices will promote the capacity of congregations to fulfill their core identity and mission at a time when too many congregations are under considerable stress.

Practicing Spiritual Integrity

When our spiritual connection is strong and secure, it can vitalize and inform the rest of our being, including our ministries, both personally and

1. On the value of "interdependence" in congregational ministry, see Lehr, *Clergy Burnout*, chap. 4.

collectively.[2] Among practices to secure and enhance spiritual integrity, we highlight the following:

- Engage regularly in prayer and meditation to clear the heart and mind for receptivity to the Spirit.

- Keep safe the precious revelations that have been entrusted to you, while recognizing when you are prompted by the Holy Spirit to share them with another.[3]

- Do not let anyone get between you and God.

- Do not interpret another's spiritual experiences. If they want your help understanding them, listen to them carefully with no preconceived ideas.

- Have some way to monitor how well you are doing at living Christ's values, such as by employing of the Prayer of Examen.

- Monitor how you are treating the least important people in your day.

- Practice common daily activities, such as driving, with spiritual mindfulness, as others' lives are entrusted into your care.

- Practice the principle of charity and speaking the truth in love.

- Keep the Sabbath to restore your soul.

- In transitioning out of Sabbath, bring the benefits of Sabbath with you; do not leave them behind.

- Foster happiness for those who have what you would like.

- Foster compassion for those who are suffering. Offer a prayer of blessing to them when you become aware of their suffering.

- Watch for consumer motives in your relationship to the church; for example, watch for the feeling of simply wanting the church to fill your own needs.[4]

- Do not use God to get what you want from others.

---

2. Harbaugh et al., *Covenants and Care*, chap. 5.
3. Blodgett, *Lives Entrusted*, chap. 2.
4. Cf. Bush, *Gentle Shepherding*, 15–16.

- Remember when you have violated a boundary that forgiveness is a gift.[5] Do not expect or demand it.

- Take seriously that people in positions of responsibility need to guard against the "negligent retention" of church staff in order to protect others and the church itself. The church has suffered by retaining people who have violated boundaries, in order to give them a second chance.

- Foster self-loving, compassionate humility.

- Watch for spiritual "bypassing," which is the use of religion and religious practices to avoid unwelcome feelings.

- Remember those to whom you are gratefully indebted, but do not allow others to leverage your gratitude for their own benefit.

- Remember that unconditional love does not mean setting limits on what should be tolerated.

- On the church calendar label the pastor's day off as "Pastor's Sabbath" to encourage others to view their own practice of Sabbath in the same way.

- Welcome preaching that challenges you and holds you accountable.

Practicing Identity Integrity

Our basic and true sense of identity flows from spiritual vitality. We are called to recognize that we are caretakers of our own identity and that another's sense of identity is fragile, like ours, given the highly relational aspect of our being. Among good practices for maintaining and enhancing identity integrity, we recommend the following:

- When meeting someone, ask what name they wish you to use and abide by that.

- When meeting someone, inform them of how you wish them to refer to you. If they deviate from that, gently remind them.

- Recognize that your impression of another person is in large part the construction of your own mind. Do not hold to or make claims about others that go beyond the facts you can be certain of.

---

5. Blodgett, *Lives Entrusted*, 39.

- Recognize that when someone gives you their impression of another person, it only has the status of a hypothesis, not a fact. Try to clear your mind of preconceived ideas and to approach the person with an open mind, expecting surprises as you delight in becoming acquainted. Do not ask for impressions of other people before meeting them.

- Avoid overgeneralizing about self and others (for example, "You always . . ." or "You never . . .").

- To avoid misrepresenting people, do not label them by associating them with others or even by a category in your own mind. Examples of unhelpful labels used by some clergy for parishioners are "alligator," "clergy killer," and "clergy wannabe."[6]

- Avoid profiling, which is treating an individual as being at higher risk than others due to the group to which they belong or life circumstances beyond their control rather than evaluating each person based on their own actions or personal qualities. Call committees and internship supervisors engage in profiling when, for example, they recommend special requirements, such as counseling, to people solely because of their background. Examples include being the child of an alcoholic parent or a person who was abused as a child. In such cases, their personal identities and characteristics are bypassed and they are treated as members of a category that others have constructed and about which generalizations are made.

- When referring to more than one person, in order to not misrepresent the situation to others or in your own mind, be precise about the number of people about whom you are talking. For example, instead of referring to an opinion you are naming as belonging to "they," say "I'm getting pushback from two people on the leadership team." Lumping people together into a "they" misrepresents a situation and the people involved.

- In order not to create false impressions, avoid speculation both in your own mind and in communication with others. Stick to the facts and do not pass along another's speculation. Clarify with others the source of their information.

6. Everist and Nessan, *Transforming Leadership*, 174.

- When you wish to raise a concern, present it as your own rather than as the concern of a group of people.

- If someone raises a concern as not their own but as something that another group of people has raised, clarify whether this is their own concern as well. Explain that you are willing to address the matter with that person insofar as it is their own concern but that you are not willing to address an issue of concern raised by others who are not present.

- In order to remain true to another person's worth and to care for their feelings, only say things that meet these four criteria: 1) is it honest? 2) is it true? 3) is it helpful? 4) is it kind? Use the same four criteria for how you think about others in your own mind. This includes thoughts that objectify the other person and therefore distract from thinking about others according to their baptismal identity and congregational roles. Sexual thoughts or thoughts about what favors the other person could do for you fall into the category of not being helpful to congregational life, if not inherently harmful.

- Avoid "You" statements, even in your own mind. Instead, use "I" statements about yourself instead. This is a basic practice for clear communication.

- Do not speak as if you have special knowledge or understanding about another person. (Avoid, for example, "I can see that you are the kind of person who . . .")

- Do not let others tell you who you are.

- Recognize the influence of your "animal nature" along with the fact that you need not let it rule you.

- You are not your role. Your role is a vehicle for doing God's work.

- Identify with the principles of Christ's contrast community to keep your sense of identity from becoming defined by prevailing and conventional social standards.[7]

- Practice identifying another person in the most inclusive way, as a child of God, like all others. This helps reduce unconscious prejudice.

7. Bailey, *Contrast Community*.

- Resist taking it personally when following congregational policies and best practices that affect you in ways you do not like. Personalizing such policies, and fearing that others will personalize them, is a major contributor to the violation of best practices.

Practicing Will Integrity

From our true identity as those tethered to God comes the will to live in accordance with how Christ taught us to live. This recognition also gives us insight into the inherent weakness of the will and helps us affirm the need for constraints on our willpower. We also recognize the value of acting for the enhancement of the healthy will of others. Among practices that protect and strengthen the will are the following.

- Practice exercising the will as you would a muscle, even doing small unnecessary things just to give the will a workout.

- Remember that self-discipline is the ability to get yourself to do things when you do not feel like it, and the ability to get yourself not to do things you would like to do.

- Address areas of your life where you feel powerless, as exactly these areas can weaken your will.

- Recognizing the weakness of the will and the limits of self-awareness, negotiate "Behavioral Covenants" in the congregation in order to constrain one's own personal will by mutual accountability.[8] It is useful to adopt congregationwide covenants as well as covenants for each committee or sub-group, including those going on trips, in order that group behavior reflect the values, principles, and purposes of the organization.

- In your designated roles, be aware of your self-interested motives that can put the welfare of others at risk.

- Whose decision is this? is a helpful question to ask before making a decision.

- Always take no for an answer and do so as respectfully and gracefully as possible.

---

8. Cf. Rendle, *Behavioral Covenants in Congregations.*

- Whenever taking no for an answer is difficult, examine carefully why you are feeling that way.

- Get comfortable saying no. Take adequate time to reflect on a request before committing to it.

- Realize that the conventional wisdom that it is "easier to ask for forgiveness than to get permission" is unfair to others.[9]

- Watch out for entrapment so that you do not do it to others or accept it when someone is doing it to you. Physical entrapment involves blocking a person's physical exit, communicating, in effect, "You won't leave till I'm ready for you to leave." Emotional entrapment involves expressing emotional consequences or threats to another person's when ending a conversation: "If you hang up, all bets are off." Verbal entrapment also consists of asking people questions in order to trap them rather than making a statement. For example, if I am upset with someone who is regularly late to a meeting and ask, "When was the last time you were on time?" I have set a trap for the person into admitting the problem. The boundary respecting alternative is simply to say, "I want to discuss the importance to me of your being on time to our meetings." If the person acts as if it is not a problem, I may say, "I can't remember the last time you were on time." The rule is: Do not ask questions when you have a statement to make. Make the statement instead."

- Unless you are the supervisor, avoid telling others what they need to do. Avoid "You need to . . ." statements.

- Express your concern, and then respect the boundary. When expressing concern for another's personal well-being, remember that they do not have to answer to you about their personal life. Express the concern and why you have it and then respect the boundary.

- When making a request of another person, do not expect an immediate answer. Instead, invite the person to think and pray about it and get back to you. This is especially helpful for those at risk of placing the pleasing of others (perhaps of you in particular) before their own needs.

- When receiving a request from others, do not decide on the spot. Instead, tell them you will consider it and get back to them. This

---

9. Blodgett, *Lives Entrusted*, 82–83.

allows for more complete consideration of the implications of the decision than can be given at the moment and under the direct pressure of the other person's desire.

- Avoid giving or requesting favors that would potentially create inequality in the relationship (for example, making another person feel like something is owed to you, such as return favors). Consider instead a verbal or written expression of gratitude.

- When giving a gift or donation, mentally and emotionally release your ownership of it so that the receiving party truly is free to do with it whatever they choose, no strings attached.[10]

- "It takes three to go." Recognizing the weakness of the human will, self-discipline and sound decision making involve controlling the environment, in order not to carelessly create temptation. Based on this strategy, it is wise to avoid being alone with someone who might theoretically become sexually or emotionally attracted to you, or you to them. It is dangerously unreliable to judge that there is no risk based on self-knowledge and of one's impression of yourself and of the other person. Here we learn from the mistakes of others. When there is legitimate ministry to be done with another person one-to-one, only do it in a place where the physical behavior could be observed by others. When alone in a room, meet in a room with an interior window so others could observe, and do so when others are present. Be alert to situations that easily evoke psychological intimacy, such as car rides. To go somewhere, take three, not two. Or go separately.

- In order to avoid temptation, the perception of carelessness, and lack of due diligence, establish "Child, Youth, and Vulnerable Adult Protection Policies and Procedures." Consistently follow such policies, in order to minimize temptation and opportunity for the mistreatment of these individuals by limiting the behavioral discretion of adult participants. Conform the selection of adult participants according to such best practices.[11]

10. Hunter, *Back to the Source*, 75 reminds us of the scene in the film *Harold and Maude*, where Harold gave Maude a gift. After expressing her delight, she kissed the present and threw it into the ocean.

11. Insurance companies often have excellent model policies.

- Identify people who are highly sensitive and aware of boundary issues and learn from them. Value their perspective.

- When thinking about not following a good boundary practice, rather than believing your own reasoning, consult with someone objective who is a good boundary keeper and who is willing to tell you what you do not want to hear. Establish that the burden of proof is always on the one who seeks to violate the good boundary practice. When you discover that you are trying to second-guess normal acceptable boundary practices, beware and consult!

- Establish as routine procedure with leadership teams, staff meetings, and colleague groups that you invite awareness about and discussion from all present on boundary issues and ethical quandaries that you and they are facing in the performance of your roles.[12] Welcome mutual accountability and feedback on boundary keeping within the conduct of these groups.

- Keep track of unmet personal needs and the risks they pose, and make a plan for meeting them appropriately.[13]

- Remember to care for your future self and let that concern override current fatigue.

- Remember the value of boundaries and best practices to protect us from our weaknesses and shadow side.[14]

- Exercise having your will be made subordinate to best practices.

- Watch out for hijacking. Hijacking is the process by which a person or persons take over a process or committee to deliberately redirect it toward a different goal and against the will of those who are already involved. The process of initiating change is not hijacking when the change agent simply uses persuasion, respects differences of opinion, and takes no for an answer. The difference is not persistence but process.

- Recognize threats as power plays, as, for example, when you realize that your congregation has an important condition on its voting membership and an upcoming meeting may force you to decide how to enforce it. Do not try to influence the vote by making a threat.

---

12. Cf. Kaptein, *Workplace Morality.*

13. Olsen and Devor, *Saying No to Say Yes,* chap. 2.

14. Lehr, *Clergy Burnout,* 106–13.

- Realize that taking things personally is emotionally coercive. When your behavior is constrained by fear that another is going to take personally what you do, you are being coerced by that fear. When you take personally what others have done, you are being coercive.

- Do not conspire with others to get your own way.

- Do not engage in secret activities. Secrecy is a means to gain power over others.[15]

- Remember that human beings behave more ethically when others can know what they are doing rather than when they believe no one will know.

- Remember, love does not insist on its own way (1 Cor 13:5).

Practicing Emotional Integrity

Feelings and emotions are a big part of ministry and the way of following Christ, with generous love being the principal component. Feelings can provide us with important information about things. For example, joy conveys important truths about life, and sometimes anger accurately tells us a person or situation is threatening or harmful. Emotions move us in important ways, engaging the vitality of life. Feelings and emotions can also mislead us, however, and their power can overwhelm other important sources of information and judgment. Consequently, we need to abide by the universally recognized need for self-control in relating to our feelings and emotions.

- Listen to feelings (your own and those of others) to see if they are telling you something important. If so, take that information and release the messenger.

- Healthy relating in congregational life can include sharing burdens and difficult feelings. This helps create bonding by strengthening caring relationships for the sake of shared ministry. Since the central value is listening and being heard, do not distract from someone else's story by telling about a similar thing that happened to you. To do so undermines trust.

---

15. Peterson, *At Personal Risk*, 80–86.

- Practice specific techniques and methods in order compassionately to listen to another person with their feelings and emotions, neither being drawn into their feelings nor being reactive to them. Anxiety, sadness, and anger are among the feelings needing the most self-differentiation for many people. In chapters 7 and 8 we discussed some methods that can help. The central point is to keep your nervous system and brain functioning independently without being controlled by the other person's emotions. Clergy, for example, are taught to be a nonanxious presence with people who are distraught. This skill has wide application.

- Support others by affirming the feelings that they have; release any thoughts that they should feel differently than they do (for example, by experiencing anger or grief).

- Appreciate that there are times and places where people do not want attention directed at how they are doing or what they are dealing with. An alternative expression of care can be, "Good to see you," rather than "How are you doing?"

- Hearing your feelings and thoughts out loud with a witness can be helpful. To make it healthy, rather than complaining about others, express what feelings are generated in you by their behavior. For example, "I just hate it when I feel I'm being ignored." Such expression can help identify the origin of the feeling. To make it about the other person is usually avoidance. Venting about another person may feel good, but that does not make it ethically good.

- Be careful to not jump to conclusions about what someone is feeling or to speculate about how they must be feeling. Invite others to give their own expression to their feelings, and use the words most meaningful to them.

- If you want someone to understand how you feel, express your feelings in an inviting way and not as an intrusion of your feelings upon them as some people do when they are venting. Emotional dumping is intruding on another's feeling space. Moderate your intensity and language to make it as easy as possible for the other person to hear and understand.

- Saying "I know how you feel" creates distance rather than closeness for most people. While this might seem to be the opposite of what you intend, some people use this expression to stop conversation rather than to open doors.

- Sharing joys also creates an important bond that can enhance ministry relationships. The person sharing creates a bubble of joy that is easily burst if the listener detracts from it in any way rather than simply entering into the joy and expanding on it.

- Understand what "too much information" (TMI) means. The issue is not simply about the quantity of information, going on and on, while capturing another person's time. It is also about the nature of the information itself. While some personal disclosure enhances role functioning in ministry on everyone's part, such as the sharing of joys and burdens does, other personal disclosure may be unwelcome and unhelpful.

- Be aware of potential manipulation through personal sharing. It can create unhelpful bonding that takes people out of their appropriate role and crosses a boundary into personal interest. Personal sharing without clear boundaries can be the verbal equivalent of "Show me yours and I'll show you mine."

- Be aware of the false intimacy that occurs through triangulation. Avoid it by directing attention to those who are present instead of attempting to deal with the nonpresent person directly.

- Be aware of the false intimacy that can occur in counseling relationships, especially when talking about someone not present.[16] Both parties risk personalizing the care that rightly belongs to the counseling relationship.

- While some socializing is important at work, during staff meetings and in staff relations, establish a disciplined limit to socializing so that such encounters are not used to compensate for a lack of social outlets beyond the job, and so that work time is spent productively.

- Parishioners do well to monitor socializing with congregational staff so that they are not used to compensate for the lack of a social life beyond the congregation. Be open to input about this.

- Use the "Get three to go" rule, whenever you find you want to spend time alone with a church member or staff member at a church

16. Regarding power dynamics and relational boundaries in pastoral counseling, see Doehring, *Taking Care*, chaps. 4 and 5.

function. In situations where inappropriate feelings theoretically could occur between two people, even if they do not have those feelings at the present time, do not enter into that situation unless a third person can be there as well. A common example involves car rides, even when it is more practical for two people to go together.

- Allow others to have their own feelings about things rather than pressuring them into feeling as you do about something. Do not establish consequences for those having different feelings.

- Ministers can help maintain boundaries with parishioners who consult or confide with them by establishing a neutral meeting space, which is not filled with objects from the minister's life or work. When the latter is the case, as with many minister offices, the parishioner has to enter into the minister's psyche, which works against maintaining their own psyche boundaries in the encounter.[17]

- Routinely assess the status of your unmet personal needs with the help of an objective, outside person, insofar as these needs will press to be met inappropriately within one's congregational roles and activities.[18]

- Routinely assess the status and activity of your personal weaknesses, including weaknesses as they relate to your role, with the help of an objective, outside person. While it is not currently popular to think in terms of personal weaknesses but instead to refer to "growing edges," the latter concept does not adequately convey the peril these personal weaknesses pose for ethical behavior.

- Healthy boundary keeping and unwelcome feelings often go together. All boundary keeping and safe practices involve forgoing something that you or someone else wants. The belief that if something is good it will feel good, or, conversely, if it is not good it will not feel good, does not hold up.

- Recognize the difference between needs and wants.

- As adults we can tolerate disappointment when our desires are not met. Being willing to disappoint others facilitates easier boundary keeping for all concerned.

---

17. Cf. Kaptein, *Workplace Morality*, 39–41.

18. Lehr, *Clergy Burnout*, Appendix 1, 128–34, provides a useful tool for personal assessment.

- Remember that there are no cliques in the body of Christ. Relate generously with those for whom you have no natural affinity.

- Foster love over jealousy and resentment.

- Get comfortable being vulnerable.

- Remember that mutual consent does not make something right or acceptable.

Practicing Mental and Speech Integrity

Thoughts and words are basic raw materials for our relationships with others and with our selves. Our thoughts are virtually constant companions, which reflect and shape our experience. We tend to identify strongly with our own thoughts and are at risk of drawing conclusions about others based on the opinions they represent. Thoughts have both inner and outer qualities. To some degree our words express our thoughts, and to some degree our words help us discover what we think. We use thoughts and words in order to do ministry together. Thoughts and words are given high significance in corporate worship and the statement of our beliefs. In fact, differences of opinion about thoughts evoke either feelings of affinity toward others whose beliefs we share or feelings of alienation and threat when beliefs are radically different. As we have emphasized throughout this book, best practices and codes of ethics are indispensable due to the unreliability of human reasoning.[19]

- If you have not told someone something, do not expect them to know it.

- Allow others to have their own thoughts about things, rather than pressuring them into agreeing with you. Do not place consequences on differences in people's thoughts, ideas, and beliefs (for example, by saying, "If that's what you think, then . . .").

- Do not expect others to trust you personally; that is the reason for best practices.

- Do not trust your own judgment. Remember the unreliability of the human mind and the ego-driven heart as demonstrated in previous chapters.

19. Regarding codes of ethics, see Trull and Carter, *Ministerial Ethics*, chap. 8.

- Do not lump events together, but see each event freshly and on its own terms. When a current event reminds you of a past event, exercise the art of letting go.

- Do not speculate; stick to the facts.

- Get comfortable with not knowing.

- When in doubt, consult.

- Remember, if you are thinking about work, you are working.

- Give exercise to the Observer self, practicing mindfulness, rather than just being swept along by your thoughts.

- Remember not to label or categorize people in your own thinking or speaking.

- Practice the use of these four criteria to decide whether or not to think something or to say it to somebody else: (1) Is it honest? (2) Is it true? (3) Is it helpful? (4) Is it kind? Carelessness with our thoughts and words is the relational equivalent of careless driving. We are responsible for the damage they cause.

- Do not personally dwell upon or pass along to others what you do not know to be true.

- Do not pass along someone else's information without their consent, unless the situation is potentially harmful. The question, whose is this? informs us about the boundary.

- Practice recognizing how your thoughts and beliefs are shaped by your feelings. One exercise is to periodically contemplate how "There are things I do not like that are nonetheless true." By letting go of your "I do not like this" response to things that have happened, it is easier to recognize the truth and accept it. Otherwise we can enter into denial and avoidance.

- If you are a church member and have romantic or other personal thoughts about a minister, or if you are clergy or a staff member and have such thoughts about a church member or fellow staff member, remember that you control where you direct your attention and need to practice the "Quick Release of Thoughts" (to coin a term). Dwelling on such thoughts and feelings makes them stronger and tempts one to seek justification for acting upon them.

- Only speak about others who are not present when they have consented, or if you are certain they would consent, if you really cannot obtain consent. Ask yourself, what if the person in question was to be able to hear the conversation? Be cautious about assuming that the other person would not mind simply because you desire to talk about that person.

- Have clear agreements in the congregation about what is confidential and what is not confidential, and review these agreements regularly. For example, if for the sake of shared ministry a staff member wants it to be policy that they inform one another about what they know is going on in members' lives, all who confide must know that this is the policy in order to decide what they choose to disclose.

- When in the presence or someone who is complaining about someone not present, remind them about triangulation and help them consider talking directly to the person with whom they have the issue.

- Adopt a congregational policy not to pass along or take action on anonymous complaints.

- Monitor your stress level, and remember how stress impairs perception and judgment.

- Do not fall prey to wishful thinking. Doing no harm includes assessing what could go wrong with a potential course of action.

- If you choose to violate a best practice, accept that the burden of proof is on you.

- Work to keep your energy high. Remain calm, with your consciousness clear and expansive, in order to be at your best.

Practicing Role Integrity

Regardless of the role you have in your congregation, that role is important to the congregation's vitality and ministry. To fulfill that role according to its purpose, practice these hallmarks of faithfulness: 1) strengthening that role while not exceeding it and 2) not weakening anyone else's role or their ability to fulfill it. In healthy congregations, people help each other in setting and keeping healthy boundaries.[20] The organization itself acts on behalf of healthy boundary keeping for the sake of healthy ministry.

- Remember that the role you are in is granted to you by others. The role is in your care and stewardship for the sake of others. Again ask the question, whose is this?

- Rank all of your roles, personal and professional, in their order of importance, and evaluate how well you are filling those roles.

- There are no role boundaries without a clear definition of each role. Establish role descriptions that are as clear and complete as possible for each major role in the congregation, paid or unpaid. Regardless of the role, it is advisable not to enter a new role without clear role definition, as this can lead to unnecessary role confusion and role conflict. Routinely review the descriptions to see whether they need to be revised.

- When someone is upset with what someone is doing or not doing in a particular role and their concern is due to lack of clarity about the role definition itself, the issue is about the role definition and not about the person filling that role. The person in that role and the dissatisfied person should refer the matter to the personnel committee, which is responsible for the role description.

- Establish accountability roles. Conduct routine evaluations about how well a person is filling their role and also about how well they are doing at not going beyond that role into someone else's area of responsibility. This is done most gracefully within the context of an overall assessment of how well the congregation is meeting its ministry goals and how well each committee or subgroup is doing its job.

- Normalize mutual accountability structures. Routinely practice addressing accountability issues. Do not take these inquiries personally.

- Remember that the role is not to benefit you personally; you are to serve the role for the sake of others.

- Meet your personal needs on your personal time by keeping track of the status of those personal needs. Make a plan for addressing them.

20. Gula, *Just Ministry*, 130–33.

- If in a committed personal relationship always know when you have your next date.

- Distinguish between reasonable expectations and realistic expectations.[21] While an expectation may be reasonable given the role description, whether it is realistic depends on circumstances that not everyone will understand unless they are informed about them.

- Make peace with the realization that there is "conduct unbecoming" a person in your role. This is a standard part of professional codes of ethics that helps professionals take responsibility for the reputation and effectiveness of their profession: professionals recognize that their personal behavior can either enhance or detract from the regard people give to that role and to those who fill that role.[22]

- To avoid questions or doubts about your full mental engagement, avoid consuming alcohol or drugs during your workday.

- When considering taking on a second role with the same person or persons, for the sake of role clarity consider all possible conflicts of interest, realizing the human tendency to deny them or minimize them. Consult with an objective, outside person who is willing to tell you things you do not want to hear. When dual roles are unavoidable (or otherwise undertaken), discuss them with those concerned so that everyone can have input and be watchful.[23]

- Recognize conflicts of interest in decision making by yourself and others. Make discussion about such possible conflicts of interest commonplace. Opt out of a decision-making role or recuse yourself when you or a person close to you has a personal stake in the decision.

- Only access information about others, including Internet and other social media searches beyond what another person has revealed to you, when it is in fulfillment of your agreed-upon role toward that person and the congregation. Being a congregation member is such a role when there is a covenant about caring community, as there should be in youth work, and as there can be with adults as well.

21. Bush, *Gentle Shepherding*, 72–73.

22. For examples of constructive "statements of ministerial commitment," see Gula, *Just Ministry*, Appendix, 240–50.

23. Gula, *Ethics in Pastoral Ministry*, 80–85.

- Respect the difference between work time and personal time so that each is done most effectively. For example, do not continue addressing domestic conflict by texting at work, and do not write work e-mails while in your personal life.

- Decision-making committees and boards do well to routinely ask if anyone is aware of conflicts of interest before proceeding to deliberate and decide on an issue. Respect those who express discomfort with any dual role that you may have.

- Recognize which roles do not mix—that is, which roles are incompatible and weaken the integrity of one's primary responsibility.

- Interim positions often call for the interim pastor or interim bishop to do unpopular things for the sake of the well-being of the church. Given that, anyone wanting to be considered for the permanent position, which follows the interim, would do well not to serve as the interim. Likewise, the church would do well to keep the interim position clear of candidates for the permanent position. The reasonable risk is that the candidate would consciously or unconsciously be more risk aversive than a noncandidate who serves as an interim, to the detriment of the church.

- Parishioners do not ask clergy or staff to take personal responsibility for their affairs, such as power of attorney. If asked to take on such roles, clergy and staff refer the parishioner to other resources for such roles.

- When you are in two roles in a situation (for example, a parent chaperone on a youth trip), explain to the others involved which is primary and which is secondary.

- In dual role situations, frequently ask these questions: What hat am I wearing now? Is this the hat according to which I am thinking and acting?

- Remember that the more a member befriends the pastor or intern, the less they will see that person as their pastor, and the more difficult it is for the pastor to think and act from the pastoral role with integrity. It is the responsibility of the pastor or intern to maintain that boundary. It is not appropriate for the member to change their membership status in order to pursue a personal relationship. If the member was to do that and the relationship went badly, they would have lost both the relationship and their congregation. The cleanest thing is for the pastor or intern to respond to personal overtures by informing the member that professional ethics do not allow such dual relationships and to help the member to accept that.[24] If the parishioner asks, "What if I leave the church?" we recommend a response like, "I'm your pastor, and my responsibility is to keep that relationship strong." By the time this question would have been posed, inappropriate-feeling interactions would already have taken place.

- For clergy, interns, and other staff, keep support functions separate from evaluation functions. An example of this problem is to have internship committees expect interns to confide in them and then to negatively evaluate them on the basis of what is disclosed. These are conflicting roles.

- Avoid conflicting roles among pastoral support groups (for example, mutual ministry committees) by not having them provide evaluation or advocacy either for the pastor or for people who are disgruntled with the pastor. Such activity is triangulating.[25] The least conflicted arrangement is for the pastor to have a support group outside the congregation, possibly with people who are not clergy themselves, in order to gain perspective from those outside the profession. This addresses the need for personal support and personal accountability beyond dual roles.

- You have assumed your role based on mutual agreement between yourself and others. Either party is free to withdraw that consent. Clergy can leave their position as they wish, and congregations can decide they wish for the pastor to leave.

- One of the most difficult and damaging conflicts of interest occurs when a person's effectiveness in their role has been compromised. Personal interest generally tends toward the desire to remain in the role, while this usually conflicts with the well-being of the congregation. Honoring the tension between these two sets of interests among all responsible parties can best lead to a decision that cares for both parties.

---

24. Gula, *Just Ministry*, 137–43.
25. Richardson, *Becoming a Healthier Pastor*, chap. 9.

- Familiarize yourself with the concept of an "impaired professional." Various medical and psychological conditions can interfere with a person's effective performance of their role. Without adequate awareness and corrective action, a congregation's ministry can suffer. In many cases, the well-being of the congregation requires that the minister be removed in order for adequate treatment to occur and for the vital functions of the congregation to continue.

- What a congregation wants from their pastor and what the pastor wants from a position may not completely coincide. Without adequate attention to the tensions, the areas not overlapping will become neglected and may spark dissatisfaction.

- In social media contacts with church members, maintain your professional role in your content and demeanor.

- Once a year review the codes of ethics, behavioral covenants, and best practices that apply to you.[26] Treat them as your allies.

- Do not ask or expect a family member, friend, or relative who is a clergyperson to perform clergy functions for you, such as counseling, weddings, or funerals. This deprives them of being a person with the same needs and desire for ministry as anyone else in those circumstances. If they volunteer, politely decline.

- In congregational gatherings and activities, do not act based on your role in life outside the congregation, such as in a business, civic, or professional role (or even in a friendship role). Stick to being a member of the body of Christ as your assigned role.

- Do not relate to others in the congregation according to their role at work. For example, do not try to get someone's professional advice, set up a business meeting, or even arrange a personal social event since this excludes others. Help others maintain their role as congregation member.

- Suspend friendship interactions during congregational events.

Practicing Transitions to Enhance the Integrity of the Whole

Each role we assume deserves our full engagement. At the same time, it is very helpful to become skillful at moving from one role to another.

---

26. See the useful checklist in Lehr, *Clergy Burnout*, 114–17.

What we learn and experience in one role can better equip us for life in other roles. Effective transitions also can assist us with the process of integration.

- Practice making effective transitions from one role to another in order to be fully present and engaged in whatever you are doing. Obviously, the most important role transition is into and out of the role you play as a member of your congregation in relation to the roles you have in other parts of your life. For clergy and staff members, this also entails transitions from one function or activity to another throughout the workday in order to remain fully engaged.

- To transition from work to your personal life, do not confuse what helps you feel relaxed (like alcohol or TV) with what helps you recover your energy and enthusiasm to enter fully into your personal life and relationships (like light exercise or meditation). Aside from meditation, most practices that help us recover energy after work actually involve some expenditure of physical energy, which the stressed brain wishes to avoid.

- Sharpen your ability to quickly and effectively shift from one state of mind and heart to another. Practice making the three-part transition each day: gain temporary closure with the role you are leaving, quickly refresh, and then turn your mind and heart into the next role and activity you are entering. In the first step of closure, consider what is wise to carry forward into future activities. Clergy must practice this role transition several times a day, given the variety of activities in which they engage. Permanent role changes involve the same three components of closure, refreshment, and turning.

- When clergy leave a call, care for the integrity and effectiveness of the role means fully disengaging from the pastoral role in that setting and from all activities that involve it in order for the congregation to disengage from the clergyperson and embrace the successor.[27] Good practice involves giving notice that the minister is leaving, which includes the directive to the congregation no longer to look to this person for ministerial services but rather to utilize other pastoral services as now designated by the congregation. Notify members on social media that you will no longer be connected with them in that way as a matter of good practice, and help them not to take it per-

27. Everist and Nessan, *Transforming Leadership*, 141–42.

sonally. The new minister supports that boundary for all concerned by not making exceptions. "All concerned" includes future ministers and ministers in other congregations, who benefit from uniformity of this practice, as they may contend with requests from members for ministry from their former ministers.

- Respect that personal contact between a former pastor and church member risks adversely affecting the bond between the new pastor and church members.

- When a congregation member leaves a role, such as a leadership role, full disengagement from that role helps the successor fill the role in their own manner.

BEST PRACTICES IN COMMUNITY BOUNDARY KEEPING

Practicing Boundaries in Times of Contrast and Conflict

Amazingly, with all the social pressure we are dealing with and are placing upon others, each of us is really quite unique. Our uniqueness gives us the advantage of benefitting from a rich variety of abilities and different points of view. Creative self-discipline is required to welcome and incorporate these differences. Helpful practices include the following:

- Make the positive assumption that points of view different from your own have value. Work to be genuinely interested in other perspectives. One such practice is to develop the habit of responding, "That's interesting. That is so different from how I look at it." This will at least keep us from reflexively disagreeing; disagreement defers attention away from the other's point of view onto our own.

- Mentally practice the method that when another person is speaking, you will not be distracted by your own thoughts or reactions but instead will discipline yourself to listen and hear.

- Seek first to understand with fresh eyes, not allowing past experience to color your perception of what is happening now.

- Pray for the capacity to see the other who disagrees with you through the eyes of Christ.[28]

28. Bonhoeffer, *Life Together*, 31–35.

- Appreciate people telling you things you do not want to hear. Thank those who have done so.

- Adopt the mindset of a mediator in your own disputes so that you can see all points of view that are represented.

- Address process before content, in order to get a better outcome. Behavioral agreements at the outset establish needed boundary safeguards. An important component of such behavioral agreements is a provision for time-outs. If any party feels another is too upset to keep the agreement, they may call a time-out for themselves. However, that person also needs to state when the process is to resume so that the time-out is not just a way to avoid dealing with the issues. Per agreement, the time-out is not negotiable once the process has begun. Whoever wants a time-out gets one.

- If process cannot be agreed upon, take the matter to the next level in the organization.

- People can get good outcomes from conflict when they actively help each other out during the conflict rather than watching out for themselves. When being criticized, try to understand what the other person is saying. Practice reframing criticism as requests and then consider the validity of the request.

- Recognize that anger is often a sign that you are engaged in a power struggle.

- Familiarize yourself with principles of fair fighting and nonviolent communication.

- Clarify and communicate carefully to others these four features of a given position: (1) the what of the position, (2) why the person holds it, (3) how strongly they feel about it, and (4) why they feel so strongly about it. Only then does everyone have adequate information to know what to do with a particular point of view.

- Remember not to take things personally even when another person tries to make things personal. Help each other out. In that process, care as much for the other persons as for yourself.

Practicing Worship Integrity

Worship is the heart of congregational identity and mission, yet few are accustomed to consider the many boundaries that are involved in effective worship. Here are some examples:

- Recognize and fulfill your role as a cocreator of the worship experience for yourself and others.

- Entering into worship, suspend your likes and dislikes in order fully to participate.

- Be on time and prepared to fully engage in worship at the time the worship leader begins the service.

- Do not distract the worship leader or fellow worshipers by telling them troubling things right before worship.

- Exercise control of attention in order to stay present and not distracted by extraneous events during worship. Is it not extraneous to care for children, unless others are already caring for them.

- Turn off mobile devices before and during worship.

- When others in the worship space are preparing themselves for worship, be careful not to distract them.

- Leave state shifting to the worship leader. Allow the worship leader to lead in making the transition from one element of worship to another. It is the worship leader's role, for example, to decide whether to applaud or not after a given part of the worship service.

- Do not distract others from worship by taking photographs.

- Strive to treat all present equally without preferences based on friendship. For example, hugging some but not all during the passing of the peace shows unequal treatment .

- Keep commercialism, promotional items, and business references out of the worship space and worship materials.

- When hearing the prayers and needs of others, consider how you might help them be met. The prayers of the people provide direction to the congregation about mission opportunities.

- During communion, set aside all differences and hold everyone in your heart.

Practicing Physical Integrity

The integrity of physical things allows them to fulfill their spiritual purpose and value. The physical property owned by the congregation is in the care of all members. While a church is not a building, the property and its well-being serves the mission of the congregation. Another dimension of the physical involves the physical bodies of people involved in the congregation. By tending to our bodies, we tend to the physical aspects of ministry. Body boundaries help us feel safe and secure. When secure, people are better equipped. When people are not secure, participation is inhibited.

- Realize that caring for your physical body helps you participate fully and contribute fully to the life and ministry of the church.[29]

- Examine congregational practices, such as what is provided for snacks, as they affect health and vitality. Appreciate that others may have health reasons for not consuming the snacks that you offer. Do not take offense.

- At church potlucks, consider taking from dishes that are being neglected by others, so that all will have their contributions valued.

- Exercise "custody of the eyes" (see chapter 3), so as not to visually intrude on another's body, even when you imagine it may be welcome.

- Exercise "Quick Release of Thoughts," which are sexualizing, objectifying, or otherwise inappropriate to your role in congregational life and ministry.

- When physical contact is an integral part of ministry activity, such as in passing the peace, in greeting and parting, or in team-building exercises, give adequate time for others to make a conscious choice about how to participate. Our own practice should be exercised uniformly, so as not to reflect or express favoritism.

- Be aware of the various ways touch can be used for the self-interest of the person initiating the contact: to establish dominance, to elicit trust, to gain reassurance or comfort for the one initiating the

29. Lehr, *Clergy Burnout*, 93–97.

touching, to generate self-arousal, or to excite arousal in the other person.[30]

- If the congregation owns the residence in which the minister lives, church officials should treat access to the property according to the same rules any landlord would need to follow in your municipality.

- When considering whether to make changes to the physical aspects of the church property, make sure you have authorization to do so. The decision-making process of the congregation should be clear. If it's not clear, get it clarified before acting.

Practicing Resource Integrity

A major source of stress is the perception that our resources are over-extended, especially the resources of our time, energy, and finances. This phenomenon adversely affects congregational health insofar as people feel unable or unwilling to contribute the resources needed for congregational vitality. How the congregation respects such resources can help all members become more adept in their stewardship.

- Do not lay claim to another's resources of time, money, or property or allow others to lay claim to your personal resources.

- In order to avoid temptation and the perception of careless behavior in the handling of money, establish and follow policies and procedures.[31] In every arena of congregational life and activity, money should always be handled by two unrelated adults. Resources for such policies and procedures include the congregation's insurance carrier, accounting firm, and denomination.

- Unsolicited donations to the church of personal items one no longer wishes to have, such as used furniture, can be burdensome to those who now have to determine what to do with them without upsetting the giver. This sort of situation can be avoided if potential donors ask in advance whether the items are wanted, and if potential donors are willing to take no for an answer.

- Avoid making personal use of congregational property.

---

30. Cf. Everist and Nessan, *Transforming Leadership*, chap. 10.

31. Trull and Carter, *Ministerial Ethics*, 103.

- Respecting the resource of another person's time includes preparing adequately for activities such as meetings. In order that time is not wasted, start on time and follow a set agenda so that others are not kept waiting, and to avoid needing to brief latecomers about what happened in their absence.

- When asking for another's time, do your best to estimate the amount of time you are requesting and to articulate what it is you are wanting from them.

- In order to be generous with what is most expressive of your core values, assess and monitor how you use your resources of time, energy, and money so that you can live and serve most consistently. Living with coherence is restorative, while living inconsistently is depleting.

- Routinely participate in the gift of Sabbath.[32]

Whew! That is a lot to take in and to work on! And yet the experience that comes down through the ages is that comprehensive disciplines that have relevance for our lives are experienced more as liberating than as oppressive once we get the hang of them. The oppressive ones are the ones that are irrelevant and useless. Relevant disciplines are liberating and life-enhancing because they are expressions of care, and care leads to many wonderful things. These disciplines bring inner equanimity along with more peaceful and productive relationships. We experience more joy, inwardly and shared with others. We are more in tune with the motivations of love and compassion.

A CHURCH ALIVE WITH INTEGRITY

The triune God is a God with a mission. God's purposes in this world involve the sending of Jesus Christ by the power of the Holy Spirit to create life-giving relationships with God, among human beings, and with all of creation.[33] The Bible employs many names to talk about God's purposes for creation: "salvation," "reconciliation," "atonement," "forgiveness," "redemption," and "shalom." While each of these metaphors accents different aspects of God's work, all of them reflect God's central purposes of

---

32. Brueggemann, *Sabbath as Resistance*, 85–89.
33. Nessan, *Beyond Maintenance to Mission*, chap. 3.

seeking to create life-giving relationships between the triune God and all creation, including human beings made in God's own image. Life-giving relationships between God and humans are fostered through God's coming to us in worship and through the spiritual practices that immerse us in the gift of Sabbath.[34] The first boundary that human beings are called upon to honor and respect involves the worship of God. This is the first of the Ten Commandments, and the premise of the Great Commandment (Matt 22:37-38). In Luther's words, "We are to fear, love, and trust in God above all things."[35]

In order to serve God's purposes of creating life-giving relationships in this world, God in Christ by the power of the Holy Spirit has called forth a community of disciples to serve as the agents of this mission in the world. This community is the body of Christ, consisting of many members with many gifts, all of which gifts have been given for the work of ministry, to build up the body of Christ for the common good of all creation (cf. Eph 4:12). Baptism is the sacrament that mediates God's promises of love, forgiveness, and eternal life in Christ to each member, incorporating them into the body of Christ. At the same time the baptized are given the vocation to serve others for Christ's sake. They are called to serve their neighbors in thought, word, and deed. Their arenas of service include the family, the school, the workplace, the local community, and the global community.

Congregations are local communities of Christian faith called to equip members to participate in serving in God's mission for the life of the world. The core identity of the congregation is to be the body of Christ in a particular context, equipping the members to claim their baptismal promises and to live out the mission of the triune God as disciples, Christ-followers, who share the good news with others and serve the needs of their neighbors. The church has a God-given identity and mission that is its very reason for existence. Church mission statements and constitutions make clear the church's explicit purpose in relation to serving the mission of the triune God in the world. These accord with the Great Tradition of the Christian faith as witnessed in the Scriptures as God's Word and in the creeds and confessions of the church throughout the ages. The church's identity and mission belong entirely to God's purposes of bringing and restoring life-giving relationships in all creation.

---

34. Gula, *Way of Goodness and Holiness*, chaps. 1 and 3.

35. Luther, *Small Catechism*, "Explanation of the First Commandment" 1160.

Because of sin, however, the historical existence of the church can and does contradict God's purposes and create many scandals that discredit not only the church but even God. This occurs not only at the level of global communions and national denominations but also at the level of local congregations. There is abundant temptation to idolatry and widespread amnesia that plague local congregations in maintaining their identity in Christ Jesus and fulfilling the mission that God has entrusted to them.[36] Wherever congregations and their members fall short of following their God-given purposes, the witness to God in Christ is contradicted, and service to neighbors is undermined. As God's way of counteracting the waywardness of the church in fulfilling its core identity and mission, God instituted a rule of law to set limits on the harm human beings can do to others. This includes laws, rules, and codes of ethics to govern the functioning of the church and its members. Such measures are necessary to safeguard the church's identity and mission so that people are not harmed and God's healing purposes for the body of Christ are promoted.

This book offers wisdom and direction to the church and its leaders about the many multifaceted and complex boundaries in thought, word, and deed that need careful stewardship, in order to preserve the God-given identity and mission of the church as the body of Christ. The church's functioning is entirely predicated on building and maintaining a climate of trust both among its members and beyond them to all the people affected by its ministry.[37] Too often the church has not recognized the expansive number and variety of boundaries that need tending in order for the church to stay on focus with its central purposes. Discussion of the topic of boundaries is often reduced to consideration of sexual boundaries.[38] As important as sexual boundaries are for the well-being of the church, its members, and all those affected by its ministry, reflection on boundaries in the church needs to become much more expansive to encompass all the kinds of issues discussed in these pages. Another common way that reflecting on boundaries gets minimized is by thinking that these are matters only of concern to church leaders, especially

36. Cf. Blodgett, *Lives Entrusted.*

37. Everist and Nessan, *Transforming Ministry*, chap. 1.

38. Ending clergy sexual misconduct remains an urgent challenge. Cf. Thoburn and Baker, *Clergy Sexual Misconduct*, chap. 1. Conscientiousness about all the other types of boundaries discussed in this book can contribute to clarity also about ethical practice in maintaining sexual boundaries.

pastors. While boundary keeping clearly belongs to the professional responsibility of church leaders, we intentionally have expanded the theme by describing boundaries as a shared endeavor on the part of all church members. Not only how church members act but also how they think and speak about things have great consequences for the success or failing of the church's identity and mission.

If the church is the body of Christ, then the ethical principles and best practices highlighted in this book belong to the skeleton of that body, providing the structure upon which all else depends for its healthy support. We have described a range of boundary questions and have proposed specific ways to address them, placing ethical responsibility on church leaders and members not only for how they act but also for the things that always precede actions: how we choose to think and speak about a given issue. It is our contention that it is possible to discipline not only how we speak but also how we choose to think about boundary questions in ways that foster God's life-giving purposes for creation. This contradicts much conventional wisdom, which claims we are not responsible for our thoughts but only for what we do with them. However, our approach more accords with the teachings of Jesus in the Sermon on the Mount (Matt 5:21–48) and with the apostle Paul's teaching that Jesus's disciples "have the mind of Christ" (Phil 2:5). This mind affects how we think about the world, including how we think about other persons.

The analysis of human behavior in this book is based not only on biblical and theological wisdom but on much clinical evidence about how human beings function and how they go astray. It is possible for congregations—both members and leaders—to attain a greater degree of insight into their behavior and to adopt practices that better preserve and accord with the core identity and mission of the church as the body of Christ. By naming best practices of boundary keeping in this chapter, we have aimed to synthesize the themes of the previous chapters in very concrete and usable terms. We, however, encourage readers to keep in mind that the impetus for this book is not so much to provide a how-to manual but rather to enhance the integrity of the body of Christ in fulfilling its God-given identity and mission. We enhance the body's integrity through reflecting upon and learning from the mistakes of others and through abiding by ethical practices that will strengthen the church's witness to God's love for the world in Jesus Christ.

Guide for Reflection and Discussion

PART 1: DEFINING AND PROTECTING INTEGRITY THROUGH BOUNDARIES

Chapter 1: The Necessity of Boundaries for Creating and Sustaining Identity and Effective Mission

1. Some good boundary keeping is invisible, while much is apparent. Who, over the course of your lifetime, has most impressed you as having good boundaries? How would you describe what impresses you about that person's boundary keeping?

2. How would you describe the feelings inside you that occur when you feel someone has disrespected your boundaries? Please note that feeling violated can bring forth strong emotions or shame, which are hard to share with others. Please respect this about yourself and others.

3. What elements of boundary keeping have you experienced in a tradition other than your own? What was it like for you to do something important to someone else but not to yourself? One example might be taking your shoes off to enter a place that is sacred to someone else.

4. It can be difficult and awkward for someone to stand up for themselves to enforce a boundary. Sometimes you might notice a difference in another's language use, or an edge to their voice when they are standing up for themselves. What has helped you learn to stand up for yourself gracefully under such circumstances?

5. In what ways is the identity of the church intended to be different from other organizations that have a different purpose?

6. What are the most hopeful and exciting insights for you from this chapter? What action items do you take from this chapter?

Chapter 2: Entrustment

1. People in positions of power or authority may tell you to trust them, which can mean that they are telling you to relinquish control to them. Entrustment, by contrast, does not take anything away from the other person. Entrustment means that the people God has entrusted to our care retain their power and rights over their well-being, not us. The question, who does this belong to? can help us keep that straight. Think of examples where this question is significant in your congregation.

2. Identify instances when people have mistreated or misrepresented what another person has said to them, including how you might have done that recently. Contrast this with examples of when someone acted to protect the integrity of what someone else said.

3. Consider people in your congregation whose service has recently gone unnoticed or was not adequately appreciated. How might you remedy that?

4. Think of an example of when someone thought there was a boundary violation that you did not agree with. Were you quick to disagree, or did you pause to inquire about and understand what they were pointing out? Why did you respond in this particular way?

5. Anticipate the next time you will be faced with an ethical or boundary issue. Identify whom you might consult with about it: someone who is good about boundary keeping and is willing to tell you things you might not want to hear.

6. What are the most hopeful and exciting insights for you from this chapter? What action items do you take from this chapter?

Chapter 3: Role Integrity

1. A diplomatic person can tell someone something they do not want to hear in such a way that the person is grateful and thanks them for it. Think of a time someone gave you input about yourself that was hard to hear but helpful in the long run.

2. Effective mutual accountability requires emotional maturity and skill. Otherwise we will give in to discomfort and will not engage in accountability practices. Or we might be harsh in how we speak or how we hear critical input. Think of the people you know who are graceful about giving and receiving mutual accountability. What are the particular characteristics you might learn from them?

3. List all of the separate roles you are in, and the functions you perform in your congregation. How well defined are these roles in ways that all those involved understand them? What might your congregation do to clarify those roles for yourself and others? Think of a situation in your congregation where you have more than one role with another person or other persons. What does it take for you to stay most faithful to your primary role?

4. How might you better set aside personal friendships for the sake of open and equal fellowship with other people at church with whom you are not friends? What relationships do you need to set aside, in order to relate to others in your role as a congregation member?

5. What has helped you get more comfortable with saying no to what someone wants from you? What could help you get more comfortable? What has helped you get more comfortable taking no for an answer from others? What could help you get more comfortable?

6. What are the most hopeful and exciting insights for you from this chapter? What action items do you take from this chapter?

PART 2: INTEGRITY OF COMMUNITY

Chapter 4: Integrity in Worship

1. What helps you transition your mind and heart so that you can fully participate in worship? What are the most challenging things for you to set aside in order to focus attentively on worship? What are

the most challenging distractions for you during worship? What is it like for you to put to voice parts of the service or parts of hymns that you do not believe or do not agree with? What can help you treat worship and the worship space as being more sacred?

2. If the members of your church exchange greetings with each other or pass the peace during worship, are there ways you treat people differently during that time based on your personal relationships with them?

3. Engaging with God during worship—through the words spoken in the service, heard in a sermon, or sung in the music—can express a wide variety of feelings, from remorse to joy and celebration. How fully do you let yourself feel and express those feelings?

4. Are there ways others try to relate to you while you are at church for worship according to a role that you have during the rest of the week? How might you redirect that back to your baptismal identity at worship and your roles with each other as Christians?

5. In what ways does the gospel you hear in church indict what you do in your daily life? In what ways does the gospel indict how you treat others? Who in your congregation is most challenging for you to see through the eyes of Christ?

6. What are the most hopeful and exciting insights for you from this chapter? What action items do you take from this chapter?

Chapter 5: Bearing Witness: Integrity in Interaction and Communication

1. The human mind does not like not knowing or leaving questions unanswered. For that reason we speculate a lot about the things that might happen, including about other people, which risks creating false images of them. Can you recall a recent incident when you or someone else engaged in speculation about another person? What would have been lost if you had resisted doing so?

2. In what ways is it difficult for you to show your own differences and uniqueness with others in the congregation? What are important spiritual experiences you have had that might benefit others if they

could hear about them? In what ways does the culture of your congregation bring out the best in you?

3. In what ways does the culture of your congregation encourage gossiping about others or other harmful behavior that involves speaking about others in ways that benefit the speaker at the expense of someone else? What role do you play when someone vents their feelings about others or otherwise portrays another negatively? In what ways does your congregation create values and ways of being that contrast with the community around you?

4. How we treat people in our own minds is as much an ethical matter as our outward behavior. Listening and understanding without interpreting or distorting what the other person is saying is both difficult and rare. How might you practice getting better at this, and who might help you with it?

5. Jesus said that how we treat the least important person is how we treat him. Which people in your day do you treat as least important or unimportant? If you were only to say things that you are sure are honest, true, kind and helpful, would you need to give up anything that is important to you?

6. What are the most hopeful and exciting insights for you from this chapter? What action items do you take from this chapter?

Chapter 6: Sabbath Shalom: A Day in the Kingdom

1. One impediment to meaningful Sabbath keeping is the belief that we need to spend our time with practical matters, so that time off from those concerns makes us uneasy. Walter Brueggemann thinks most of us simply "go through the motions" of keeping Sabbath without getting into it deeply. What does "going through the motions" mean for you?

2. Numbing out is one way to reduce the feeling of stress, though it clouds our awareness. What are your preferred ways of numbing out? What might be the benefit of entering into the practices of Sabbath rather than numbing out? What benefits of Sabbath practice described in this chapter are you most drawn to at this point in your life?

3. Think of a time you and another person had the freedom to go deeply into a conversation, getting to know each other and yourselves better. How can your Sabbath time regularly create the conditions for such encounters?

4. Thinking about work is work. Pastor Rob Bell and others have found that they need to get through a zone of depression or other types of discomfort before they arrive into deeper levels of Sabbath freedom. How are you doing at getting closure with thoughts about work so you can get deeply into other parts of your life? What could help you better do this?

5. Meaningful Sabbath helps us keep our bearings on the "true north" that Jesus points toward. How disruptive is true north for you at this point, given how you are living your life? If you had more courage, what changes would you make in your work or life?

6. What are the most hopeful and exciting insights for you from this chapter? What action items do you take from this chapter?

PART 3: INTEGRITY OF PERSONS

Chapter 7: The Pastor as Person

Questions for Clergy:

1. The pastor's personal life can get neglected when there is not enough time or psychological distance from pastoral responsibilities. What feelings and thoughts occur to you with the idea of receiving a Pastor-of-the-Year award? How are you doing at taking your weekly personal days and annual vacation time?

2. In what ways do you allow your personal life and personal concerns to encroach on the time designated for your pastoral role? How do your continuing education choices directly benefit your congregation rather than your personal interests?

3. What aspects of your early life led you to pastoral ministry? What unhealthy dynamics in your family of origin are you still carrying and perpetuating? Are there ways that serving as a pastor perpetuates certain roles you played in your family of origin? Are there ways that the ministry compensates for what was missing in your

childhood? In what ways are you at risk of shaping your ministry to meet your own needs?

4. How are you doing at dealing with criticism objectively? What practices can help you with this? What blind spots have others claimed that you have? How do you go about trying to solicit input on your blind spots? Who do you have available to confide in, who can help you be objective about yourself, your congregation, and pastoral ministry?

5. How are you doing at gracefully and effectively initiating conflict or contrast in your ministry? In your personal life? How are you doing at cultivating compassionate awareness of yourself rather than resorting to shaming or blaming awareness of yourself?

6. What are the most hopeful and exciting insights for you from this chapter? What action items do you take from this chapter?

Questions for Church Members:

1. As an individual, what boundary keeping helps you support the personal well-being of your pastor?

2. As a congregation, what boundary keeping helps you support the personal well-being of your pastor?

3. What are the most hopeful and exciting insights for you from this chapter? What action items do you take from this chapter?

Chapter 8: Boundaries as Shared Responsibility by Church Members

1. Do you think of your participation in the life of the congregation as a volunteer—as something you could do or not do as it suits you? Or do you consider your congregational participation as a responsibility that comes with being a part of the ministry of the congregation? How can you tell when your actions in congregational life are overly self-motivated? How might you apply the principle that the conduct you expect of your pastor is also what you expect of yourself?

2. Are there ways that your church involvement perpetuates the roles you played in the dynamics of your family of origin? Are there ways

that your church involvement is attempting to compensate for what is otherwise missing in your life? What helps you say no when that is the healthiest decision? What helps you take no for an answer from someone else?

3. How are you doing at dealing with criticism objectively? What role do you play in anonymous complaints or anonymous input? How are you doing at gracefully and effectively initiating conflict or contrast in your congregational life? In your personal life? What practices can help you with this?

4. How comfortable are you dealing with those in the congregation who insist on getting their own way? How comfortable are you taking charge in the congregation when the situation calls for it? How comfortable are you at yielding to others in the congregation when the situation calls for it?

5. How are you doing at cultivating compassionate awareness of yourself rather than resorting to shaming or blaming awareness of yourself? When and how do you most strongly feel God's love and acceptance toward you and toward everyone else? How can you connect with this more often?

6. What are the most hopeful and exciting insights for you from this chapter? What action items do you take from this chapter?

Chapter 9: Being the Body of Christ with Integrity: Toward Best Practices in Boundary Keeping

1. How do your personality and temperament relate to the recommended best practices? With which recommended best practices do you disagree? Why?

2. Which of the practices in this book do you think are most helpful for your congregation? Why?

3. Which of the practices in this book are the most important for you to adopt personally? Why?

4. What are some other practices not described in this book that can help you to keep healthy boundaries? How do they do so?

5. This book makes the case that a faithful congregation will proclaim and do things that make you and others uncomfortable. In what ways do consumer motives affect your congregation and your role in it? How do the needs of your congregation challenge you to be different than you would be if you just let your personal preferences control you?

6. What are the most hopeful and exciting insights for you from this chapter? What action items do you take from this chapter?

Bibliography

Albers, Robert H. *Shame: A Faith Perspective*. Binghamton, NY: Haworth, 1995.

Anderson, T. Carlos. *Just a Little Bit More: The Culture of Excess and the Fate of the Common Good*. Austin: Blue Ocotillo, 2014.

Armstrong, Karen. *Through the Narrow Gate: A Memoir of Spiritual Discovery*. New York: St. Martin's, 2005.

Assagioli, Roberto. *Psychosynthesis: A Collection of Basic Writings*. Amherst, MA: Synthesis Center, 2000.

Bacher, Robert N., and Michael L. Cooper-White. *Church Administration: Programs, Process, Purpose*. Minneapolis: Fortress, 2007.

Bailey, James L. *Contrast Community: Practicing the Sermon on the Mount*. Eugene, OR: Wipf & Stock, 2013.

Bash, Anthony. *Forgiveness: A Theology*. Cascade Companions 19. Eugene, OR: Cascade Books, 2015.

Batchelor, Valli Boobal, ed. *When Pastors Prey: Overcoming Clergy Sexual Abuse of Women*. Geneva: World Council of Churches Publications, 2013.

Bates, Brian, and John Cleese. *The Human Face*. New York: Dorling Kindersley, 2001.

Bazerman, Max H., and Ann E. Tenbrunsel. *Blind Spots: Why We Fail to Do What's Right and What to Do about It*. Princeton: Princeton University Press, 2011.

Bazerman, Max H. et al. "Negotiating with Yourself and Losing: Making Decisions with Competing Internal Preferences." *Academy of Management Review* 23 (1998) 225–41

Beck, Ulrich. *A God of One's Own: Religion's Capacity for Peace and Potential for Violence*. Cambridge: Polity, 2010.

Bell, Rob. *Velvet Elvis: Repainting the Christian Faith*. New York: HarperCollins, 2005.

Blodgett, Barbara J. *Lives Entrusted: An Ethic of Trust for Ministry*. Prisms. Minneapolis: Fortress, 2008.

Bonhoeffer, Dietrich. *Life Together; Prayerbook of the Bible*. Translated by Daniel W. Bloesch and James H. Burtness. Dietrich Bonhoeffer Works 5. Minneapolis: Fortress, 1996.

Borgmann, Albert. *Crossing the Postmodern Divide*. Chicago: University of Chicago, 1992.

Brown, Brené. *Daring Greatly: How the Courage to Be Vulnerable Transforms the Way We Live, Love, Parent, and Lead*. New York: Gotham, 2012.

Brown, Robert McAffe, ed. *The Essential Reinhold Niebuhr: Selected Essays and Addresses*. New Haven: Yale University Press, 1986.

Browning, Don S. *Religious Ethics and Pastoral Care*. Theology and Pastoral Care Series. Minneapolis: Fortress, 2009.

Brueggemann, Walter. *The Covenanted Self: Explorations in Law and Covenant*. Minneapolis: Fortress, 1999.

———. *Sabbath as Resistance: Saying No to the Culture of Now*. Louisville: Westminster John Knox, 2014.

Buber, Martin. *I and Thou*. Translated by Ronald Gregor Smith. 2nd ed. New York: Scribner, 1958.

Burns, David D. *The Feeling Good Handbook: Using the New Mood Therapy in Everyday Life*. New York: Morrow, 1989.

Bush, Joseph E., Jr. *Gentle Shepherding: Pastoral Ethics and Leadership*. St. Louis: Chalice, 2006.

Campbell, Troy H., and Aaron C. Kay. "Solution Aversion: On the Relation between Ideology and Motivated Disbelief." *Journal of Personality and Social Psychology* 107 (2014) 809–24.

Cannon, Katie Geneva et al., eds. *Womanist Theological Ethics: A Reader*. Louisville: Westminster John Knox, 2011.

Ched, Graham, writer and producer; with Larry Engel, dir. of photography, et al. *The Human Spark, with Alan Alda*. Originally produced in 2007. Originally broadcast as a three-part miniseries on PBS in 2009. Produced by Ched-Angier-Lewis Productions. DVD. Boston: PBS Productions, 2010.

Chopp, Rebecca S. *The Power to Speak: Feminism, Language, God*. New York: Crossroad, 1989.

Center for Faith and Giving. "Building a Narrative Budget." http://www.centerforfaithandgiving.org/Resources/AdministrativeResources/BuildingaNarrativeBudget/tabid/950/Default.aspx/

Cloud, Henry. *Boundaries for Leaders: Results, Relationships, and Being Ridiculously in Charge*. New York: HarperCollins, 2013.

Cooper-White, Pamela. *The Cry of Tamar: Violence against Women and the Church's Response*. Minneapolis: Fortress, 1995.

———. *Shared Wisdom: Use of the Self in Pastoral Care and Counseling*. Minneapolis: Fortress, 2004.

Darley, J. M., and C. D. Batson. "From Jerusalem to Jericho: A Study of Situational and Dispositional Variables in Helping Behavior." *Journal of Personality and Social Psychology* 27 (1973) 100–108.

Davidson, Donald. *The Essential Davidson*. Oxford: Clarendon, 2006.

Dickhart, Judith McWilliams. *Church-Going Insider or Gospel-Carrying Outsider? A Different View of Congregations*. Chicago: ELCA Division for Ministry, 2002.

Doblmeier, Martin, dir. *The Power of Forgiveness*. Produced by Dan Juday and Adele Schmidt. DVD. Alexandria VA: Journey Films, 2007 (New York: First Run Features, distributor).

Doehring, Carrie. *Taking Care: Monitoring Power Dynamics and Relational Boundaries in Pastoral Care and Counseling*. Nashville: Abingdon, 1995.

Epley, Nicholas, and Eugene M. Caruso. "Egocentric Ethics." *Social Justice Research* 17 (2004) 171–87.

Evangelical Lutheran Church in America. "Affirmation of Baptism." In *Evangelical Lutheran Worship*, 234–37. Minneapolis: Augsburg Fortress, 2006.

———. *Small Catechism*, by Martin Luther. In *Evangelical Lutheran Worship*, by the Evangelical Lutheran Church in America, 1160–67. Minneapolis: Augsburg Fortress, 2006.

———."A Social Statement on Sufficient, Sustainable Livelihood for All." Adopted by a more than two-thirds majority vote by the sixth Churchwide Assembly of the Evangelical Lutheran Church in America, meeting in Denver, Colorado, August 16–22, 1999. http://download.elca.org/ELCA%20Resource%20Repository/Economic_LifeSS.pdf/.

Everist, Norma Cook. *The Church as Learning Community: A Comprehensive Guide to Christian Education.* Nashville: Abingdon, 2002.

———. *Church Conflict: From Contention to Collaboration.* Nashville: Abingdon, 2004.

Everist, Norma Cook, and Craig L. Nessan. *Transforming Leadership: New Vision for a Church in Mission.* Minneapolis: Fortress, 2008.

Fortin, Jack. *The Centered Life: Awakened, Called, Set Free, Nurtured.* Minneapolis: Augsburg Fortress, 2006.

Fortune, Marie M. *Is Nothing Sacred? The Story of a Pastor, the Women He Sexually Abused, and the Congregation He Nearly Destroyed.* 1999. Reprinted, Eugene: Wipf & Stock, 2008.

———. *Love Does No Harm: Sexual Ethics for the Rest of Us.* New York: Continuum, 1998.

Foss, Michael W. *From Members to Disciples: Leadership Lessons from the Book of Acts.* Nashville: Abingdon, 2007.

Frankl, Viktor E. *Man's Search for Meaning.* 4th ed. Boston: Beacon, 1992.

Franklin, Robert M. *Crisis in the Village: Restoring Hope in African American Communities.* Minneapolis: Fortress, 2007.

Friberg, Nils C., and Mark R. Laaser. *Before the Fall: Preventing Pastoral Sexual Abuse.* Collegeville, MN: Liturgical, 1998.

Gaede, Beth Ann, ed. *When a Congregation Is Betrayed: Responding to Clergy Misconduct.* Bethesda, MD: Alban Institute, 2006.

Gentile, Mary C. *Giving Voice to Values: How to Speak Your Mind When You Know What's Right.* New Haven: Yale University, 2012.

Giere, Samuel D. *With Ears to Hear.* http://www.withearstohear.org/.

Grenz, Stanley J., and Roy D. Bell. *Betrayal of Trust: Confronting and Preventing Clergy Sexual Misconduct.* Grand Rapids: Baker, 2001.

Güggenbühl-Craig, Adolf. *Power in the Helping Professions.* Translated by Myron Gubitz. Thompson, CT: Spring, 2009.

Gula, Richard M. *Ethics in Pastoral Ministry.* Mahwah, NJ: Paulist, 1996.

———. *Just Ministry: Professional Ethics for Pastoral Ministers.* Mahwah, NJ: Paulist, 2010.

———. *The Way of Goodness and Holiness: A Spirituality for Pastoral Ministers.* Collegeville, MN: Liturgical, 2011.

Halstead, Kenneth A. *From Stuck to Unstuck: Overcoming Congregational Impasse.* Bethesda, MD: Alban Institute, 1998.

Harbaugh, Gary L. *The Pastor as Person: Maintaining Personal Integrity in the Choices and Challenges of Ministry.* Minneapolis: Augsburg, 1984.

Harbaugh, Gary L. et al. *Covenants and Care: Boundaries in Life, Faith, and Ministry.* Minneapolis: Fortress, 1998.

Hedahl, Susan K. *Listening Ministry: Rethinking Pastoral Leadership.* Minneapolis: Fortress, 2001.

Hess, Carol Lakey. *Caretakers of Our Common House: Women's Development in Communities of Faith.* Nashville: Abingdon, 1997.

Heyward, Carter. *When Boundaries Betray Us: Beyond Illusions of What Is Ethical in Therapy and Life*. San Francisco: HarperSanFrancisco, 1994.

Hinrichs, Jonathan, Jared DeFife, and Drew Westen. "Personality Subtypes in Adolescent and Adult Children of Alcoholics: A Two Part Study." *Journal of Nervous and Mental Disorders* 199 (2011) 487–98.

hooks, bell. *Killing Rage: Ending Racism*. New York: Holt, 1995.

Hopkins, Dwight N. *Being Human: Race, Culture, and Religion*. Minneapolis: Fortress, 2005.

Hopkins, Nancy Myer, and Mark Laaser, eds. *Restoring the Soul of a Church: Healing Congregations Wounded by Clergy Sexual Misconduct*. Collegeville, MN: Liturgical, 1995.

Hunter, Mic. *Back to the Source: The Spiritual Principles of Jesus*. Amazon: CreateSpace Independent Publishing, 2011.

Jameson, Frederic. *Postmodernism, or The Cultural Logic of Late Capitalism*. Durham: Duke University Press, 1991.

Jennings, Willie James. *The Christian Imagination: Theology and the Origins of Race*. New Haven: Yale University, 2010.

Jung, Patricia Beattie, and Darryl W. Stephens, eds. *Professional Sexual Ethics: A Holistic Ministry Approach*. Minneapolis: Fortress, 2013.

Kanyoro, Musimbi R. A. *Introducing Feminist Cultural Hermeneutics: An African Perspective*. Cleveland: Pilgrim, 2002.

Kaptein, Muel. *Workplace Morality: Behavioral Ethics in Organizations*. Bingly, UK: Emerald Group, 2013.

Karjala, Lynn Mary. *Understanding Trauma and Dissociation*. Atlanta: ThomasMax, 2007.

Kerns, Charles D. "Why Good Leaders Do Bad Things: Mental Gymnastics behind Unethical Behavior." *Grazaido Business Review* 6.4 (2003). <http://gbr.pepperdine.edu/2010/08/why-good-leaders-do-bad-things/. September 8, 2015.

Kerper, Michael. "Loss of Leisure Time, Loss of Faith." <http://universespirit.org/loss-of-leisure-time-loss-of-faith> July 14, 2015.

Kierkegaard, Søren. *Concluding Unscientific Postscript*. Translated by David F. Swenson. Princeton: Princeton University Press, 1944.

Kolodiejchuk, Brian, ed. *Mother Teresa—Come Be My Light: The Private Writings of the "Saint of Calcutta."* New York: Doubleday, 2007.

LaCugna, Catherine Mowry. *God for Us: The Trinity and the Christian Life*. New York: HarperCollins, 1993.

Lathrop, Gordon W. *Holy Things: A Liturgical Theology*. Minneapolis: Fortress, 1993.
———. *The Pastor: A Spirituality*. Minneapolis: Fortress, 2006.

Law, Eric H. F. *Sacred Acts, Holy Change: Faithful Diversity and Practical Transformation*. St. Louis: Chalice, 2002.
———. *The Wolf Shall Dwell with the Lamb: A Spirituality for Leadership in a Multicultural Community*. St. Louis: Chalice, 1993.

Lebacqz, Karen. *Professional Ethics: Power and Paradox*. Nashville: Abingdon, 1985.

Lebacqz, Karen, and Joseph D. Driskill. *Ethics and Spiritual Care: A Guide for Pastors, Chaplains, and Spiritual Directors*. Nashville: Abingdon, 2000.

Lehr, Fred. *Clergy Burnout: Recovering from the 70-Hour Work Week and Other Self-Defeating Practices*. Prisms. Minneapolis: Fortress, 2006.

Levine, Robert A. *A Geography of Time: The Temporal Misadventures of a Social Psychologist*. New York: Basic Books, 1998.

Luther, Martin. *The Freedom of a Christian*. Translated and introduced by Mark D. Tranvik. Minneapolis: Fortress, 2008.

Marty, Martin. *Baptism: A User's Guide*. Minneapolis: Augsburg, 2008.

McGonigal, Kelly. *The Willpower Instinct: How Self-Control Works, Why It Matters, and What You Can Do to Get More of It*. New York: Penguin, 2012.

McLaren, Brian D. *A New Kind of Christian: A Tale of Two Friends on a Spiritual Journey*. San Francisco: Jossey-Bass, 2001.

Menking, Wayne L. *When All Else Fails: Rethinking Our Pastoral Vocation in Times of Stuck*. Eugene, OR: Wipf & Stock, 2013.

Merton, Thomas. *Conjectures of a Guilty Bystander*. New York: Doubleday, 1965.

———. *New Seeds of Contemplation*. New York: New Directions, 1961.

———. *Seeds of Contemplation*. 1949. Reprinted, New York: Dell, 1960.

Mockenhaupt, Brian. "Confessions of a Whistleblower." *AARP Bulletin* (September 2014). http://www.aarp.org/politics-society/advocacy/info-2014/dr-sam-foote-va-whistleblower.2.html/.

Nessan, Craig L. *Beyond Maintenance to Mission: A Theology of the Congregation*. 2nd ed. Minneapolis: Fortress, 2010.

———. "Sex, Aggression, and Pain: Sociobiological Implications for Theological Anthropology." *Zygon* 33 (1998) 443–54.

———. *Shalom Church: The Body of Christ as Ministering Community*. Minneapolis: Fortress, 2010.

———. "Surviving Congregational Leadership: A Theology of Family Systems," *Word and World* 20 (200) 390–99.

Nouwen, Henri J. M. *Life of the Beloved: Spiritual Living in a Secular World*. New York: Crossroad, 1992.

———. *Making All Things New: An Invitation to the Spiritual Life*. New York: Harper-Collins, 1981.

Nussbaum, Martha C. *Upheavals of Thought: The Intelligence of Emotions*. New York: Cambridge University Press, 2001.

Olsen, David C., and Nancy G. Devor. *Saying No to Say Yes: Everyday Boundaries and Pastoral Excellence*. Lanham, MD: Rowman & Littlefield, 2015.

Perrin, Norman. *Jesus and the Language of the Kingdom: Symbol and Metaphor in New Testament Interpretation*. Philadelphia: Fortress, 1976.

Peterson, Marilyn R. *At Personal Risk: Boundary Violations in Professional-Client Relationships*. New York: Norton, 1992.

Putnam, Robert D. *Bowling Alone: The Collapse and Revival of American Community*. New York: Simon & Schuster, 2000.

Ragsdale, Katherine Hancock, ed. *Boundary Wars: Intimacy and Distance in Healing Relationships*. Cleveland: Pilgrim, 1996.

Rendle, Gil. *Behavioral Covenants in Congregations: A Handbook for Honoring Differences*. Bethesda, MD: Alban, 1998.

Richardson, Ronald W. *Becoming a Healthier Pastor: Family Systems Theory and the Pastor's Own Family*. Minneapolis: Fortress, 2005.

Ridley, Matt. *The Red Queen: Sex and the Evolution of Human Nature*. New York: Perennial, 2003.

Riggs, Marcia. "Living as Religious Ethical Mediators: A Vocation for People of Faith in the Twenty-first Century." In *Womanist Theological Ethics: A Reader*, edited by Katie Geneva Cannon et al., 247–53. Louisville: Westminster John Knox, 2011.

Roberto, Michael A. *The Art of Critical Decision Making*. The Great Courses DVD. Chantilly, VA: Teaching Company, 2009.

Romero, Oscar A. *The Violence of Love: The Pastoral Wisdom of Archbishop Oscar Romero*. Compiled and translated by James R. Brockman. New York: Harper & Row, 1988.

Salter, Daniel et al. "Development of Sexually Abusive Behaviour in Sexually Victimised Males: A Longitudinal Study." *The Lancet* 361 (2003) 471–76.

Schmit, Clayton J. *Sent and Gathered: A Worship Manual for the Missional Church*. Grand Rapids: Baker Academic, 2009.

"Sensory Illusions in Aviation." https://en.wikipedia.org/wiki/Sensory_illusions_in_aviation.

Sevig, Julie B., and Michael D. Watson. "Bullying the Pastor." *The Lutheran* 24 (January 2011): <http://www.thelutheran.org/article/article.cfm?article_id=9636&key=92852494> July 26, 2015.

Snow, Luther K. *The Power of Asset Mapping: How Your Congregation Can Act on Its Gifts*. Herndon, VA: Alban Institute, 2004.

Sternberg, Robert J., and Susan T. Fiske, eds. *Ethical Challenges in the Behavioral and Brain Sciences*. New York: Cambridge University Press, 2015.

Substance Abuse and Mental Health Services Association. *Spiritual Caregiving to Help Addicted Persons and Families*. Rockville, MD: SAMHSA, 2007.

Sue, Derald Wing, ed. *Microaggressions and Marginality: Manifestation, Dynamics, and Impact*. Hoboken, NJ: Wiley, 2010.

Tanner, Kathryn. *Theories of Culture: A New Agenda for Theology*. Guides to Theological Inquiry. Minneapolis: Fortress, 1997.

Taylor, Barbara Brown. *Leaving Church: A Memoir of Faith*. New York: HarperOne, 2006.

Tenbrunsel, Ann E., and David M. Messick. "Ethical Fading: The Role of Self-Deception in Unethical Behavior." *Social Justice Research* 17 (2004) 171–87.

Tillich, Paul. *Love, Power, and Justice: Ontological Analyses and Ethical Implications*. Galaxy Book. New York: Oxford University Press, 1960.

Thoburn, John, and Rob Baker, with Maria Dal Maso, eds. *Clergy Sexual Misconduct: A Systems Approach to Prevention, Intervention, and Oversight*. Carefree, AZ: Gentle Path, 2011.

Thomas, Kim. *Even God Rested: Why It's Okay for Women to Slow Down*. Eugene, OR: Harvest House, 2003.

Trull, Joe E., and James E. Carter. *Ministerial Ethics: Moral Formation for Church Leaders*. Grand Rapids: Baker Academic, 2004.

Ubeda, Paloma. "The Consistency of Fairness Rules: An Experimental Study." *Journal of Economic Psychology* 41 (2014) 88–100.

Vaughan, Judith. *Sociality, Ethics, and Social Change: A Critical Appraisal of Reinhold Niebuhr's Ethics in the Light of Rosemary Radford Ruether's Works*. Lanham, MD: University Press of America, 1983.

Vingerhoets, A. J., M. Van Huijgevoort, and G. L. van Heck. "Leisure Sickness: A Pilot Study on Its Prevalence, Phenomenology, and Background." *Logo Psychotherapy and Psychosomatics* 71 (2002) 311–17.

Walsh, James, ed. *The Cloud of Unknowing*. Mahwah, NJ: Paulist, 1981.

Wedel, Theodore O. "Evangelism—the Mission of the Church to Those Outside Her Life." *Ecumenical Review* 6 (1953) 19–25.

Whitehead, James D., and Evelyn Eaton Whitehead. *Transforming Our Painful Emotions: Spiritual Resources in Anger, Shame, Grief, Fear, and Loneliness*. Maryknoll, NY: Orbis, 2010.

Wilson, Michael Todd, and Brad Hoffmann. *Preventing Ministry Failure: A ShepherdCare Guide for Pastors, Ministers and Other Caregivers*. Downers Grove, IL: InterVarsity, 2007.

Wingren, Gustav. *Creation and Law*. Translated by Ross MacKenzie. Philadelphia: Muhlenberg, 1961.

———. *Luther on Vocation*. Translated by Carl C. Rasmussen. Philadelphia: Muhlenberg, 1957.

Woititz, Janet Geringer. *Adult Children of Alcoholics*. Deerfield Beach, FL: Health Communications, 1983.

Woodley, Randy S. *Shalom and the Community of Creation: An Indigenous Vision*. Grand Rapids: Eerdmans, 2012.

Index of Names

Index of Subjects

dual role, 48, 130, 183, 184, 185; *see also* multiple roles
due diligence, 58, 87, 166, 173

emotions/emotional, 30, 34, 40–41, 50, 61, 75, 80, 81, 88, 93, 104, 109, 110, 124, 129–30, 133, 140, 152, 156, 158, 159, 162, 172–76, 197, 199, 211, 213
emotional boundaries, 93, 129, 159; *see also* feeling boundaries
enduring institutions, 57
entrapment, 172
entrustment, 29–36, 198
ethics, xii, 4–7, 19, 39–40, 42, 48–49, 67n1, 126n5, 155, 179, 183, 185–86, 192n31, 195, 207–10, 212
evolution, 81–84, 211
expectations, 49, 55–56, 60–61, 65, 71, 125, 128, 151, 183
exploit/exploitation, xii, 19, 21, 53, 68, 90, 93, 99, 116, 118, 157

fall, 81, 155, 209
false, 13–14, 22, 39, 77, 86, 89, 93–94, 157, 169, 177, 200
family, 25, 51, 57, 69, 72, 76, 78, 80, 86, 90–91, 109, 111, 124, 126, 128, 131–32, 135–38, 144–46, 151–52, 186, 194, 203, 211
family systems, 17, 80, 131, 134, 211
favoritism, 48, 154, 191
feelings, 2, 4, 7, 18, 21, 28–29, 32, 38, 40–41, 43, 47, 50, 53–55, 75, 89–91, 93, 97, 103–4, 109, 130, 133, 138, 140, 145, 148, 156, 159–62, 168, 170, 175–76, 178–80, 197, 200–202
fidelity/infidelity, 14, 61, 92
fishbowl, 56
fixing, 135

forgiveness, 23, 35–36, 40, 66, 71–72, 74, 84, 91–92, 124, 142, 168, 172, 193–94, 207–8
freedom, vii, 3, 5, 72, 81, 105–8, 125, 144, 153, 157, 202, 211
friend/friendship(s), xi, 3, 7, 21, 43, 46–47, 53, 57–59, 61, 65–66, 72, 96, 110–11, 114, 124, 126–28, 137–38, 152, 155, 184, 186, 190, 199, 211
funerals, 150–52, 186
future self, 155–56, 174

gift/donation, 173, 192
gospel, 6, 16, 19, 22–23, 34, 96, 119, 124–25, 200, 208
gossip, 16, 25, 42, 57–58, 94, 201
gratitude, 25, 36, 55, 71–72, 74–75, 105, 142, 168, 173
Great Commandment, 22–23, 45, 50, 61, 67, 85, 126, 194
Great Commission, 30, 55–56, 60
groupthink, 42

habituation, 17, 113
happiness, 36, 79, 115–16, 145, 167
harm/harmful, xi, 1–3, 16n7, 17–18, 27, 36, 41, 43–44, 47n2, 50, 57, 82, 84
hijack/hijacking, 29–31, 70, 174
HIPAA, 58
holy/holiness, 100, 102–8, 111–12, 194n34, 209
Holy Spirit, 17, 22, 73, 76, 124, 167, 193–94
holy things, 20–21, 68n3, 71n7, 210
honest/honesty, 87, 91, 97, 113–14, 118, 157, 170, 180, 201
humility, 36–37, 40, 168
hypocrisy, 23

I statements, 97, 132, 170
identity/identities/identity boundaries, 11–14, 18–29, 35, 44, 46–48, 54, 59, 71, 76, 93, 99, 108, 118, 120, 124, 126, 132, 136, 138, 142–44,

How can we help
parishioners develop
better boundaries?

How do we respond
when parishioners react
extremely negatively to
our setting a boundary?

CPSIA information can be obtained
at www.ICGtesting.com
Printed in the USA
BVHW031954240119
538609BV00001B/73/P

9 781498 235365